MERTHYR TYDFIL COLLEGE
KU-696-046
25053

Thinking Through Religion

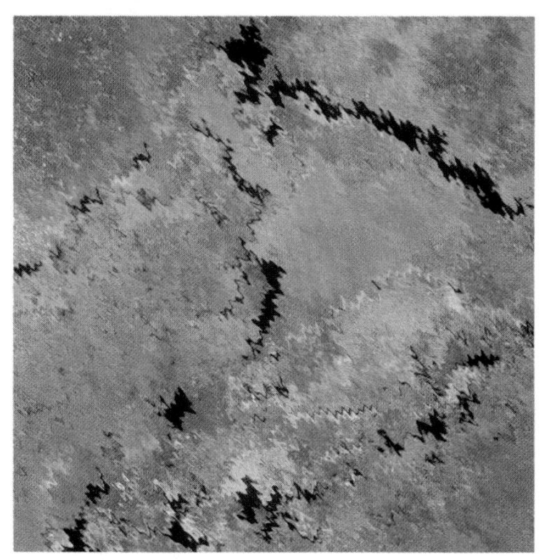

Chris Wright
Carrie Mercier
Richard Bromley
David Worden

OXFORD

Great Clarendon Street, Oxford OX2 6DP

Oxford University Press is a department of the University of Oxford. It furthers the University's objective of excellence in research, scholarship, and education by publishing worldwide in

Oxford New York
Athens Auckland Bangkok Bogotá Buenos Aires
Calcutta Cape Town Chennai Dar es Salaam Delhi
Florence Hong Kong Istanbul Karachi Kuala Lumpur
Madrid Melbourne Mexico City Mumbai Nairobi Paris
São Paulo Singapore Taipei Tokyo Toronto Warsaw

with associated companies in Berlin Ibadan

Oxford is a registered trade mark of Oxford University Press in the UK and in certain other countries

© C Wright, C Mercier, R Bromley, D Worden 2000

Database right Oxford University Press (maker)

First published 2000

ISBN 0 19 917257 9

A CIP catalogue record for this book is available from the British Library.

All rights reserved. No part of this publication may be reproduced, stored in a retrieval system, or transmitted, in any form or by any means, without the prior permission in writing from Oxford University Press.

Within the UK, exceptions are allowed in respect of any fair dealing for the purpose of research or private study, or criticism or review as permitted under the Copyright, Designs and Patents Act, 1988, or in the case of reprographic reproduction in accordance with the terms and licences issued by the Copyright Licensing Agency. Enquiries concerning reproduction outside the scope of the above should be sent to the Rights Department, Oxford University Press, at the above address.

Printed in Spain by Graficas Estella.

The Authors and Publisher thank the following for their permission to reproduce photographs:

Carol Bomer: 17; Bridgeman Art Library: 40 (Oriental Museum, University of Durham), 147t (Vatican Museums and Galleries), 211l, 211r (Andreas Cellarius), 212l (Ottavio Mario Leoni), 212c (Charles Robert Leslie), 213l (George Richmond); Camera Press: 6b, 39, 92, 104, 126, 132l, 137, 142, 143, 189, 199; Circa Photo Library: 23b, 24 (John Smith), 34, 42 (William Holtby), 50t (William Holtby), 50b (John Smith), 56 (William Holtby), 63 (Barrie Searle), 64, 68 (Barrie Searle), 81 (Bipin J. Mistry), 85 (Martin Palmer), 88 (John Fryer), 107 (William Holtby), 110 (Martin Palmer), 147b, 153, 156 (Bipin J. Mistry), 178 (John Smith), 190 (William Holtby), 195b (John Smith); Corbis Images: 10l (Nik Wheeler), 10r (Lowell Georgia), 11 (Joseph Sohm; ChromoSohm Inc.), 12 (Burstein Collection), 16, 18 (Archivo Iconografico, S. A.), 21 (Roger Wood), 22 (Nik Wheeler), 31 (Paul A. Souders), 36 (Dewitt Jones), 67 (David H. Wells), 69t (Hanan Isachar), 69b (Philip Gould), 71t (David H. Wells), 71b (David H. Wells), 82 (Owen Franken), 83, 93t (David Turnley), 94 (Danny Lehman), 98 (Dean Conger), 100l (Gianni Dagli Orti), 100r (Wolfgang Kaehler), 105, 116l (Joseph Sohm; ChromoSohm Inc.), 130 (Bettmann), 134 (Bettmann), 135, 140 (Bettmann), 145, 152t (Owen Franken), 159 (Bettmann), 184 (Catherine Karnow), 191 (Bob Krist), 192 (Alison Wright), 201 (David Turnley), 202 (Bettmann), 206tl (Richard T. Nowitz), 217t (Richard T. Nowitz), 218t (Dave G. Houser), 218bl (Dave Bartruff); Sally and Richard Greenhill: 35, 93b, 128, 172, 174, 176, 180t, 188, 197; Robert Harding Picture Library: 152b, 187t, 218br; Image Bank: 214c, 214r; IPC Magazines Ltd: 166; Christine Osborne: 8, 9t, 9b, 14, 23t, 30, 33, 37, 38, 45, 47, 48, 55b, 57, 73, 75, 76, 78t, 78b, 86, 102, 108, 139, 161, 163, 186, 204, 206br, 207, 210, 216, 217b; PA News Photo Library: 165; Panos Pictures: 26 (Pietro Cenini), 95 (Chris Sattlberger), 96 (Daniel O'Leary), 113t (R. Berriedale-Johnson), 113b (Dermot Tatlow), 116r (Eric Miller), 151 (Howard Davies), 195t; Popperfoto: 6t, 27, 28, 89, 90, 91, 99, 119, 124, 132r, 136, 141, 144, 149, 157, 171, 175, 180b, 198; Royal Signals Museum: 15; Peter Sanders: 46, 52, 53, 55t, 59, 61, 97, 121, 182, 209; Science Photo Library: 114, 211c, 212r, 213r, 214l, 215l, 215c, 215r, 221; Still Pictures: 155 (John Newby), 187b (Christian Aid/Elaine Duigenan); Stock Directory: 4, 32, 49, 112, 122, 162, 173, 206tr, 206bl; War Child/Keith Brame 138.

The illustrations are by:
Jeff Anderson, Philip Burrows, and Peter Jones.

The Authors and Publisher are also grateful for permission to reproduce extracts from various publications as annotated in the text. Every effort has been made to reach copyright holders, but the Publisher will make amendments at the next reprint, if necessary.

Contents

Introduction

UNIT ONE

Thinking

1 Write a statement of your beliefs – perhaps as a list of points beginning "I believe". For example, what do you believe about the environment, or about abortion, or about the way people should treat each other? Try to include beliefs which answer the "big questions" in life, such as "Why are we here?"

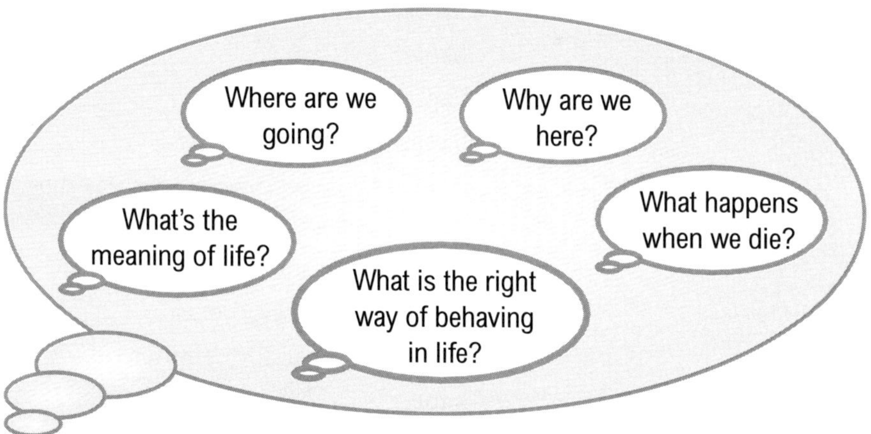

Think about the comparison that is often made between life and a journey. For example, these cars on a motorway could be seen as a picture of the idea that being in a rush makes people one-track-minded. What other kinds of journey images can you think of, to represent how people think and act through their lives?

You probably found exercise Q1 quite difficult! We tend to get so caught up in the rush of modern life that we don't find time to think about what we believe. This book offers you the opportunity to stop rushing and think about some of the "big questions".

The book will introduce you to the thinking of six of the principal world religions on some of the key issues facing people today. For example:

- Is it ever right to go to war?
- Why are some people very rich and yet many others dying of starvation?
- How should we care for our planet?

The book's main aim is to enable you to work out your own beliefs and values, as you study the religious traditions and issues presented. Although your examination syllabus may require you to study [illegible] religions, we encourage you to dip into all the "Religion Files" in the book, to discover other ways of seeing the world and of answering the big questions in life.

2 Consider the following situation. Then, in small groups, discuss questions (a), (b), and (c), and write a brief summary of your conclusions to report back to the class.

There are five people in a hot-air balloon that is quickly losing height. They have miraculously survived a nuclear explosion. To prevent the balloon from crashing to the ground, two people must jump out, sacrificing their lives so that the remaining three can survive. The five people are: a new-born baby, a doctor, a young mother, a wise elderly person, and a clever university student.

(a) Would it be possible to decide which two people should be lost?

(b) Is there further information you would want in order to make a decision?

(c) Is it ever justifiable to encourage the taking of life?

There are no easy answers

You will soon find out that there are no easy answers to many of the questions we will be exploring. For example, look at exercise Q2. Many situations occur where it is difficult to decide which is the right thing to do. In looking at the ideas of the religions covered in this book, you will discover that even believers within the same religion often have differing answers to a question. We have tried to give a range of views from within each religion. And yet you may well find another member of the religion who has another idea.

Thinking about yourself

Who am I? What makes me different from others? Where do I fit into the big scheme of things? Do I count? When was the last time you asked yourself any of these questions? Sometimes we ask these questions when we are trying to work out what we should do with our lives – for example, which career to pursue. Sometimes we start to ask these questions when we are feeling sad or depressed. The religions of the world encourage and help each person to "look within", to think about these questions.

"You are what you think most about; the good, the bad, and everything in between that we think or don't think about tells much about who we are." [M. Scott Peck, *The Road Less Travelled and Beyond*, Rider Books, 1997]

People see what they think they are going to see. Depending on what they are expecting, people will see this picture as a rabbit or as a duck.

THINKING AND SEEING

Anthony de Mello was a spiritual teacher who lived in India. In his teaching he drew on the spiritual traditions of many countries, cultures, and religions. He often used the title "Master" when describing a religious teacher. Here he points out that the way you think affects the way you see the world:

"The Master was certainly no stranger to what goes on in the world. When asked to explain one of his favourite sayings, 'There is no good or ill but thinking makes it so', this is what he said: 'Have you ever observed that what people call congestion in a train becomes atmosphere in a nightclub?'" [Anthony de Mello, *One Minute Nonsense*, 1992]

UNIT TWO

Thinking about morality

Schools must teach new code of values

[*The Times*, Monday, 15 January 1996]

Teach children right from wrong

[*Daily Telegraph*, 5 July 1996]

New bishop warns of moral vacuum threatening cities

[*The Times*, 27 January 1996]

A soldier of the peace-keeping United Nations Protection Force (UNPROFOR) in Sarajevo, Bosnia, 1994.

Anti-abortion campaigners in Washington, D.C., 1996.

In the 1990s debate raged about the moral state of the UK. Some horrifying events raised the question: Have people lost the understanding of what is right and acceptable behaviour and what is wrong and unacceptable? In 1993, ten-year-olds Robert Thompson and Jon Venables brutally murdered two-year-old James Bulger. They kidnapped James in a shopping centre, took him to a deserted railway track, and punched and kicked him to death. In 1995 a sixteen-year-old killed headteacher Philip Lawrence at his own school gates. In the same year Frederick and Rosemary West were sentenced for the murder of at least twelve young women in their house in Gloucester. And in 1996 a gunman, Thomas Hamilton, opened fire in a school gym in Dunblane, killing sixteen children.

Politicians and religious leaders called for a moral campaign in UK schools, to teach standards of right and wrong and so prevent such dreadful events in the future. Educationalists were asked to draw up a code of values to introduce to schools in the year 2000. Their statement of values covered: Self; Relationships; Society; and the Environment. Discussion centred on what type of moral system should be introduced. Can absolute moral guidelines be given, or is all morality relative? In other words, is it possible to say that some things are always right or wrong, or does what is "right" depend on circumstances?

Q

1 Think about how you decide what is right or wrong. Do you decide by gut feeling, on the basis of what affects you personally, by what your friends and peers say, by what you have been taught by your parents, by what you are taught by your teachers, by what sacred books say, by listening to religious leaders, or in other ways?

Information File: Absolute and relative morality

People who accept that there is **absolute morality** believe that certain actions are always good or bad, in whatever situation. They believe that a person's motives for carrying out an action, and the consequences of an action, don't make any difference to whether the action is good or bad.

People who accept that there is **relative morality** believe that an action that is wrong in some situations can be right in another situation. They believe that what is right or wrong, or good or bad, for a person may vary according to the cultural group to which he or she belongs.

2 (a) Is it always wrong to kill? Think about the situations suggested by the two photographs on page 6.
(b) Describe how someone who accepts absolute morality and someone who accepts relative morality would respond to question (a).

3 (a) Do you think there are actions which do not always fall easily into "right" or "wrong"? For example, can you think of occasions where lying and stealing might be the right things to do?
(b) Do you think a person's motives make a difference to whether an action is right or wrong?

How do you decide?

Some situations are confusing and it is hard to know what to think, how to decide what is right and what is wrong, and how to explain our views. It is helpful then to have rules or guidelines, against which to compare situations. Each religion we shall be studying provides guidance to its followers on what is right and wrong. You will discover that there are many areas on which the religions agree. For example, all of the major world religions contain a version of "The Golden Rule". You will also find that there are important differences between the religions. The more you understand a religion's beliefs, the more you will understand its moral stance on issues. In Parts B and C of this book you will be able to find out about the religions' moral stances, in the "Religion Files".

THE GOLDEN RULE

Buddhism:	"Hurt not others with that which pains yourself." [Tripitaka, Samyutta Nikaya 353]
Christianity:	"Treat others as you want them to treat you." [Matthew 7: 12]
Hinduism:	"Do not do to others that which, if done to you, would cause you pain." [Mahabharata, Anusasana Parva 113: 8]
Islam:	"No one of you is a believer until he loves for his brother what he loves for himself." [Forty Hadith of an-Nawawi 13]
Judaism:	"And what you hate, do not do to anyone." [Book of Tobit 4: 15]
Sikhism:	"As you regard yourself, so regard others." [Guru Granth Sahib]

4 What do you think the Golden Rule means? How might it be put into practice?

5 Libby Purves wrote: "To think most school RE will make children behave is as stupid as thinking that TV football will make them fit." [*Holy Smoke*, Hodder & Stoughton, 1998]. What do you think? Is it the role of schools to teach morality?

6 "Society today is very plural – it is like a large supermarket full of ideas. Within the supermarket each of the major religions advertises its values. It doesn't really matter which one you go for – it's just a matter of personal choice."
(a) What do you think?
(b) How should a school decide which set of moral values to teach and live by?

PART A: BELIEVING

INTRODUCTION

Human beings differ from all other animals in one specific respect: they have always been religious. Part A of this book provides an introduction to six of the principal world religions. Before you read the chapters in this section, it is useful to consider what "religion" is and in what ways humans are "religious".

Thinking about religion

1 What do you think religion is? Try writing a definition.

2 Chief Rabbi, Dr Jonathan Sacks, wrote in the *Daily Telegraph* on 22 December 1998: "If an anthropologist visited this country from Mars and looked at the buildings in the average English town, he would be bound to assume that the places of worship were the supermarkets." What do you think Dr Sacks means? What makes shopping look like worshipping? What god might the shoppers be worshipping? Do you agree with Dr Sacks? Give your reasons.

Did your answer to question 1 include words like "belief", "worship", or "rituals"? Religion contains all those, but so do other activities. You can listen to political speeches and hear people talk about what they believe, or go to a football match and see people following a set of rituals. So what else defines religion?

The spires of the Sagrada Familia (the Church of the Holy Family) in Barcelona, Spain, seem to reach out beyond everyday reality.

Contacting the spiritual world

Belief in a spiritual life beyond our physical existence on earth, and in a life after death, is common to many religions. Much religious ritual is concerned with establishing links with the spiritual realm. (A religious ritual is a service or other ceremony involving a series of actions performed in a fixed order.) Religious leaders have often acted as intermediaries and communicators between the earthly and the spiritual worlds. Temples, churches, mosques, and sacred mountains symbolise the attempt of believers to reach out and touch the spiritual realm.

Searching for more

A belief common to many religions is that human beings are imperfect and incomplete creatures struggling for "salvation" and completion:

"Most animals are perfectly content if they find food, drink, and shelter. Humans are the only animals who are driven by an obscure need to change themselves . . . This desire to change and evolve seems to be fundamental to all human beings, regardless of intelligence." [Colin Wilson, *The Atlas of Holy Places and Sacred Sites*, Dorling Kindersley, 1996]

Nature may make us aware of a mysterious power or presence.

Inspiration and revelation

Some of the world's great artists and scientists have said that their best ideas have come in flashes of "inspiration". The ideas seem to have come from outside themselves or from an intuition deep within. In the histories and sacred books of all religions there are accounts of people who are aware of an unseen spiritual force acting in their lives, which inspires them to do great things.

A "revelation" is an experience in which some truth that was hidden becomes clear, or is "revealed". Many people have felt that God has revealed Himself or His truths to them – in a very personal way, or perhaps through the natural world, which they believe God created.

“The true believers are those whose hearts are filled with awe at the mention of God, and whose faith grows stronger as they listen to His revelations.” [Islam, Qur'an 8: 2-4]

3 (a) Have you ever felt that something outside yourself was inspiring you to think or do something in a way that you could not do on your own?
(b) Have you ever had an experience which you would say was "religious"?
(c) Have you ever felt that you were in the presence of something "holy" (i.e. special because it is connected with God)?

Religion as a life of faith

Religion is a response to revelation and inspiration. It is more than believing a set of statements. Religious people show faith by putting their trust in the revelation, and living their lives according to the insights they have received.

Viewing the world from a religious perspective has an effect on the way a person lives. Each religion has its own perspective – that is, its own particular way of seeing the world. The following chapters (pages 10-81) will introduce you to the major beliefs and ideas of six religions, and help you to understand what it is like to belong to each of those. In Part B (pages 82-161) you will look at how the six religions answer some of the fundamental questions in life. In Part C (pages 162-221) you will explore how religious people's world views affect their actions.

These Buddhist nuns from a monastery in the mountains of Nepal have chosen to commit their lives to following their religion.

“Faith is verification by the heart; confession by the tongue; action by the limbs.” [Sufi proverb, quoted in *God's Big Book of Virtues*, One World, 1998]

4 Do you think you can tell whether people have a religious belief from the way they behave day-to-day? Give examples to explain your answer.

CHAPTER

Christianity

UNIT ONE

If you are not Christian, when did you first hear about Christians? What impression do you have of Christianity? If you are Christian, when did you first realise it and what does being Christian mean to you? The seven units in this chapter focus on Christian beliefs and on how they influence the Christian world view.

Looking at Jesus

God with a human face

Christians are sometimes described as people who follow the teachings and example of Jesus Christ. But, for Christians, Jesus is more than a powerful teacher and a "good" person. Christians believe that Jesus is "the Son of God", who was sent to earth for a particular purpose. He was born and lived on earth as a human being. This is called the Incarnation (becoming flesh). In his life on earth, Jesus was somehow both human and divine.

❝When God became a human being in Jesus and lived like one of us, He showed that He really cared about us, so much that He was willing to give up all the riches of heaven and live like us. In Jesus we know that God understands what it feels like to be human and to suffer. I know I can trust a God who knows more about life than I do. One of Jesus's names is Emmanuel, which means 'God with us'. In Jesus God comes close to us. Jesus is the human face of God.❞ [Sue]

Christians believe that by looking at Jesus – what he was like, the values he thought were important, the work he did, the way he related to people, and the content of his teaching – a person can see what God is like. One Christian described Jesus as a "window into God".

1 (a) Explain the meaning of "Incarnation" and "Emmanuel".
(b) Using your own words, explain why Sue thinks it is important that God became a human being in the person of Jesus.
(c) What does it mean that Jesus is "a window into God"?

Around the world, people picture Jesus in ways which make sense to them. This child in Mexico City holds a Jesus doll, as he watches a parade for Candlemas (a festival celebrating the purification of the Virgin Mary after the birth of Jesus and the presentation of Jesus in the temple at Jerusalem, Luke 2).

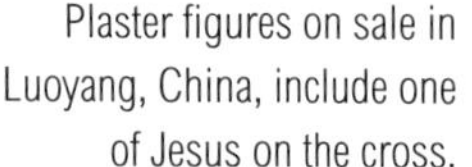

Plaster figures on sale in Luoyang, China, include one of Jesus on the cross.

Jesus the Messiah

At the time of Jesus, the land in which he lived had been ruled for over 300 years by foreign powers – first the Greeks and then the Romans. A number of Jews looked forward to a time when God would send His Messiah (or Christ), His chosen one, to free them from oppression.

This graffiti appeared in Los Angeles, California, in 1992, after a not-guilty verdict had been announced in the trial of some police officers accused of beating a black motorist, Rodney King. If you were to commission a picture of Jesus, what would you want him to look like? How would you show both his divinity and his humanity?

The Jews of the time had a good idea who they were looking for. The Hebrew Bible (which Christians often call the Old Testament) contains numerous references to the Messiah. Many thought he would be a king, like the old kings of Israel, who would lead his people into battle against the Romans. Some thought that the Messiah would have special powers from God. They believed that there would be a final battle at the end of the world. God would then recreate everything and there would be a reign of peace [Isaiah 11: 6-9].

Jesus was born to Jewish parents and brought up to be an observant Jew. He knew the Hebrew Bible well and often quoted from it in his teaching. His closest disciples came to believe that Jesus was the Messiah, the one they had been looking for [Luke 9: 20]. However, Jesus went on to broaden their view of who the Messiah would be.

At the beginning of his teaching, he announced that the following passage from the prophet Isaiah was being fulfilled: "The Spirit of the Lord is upon me, because He has chosen me to bring good news to the poor. He has sent me to proclaim liberty to the captives . . . to set free the oppressed and announce that the time has come when the Lord will save His people." [Luke 4: 18-21]. This clearly fell within the common understanding of what the Messiah would do.

However, Jesus also drew attention to passages in Isaiah (known as the "Suffering Servant" passages) that speak of God's servant being rejected and enduring suffering and pain: "he endured the suffering that should have been ours, the pain that we should have borne . . . Because of our sins he was wounded, beaten because of the evil we did. We are healed by the punishment he suffered." [Isaiah 53]

Once his disciples had declared that they believed he was the Messiah, Jesus went on to teach them that "The Son of Man must suffer much and be rejected . . . He will be put to death, but three days later he will be raised to life." [Luke 9: 22]. The "Son of Man" is a title that Jesus used for the Messiah.

2 In what ways did Jesus extend his disciples' views of the Messiah?

After three years of public ministry, Jesus was crucified. The prophecies in the Hebrew Bible had come true. Jesus was rejected, he suffered, and he was killed. His disciples came to believe that Jesus's death was full of meaning.

UNIT TWO

Jesus's death and resurrection

Jesus was crucified and buried on a Friday. The following Sunday he was raised from the dead: this is called the Resurrection. It is celebrated at Easter, which is the most important Christian festival. In this unit you will read accounts of Jesus's resurrection appearances and learn why his death and resurrection are so important for Christians.

The Crucifixion, painted by British artist Graham Sutherland in 1946. It was commissioned by Canon Walter Hussey, later Dean of Chichester, who described the finished work as "profoundly disturbing and purging". Why do you think he said this? How would you describe the painting?

Christians believe that Jesus's death was not the end of the story. The gospels contain accounts of Jesus's resurrected body appearing to many people. Although there is no description of the Resurrection, three things convinced members of the Early Church that Jesus had risen from the dead: (a) the tomb in which Jesus had been buried was empty; (b) Jesus appeared to people after his death; (c) they felt his presence among them.

JESUS APPEARS TO WOMEN AT THE TOMB [Luke 24: 1-12]

Narrator: Very early on Sunday morning the women went to the tomb, carrying spices they had prepared. They found the stone rolled away from the entrance to the tomb, so they went in; but they did not find the body of the Lord Jesus. They waited there puzzled, when suddenly two men in bright shining clothes stood by them. Full of fear, the women bowed down as the men spoke.

Man 1: Why are you looking among the dead for one who is alive?

Man 2: He is not here; he has been raised.

Man 1: Remember what he said to you while he was in Galilee:

Man 2: "The Son of Man must be handed over to sinful men, be crucified."

Man 1: "And three days later rise to life."

Narrator: Then the women remembered his words, returned from the tomb, and told all these things to the eleven disciples and all the rest. The women were Mary Magdalene, Joanna, and Mary the mother of James; they and the other women with them told these things to the apostles. But the apostles thought that what the women said was nonsense, and did not believe them. However, Peter ran to the tomb; he bent down and saw the linen wrappings but nothing else. Then he went back home amazed at what had happened.

Over the forty days after his appearance to the women at the tomb, Jesus appeared to people in the most ordinary circumstances: at a private dinner, to two men walking along a road, to a woman weeping in a garden, to some fishermen working on a lake. The texts indicate that Jesus didn't appear as a ghost, but in flesh and blood. When Jesus appeared to the disciples he still had the holes in his hands and feet from the nails of his crucifixion. Christians interpret this as showing that God did not take away suffering. Jesus's suffering body was transformed into a resurrection body. God raised Jesus from the dead.

"Because Jesus rose from the dead I know that death is not the end for me." [Peter]

"I know Jesus rose from the dead, because he is alive today. When I pray I know he listens. I have seen a miracle performed in a church because of Jesus." [Tom]

JESUS APPEARS TO CLEOPAS AND HIS FRIEND AND THEN TO THE DISCIPLES [Luke 24: 13-49]

On the same day [Sunday], Cleopas and a friend were travelling from Jerusalem to Emmaus. They were feeling very sad that Jesus had been crucified. A stranger joined them on their walk and started to explain what the Bible had said about the Messiah. It was late afternoon and the two friends invited the stranger to stay with them for a meal.

"When he was at the table with them, he took bread, gave thanks, broke it and began to give it to them. Then their eyes were opened and they recognised him, and he disappeared from their sight." [Luke 24: 30-31]

Cleopas and his friend returned immediately to Jerusalem to tell the disciples that Jesus had risen. The disciples replied: "The Lord is risen indeed! He has appeared to Simon!" [Luke 24: 33-34]

"While the two were telling them this, suddenly the Lord himself stood among them and said to them, 'Peace be with you.' They were terrified, thinking that they were seeing a ghost. But he said to them, 'Why are you alarmed? Why are these doubts coming up in your minds? Look at my hands and my feet, and see that it is I myself. Feel me, and you will know.'" [Luke 24: 36-39]. He ate a piece of cooked fish.

Then Jesus taught them that "the message about repentance and the forgiveness of sins must be preached to all nations, beginning in Jerusalem." [Luke 24: 47]

Christians believe that the Resurrection was proof that Jesus was the Messiah and the Son of the Living God. They also say that it proved that good is greater than evil, and that life is stronger than death. Death is not the end. The Resurrection offers Christians the hope that they too will be raised from the dead.

"Christ has been raised from death, as the guarantee that those who sleep in death will also be raised." [St Paul, 1 Corinthians 15: 20]

Q

1. Some people find it difficult to believe that Jesus rose from the dead. They explain the disappearance of the body in different ways, for example:
   (i) Jesus became unconscious on the cross and later recovered in the tomb;
   (ii) the disciples stole the body and later told people that Jesus had been raised from the dead;
   (iii) the women went to the wrong tomb.
   In groups, consider each of these theories in turn. List the arguments you can find (a) in support of and (b) against the theory. What conclusions do you draw from this exercise?
2. Why were members of the Early Church convinced that Jesus had risen from the dead?
3. For Christians, what did Jesus's resurrection prove?

Easter people

For many Christians the most convincing evidence for the Resurrection is the dramatic effect it had on Jesus's disciples at the time. Before the risen Jesus appeared to them they were a frightened group, hiding from the authorities. But after seeing him they were transformed into people willing to spread the "good news" even if doing so brought suffering and death. Many of Jesus's early followers were crucified, stoned, or thrown to lions. The belief that Jesus had overcome death gave these early Christians hope when they were being persecuted.

The Acts of the Apostles provides further clues as to why the disciples changed into brave preachers. It records that the believers were all together at Pentecost (the Jewish festival of Shavuot). Suddenly a noise from the sky, which sounded like a strong wind, "filled the whole house where they were sitting. Then they saw what looked like tongues of fire which spread out and touched each person there. They were all filled with the Holy Spirit." [Acts 2: 2-4]. Before Jesus died, he had promised his disciples that he would send the Holy Spirit to help and guide them [John 14: 25-26]. At Pentecost this promise was kept.

4 What effect did Jesus's resurrection have on the disciples? How did it encourage the early Christians?

5 What happened on the day of Pentecost? Why do you think this was important?

Like this girl in Ethiopia, many people around the world choose to wear a cross.

The meaning behind Jesus's death on the cross

The most commonly used Christian symbol is the cross. Many people wear a cross on a chain, as a necklace. We think of this as a normal piece of jewellery, and yet it is like wearing a symbol of an electric chair or a syringe full of cyanide. All are means of execution. Jesus was killed by being nailed to the cross. So why has the cross become the central Christian symbol?

"Jesus suffered in every imaginable way on the cross. He had been rejected by his closest followers – they had all fled. He was rejected by his own people – they jeered at him. He suffered humiliation by the Roman soldiers who whipped him and put a crown of thorns on his head. He also felt abandoned by God his father. Because Jesus suffered in this way I know that he understands my suffering. This sort of God I can trust. This sort of God understands me when I suffer." [Susan]

"On the cross, God says, 'Not only do I know about your suffering. I have shared in it.'" [Issa]

6 (a) What does it mean to say that Christians believe in a suffering God?
(b) Read Matthew 27: 46. Why do you think Jesus felt that God had forsaken him?
(c) Explain how the understanding of God as a suffering God helps Christians in their daily lives.

The cross is also important because of the belief that Jesus's death on the cross mended the broken relationship between God and humanity. The relationship had been broken when humanity rebelled against God [Genesis 3]. The painting below, entitled "Through", helps to explain the idea of Jesus as reconciler.

St Paul wrote to the Corinthians:

"I passed on to you what I received, which is of the greatest importance: that Christ died for our sins, as written in the Scriptures [i.e. in the prophecies of the Hebrew Bible]; that he was buried and that he was raised to life three days later, as written in the Scriptures; that he appeared to Peter and then to all twelve apostles." [1 Corinthians 15: 3-5]

This picture, entitled "Through", was painted during the First World War (1914-18). The signaller has been sent out to repair a cable broken down by shellfire. There he lies, cold in death, but with his task accomplished; for beside him lies the rejoined section of cable. For Christians, this picture can be seen as a representation of what Jesus accomplished on the cross: the mending of the relationship between God and humanity.

To explain the idea that Jesus died on the cross for "our sins", some Christians liken Jesus to the scapegoat or substitute used by the Jewish people to atone for their sins. The Hebrew Bible [Leviticus 16: 21] describes how once a year, on the Day of Atonement, a goat was sent off into the wilderness, symbolically carrying away all the people's sins. Today, some Jewish people use a chicken. Before the Day of Atonement, people go to the market to buy a chicken. Before the chicken is killed, the butcher waves it over the heads of the people; their sins symbolically go into the chicken. The chicken is then killed as a substitute.

Christians use the word atonement to describe what Jesus's death on the cross accomplished for all time: the reconciliation (the making "at one") of God and humanity. Another word used is redemption. In the context of Christian belief, to redeem someone means to save them by freeing them from the power of sin and evil in their lives. Christians believe that Jesus redeemed people when he died on the cross. He paid the price for their sins. His rising from the dead showed that the power of sin and evil had been broken.

"Jesus is the One whom God raised to be on his right side, as leader and Saviour. Through him all people can change their hearts and lives and have their sins forgiven." [Acts 5: 31]

"If Christ has not been raised from death, then we have nothing to preach and you have nothing to believe." [1 Corinthians 15: 14]

7 (a) What do Christians mean by atonement?
(b) Explain why Christians think it was important for Jesus to die.

Gracious God

Jesus and his first followers were Jews. Their understanding of God came from the Hebrew Bible. In this unit you will find out what Jesus taught about the nature of God, and how Christians today think of God.

1 (a) How do you describe something you cannot see? For example, try writing a description of the wind. How difficult did you find it?
(b) How should a religious believer go about describing God, who cannot be physically seen? What kind of language is most appropriate for talking about God?

Christians use a variety of images when they talk about God, many from the Hebrew Bible (the Old Testament). As a Jew, Jesus knew the Hebrew Bible well and used many of the images of God contained in it. God is the creator [Genesis 1: 1; Deuteronomy 32: 6]. God protects as a father cares for his child [Deuteronomy 1: 31] and as a fortress protects a city [Psalm 18: 2]. Jesus used the term "Abba" [Mark 14: 36] – the equivalent of "Daddy", though it also carried the idea of authority. God is described as a mother who never forgets her children [Isaiah 49: 15] and who nurses her young children [Isaiah 66: 13]. God is a shepherd who cares for his flock [Psalm 23: 1]. God is also pictured as a king [I Timothy 6: 15] and a judge [1 Corinthians 4: 5].

One of the Christian descriptions of God is Creator. This is a representation of God creating Eve from Adam's rib [Genesis 2: 21-22].

In his teaching, Jesus told stories, like that of the Loving Father and His Two Sons (page 17), to help people understand God. The stories emphasise that God is merciful and forgiving. God is described in the Hebrew Bible as "a compassionate and gracious God, slow to anger, abounding in love and faithfulness" [Exodus 34: 6]. Gracious means full of grace – undeserved mercy and kindness. When they describe God as gracious, Christians mean that there is nothing that people can do to make God love them more, or less; God already loves people so much. Christianity is a celebration of God's grace.

❝Ask people what they must do to get to heaven and most reply, 'Be good'. Jesus's stories contradict that answer. All we must do is cry, 'Help!' God welcomes home anyone who will have him and, in fact, has made the first move already.❞ [Yancey, *What's so amazing about grace?*, Zondervan Publishing Company, 1997]

THE LOVING FATHER AND HIS TWO SONS [Luke 15: 11-32]

Once a man had two sons. The younger said to him: "Give me my share of the property now." The son sold the property and left home with the money. He spent it all on wild living. Then he had to find work and was given a job looking after pigs. No one gave him anything to eat. At last he came to his senses ... "All my father's hired workers have more than they can eat, and here I am about to starve!"

He decided to go home and say sorry to his father. He would ask for a job as one of his hired workers. He was still a long way from home when his father saw him and ran to meet him. "Father, I have sinned against God and against you. I am no longer fit to be called your son." But the father called his servants, saying "Let us celebrate with a feast!"

The elder son heard the sound of feasting and asked a servant what was happening. "Your brother has come home." The elder brother was so angry that he would not go into the house. He told his father: "Look, all these years I have worked for you like a slave. What have you given me? Not even a goat for me to have a feast with my friends!" "My son," the father replied, "you are always here with me, and everything I have is yours. But we had to celebrate and be happy, because your brother was dead, but now he is alive; he was lost, but now he has been found."

2 What strikes you as you read the story of the Loving Father and His Two Sons? What do you think about the behaviour of the sons? What do you think of the father? Was he a strong or a weak person?

3 In the story, the father represents God. How does the father show grace towards his younger son? Do you think he was right to do so? What does the story teach about the nature of God?

The artist who created this picture of the son who is forgiven entitled her work "Weeping for the Wiping of Grace". What do you understand by that title?

"Just as a person can be a mother, a sister, and a nurse, so you can also say that God is Father, Son, and Holy Spirit." [Carl]

God as Three in One – The Trinity

Christians talk about God as a Father who is creator of the universe and father of humankind [Genesis 1: 1]. They talk about God the Son: this is the person Jesus Christ. And they talk about God the Holy Spirit, who guides and comforts them. The idea of One God who makes Himself known in three persons is called the Trinity – "three in one".

Christians believe that the Holy Spirit is God's living presence with people today. It cannot be seen, so a number of images are used to describe it. The Holy Spirit is like wind – you cannot see it but you can see the results of its power. It is like water that gives life and cleanses. It is like fire that burns away things wrong in you. The Holy Spirit is also often shown as a dove, because it brings peace between people and God.

"Come, you people, let us adore God in three persons:
The Father in the Son, with the Holy Spirit.
For the Father from everlasting begete the Word,
Who shares his Kingdom and his eternity,
And the Holy Spirit is in the Father,
Glorified with the Son,
A single power,
A single essence,
A single godhead."
[*Great Vespers of Pentecost*]

Q

4 How does the painting show the Trinity?

5 What does the Russian Orthodox prayer, "Come, you people . . ." tell you about the Trinity?

6 Read the account of Jesus's baptism in Mark 1: 9-11. How is the Trinity shown at work in this passage?

A representation of the Trinity, painted in 1471. Which event in Jesus's life is this picture illustrating? What do you think the painter is saying about where God is in this event by (a) the position of the Father to the Son; (b) the presence of the Holy Spirit in the form of the dove?

UNIT FOUR

Salvation and eternal life

Christians believe that the aim of all life is to be at one with God in heaven. But how does a person get to heaven? In this unit you will be considering Jesus's teaching on this issue.

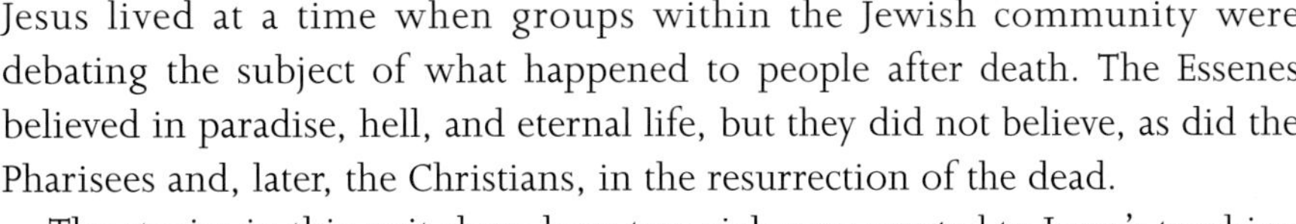

Jesus lived at a time when groups within the Jewish community were debating the subject of what happened to people after death. The Essenes believed in paradise, hell, and eternal life, but they did not believe, as did the Pharisees and, later, the Christians, in the resurrection of the dead.

The stories in this unit show how two rich men reacted to Jesus's teaching about salvation and eternal life. "Salvation" (being saved) refers to the idea of God saving people from eternal death, to be with Him in heaven. When Christians talk about eternal life, they are referring to life with God, which never ends.

JESUS AND ZACCHAEUS [Luke 19: 1-10]

Narrator: Jesus went on into Jericho and was passing through. There was a chief tax collector there named Zacchaeus, who was rich. He was trying to see who Jesus was, but he was little and could not see because of the crowd. So he ran ahead and climbed a sycamore tree to see Jesus, who was going to pass that way. When Jesus came to that place, he looked up.

Jesus: Hurry down, Zacchaeus, because I must stay in your house today.

Narrator: Zacchaeus hurried down and welcomed him with great joy. All the people who saw it started grumbling:

Grumbler: This man has gone as a guest to the home of a sinner!

Narrator: Zacchaeus stood up and said to the Lord:

Zacchaeus: Listen, sir! I will give half my belongings to the poor, and if I have cheated anyone, I will pay him back four times as much.

Jesus: Salvation has come to this house today, for this man, also, is a descendant of Abraham. The Son of Man came to seek and to save the lost.

Comments on the story

- Tax collectors were disliked and treated as outcasts because they collected money from their fellow Jews for the occupying Roman power. Respectable Jews did not mix with tax collectors, so Jesus was criticised as a Jew and as a teacher of the law for befriending Zacchaeus.
- The Hebrew word for "sycamore" means "rehabilitation". When Jesus called Zacchaeus to come with him, he was calling him to a new life, eternal life.
- In the Middle East eating a meal together is a sign of forgiveness.

1 Imagine that you were Zacchaeus. Write your diary account of meeting Jesus. Record your feelings before and after the meeting.

2 (a) Compare the story of Zacchaeus with the story of the rich man on page 20. How is the reaction of Zacchaeus to Jesus different from that of the rich man?
(b) Why do you think Zacchaeus reacted differently?

JESUS AND THE RICH MAN [Luke 18: 18-30]

Narrator: A Jewish leader asked Jesus:

Leader: Good Teacher, what must I do to receive eternal life?

Narrator: Jesus asked him:

Jesus: Why do you call me good? No one is good except God alone. You know the commandments: "Do not commit adultery; do not commit murder; do not steal; do not accuse anyone falsely; respect your father and your mother."

Leader: Ever since I was young, I have obeyed all these commandments.

Jesus: There is still one more thing you need to do. Sell all you have and give the money to the poor, and you will have riches in heaven; then come and follow me.

Narrator: But when the man heard this, he became very sad, because he was very rich. Jesus saw that he was sad.

Jesus: How hard it is for rich people to enter the Kingdom of God! It is much harder for a rich person to enter the Kingdom of God than for a camel to go through the eye of a needle.

Narrator: The people who heard him asked:

Person: Who, then, can be saved?

Jesus: What is impossible for man is possible for God.

Narrator: Then Peter said:

Peter: Look! We have left our homes to follow you.

Jesus: Yes, and I assure you that anyone who leaves home or wife or brothers or parents or children for the sake of the Kingdom of God will receive much more in this present age, and eternal life in the age to come.

Comments on the story

- In the Christian Bible the "Kingdom of God" is another phrase for the "Kingdom of Heaven".
- The camel was the largest animal in the land of Israel, and the eye of a needle is one of the smallest possible openings. Jesus is saying that even something that seems quite impossible to us is possible for God: if a person is willing to turn to God, God in his mercy will accept the person and help him or her to go the rest of the way.
- Jesus teaches that to enter the Kingdom of God you must want it more than anything else. A person must be willing to make a break with worldly things, and to sacrifice everything for God. The rich man became sad. It was a difficult decision to turn fully to God, and not to trust in his riches.
- There is a danger for wealthy people that they put so much trust in their riches, that they neglect to put their trust in God. Jesus drew attention to the need for everyone to put complete trust in God. He promised the rich man "treasure in heaven" for giving his wealth to the poor.

3 (a) In the story of the rich man, where do the commandments about adultery, murdering, stealing, etc., come from?

4 Imagine that you were an onlooker of the conversation between Jesus and the rich man. You are too far away to hear, but you can see their faces. What emotions would their faces express? From their expressions what do you think are the turning points in the conversation?

In both encounters with rich people Jesus teaches that all a person needs to do to receive salvation and enter eternal life is to turn back to God, to repent. God is gracious and will welcome the person with open arms. This turning back to God will also affect how people treat their fellows: they will care for the poor.

Life as a journey

A Russian Orthodox Christian icon shows a "Ladder to Heaven". Nadya explains:

"It is a vision of the Christian life as a journey towards heaven. Throughout our life we climb this ladder. Sometimes we climb two steps and fall back one, but we are still climbing. God is love, and He calls us to live a life of love. The ladder to heaven is a road of selfless love – the same love that drives you to go without your dinner to help a family who has no food at all."

Many Christians see their life as a journey, and describe their religion as a path along which they travel. One of the earliest names used for Christianity was simply "the Way" [Acts 19: 23 and 24: 22].

5 (a) In what ways is the image of life as a journey a useful one?
(b) The icon of the "Ladder to Heaven" shows devils trying to pull people off. What things in life pull people down?
(c) In what ways do people struggle in life?
(d) What is the goal of life, according to this icon?

This icon of the Ladder to Heaven (or "The Ladder of Climax") was painted in the 12th century.

UNIT FIVE

Christian worship

After the Resurrection, the "good news" about Jesus was spread throughout Asia Minor and Europe, by St Paul and other early Christian missionaries. Today Christians are found all over the world. Over the centuries the Christian Church has divided into many branches. They hold much in common, but express their beliefs and worship in different ways. This unit explores some of the different ways in which Christians respond to God in worship.

Worship is giving worth to something – celebrating its value. In Christian worship, people stand before God and celebrate His very existence.

❝Worship celebrates the beauty of God, the sheer fact of His existence. It could be described as doing something beautiful for God. We believe that when we worship we are in the presence of angels and all the heavenly host. At times worship is like being in the middle of a beautiful theatrical set. At other times it has the quietness and intimacy of a lover's kiss.❞ [Richard, a Greek Orthodox Christian]

Christians worship God in many ways. Worship can be a private activity, when the person spends time alone with God, in prayer and praise. It can be a public activity, when Christians meet together as the "body of Christ" at work in the world. Public worship can be liturgical – that is, it follows a set form, approved by the church and written down in a prayer book; or non-liturgical – when it is more informal and does not follow set words.

Most Christians meet for worship on a Sunday, because this is the day when Jesus rose from the dead. Christians celebrate his victory over the grave and the hope of their own resurrection. A central part of the worship is prayer.

❝We believe that when we pray we are standing before God our Maker.❞ [Kelly, a Roman Catholic]

❝The way we worship has been the same for hundreds of years. Whichever Orthodox Church I go to in the world, I know that I will be able to understand what is happening because it will be the same service which has been approved by our tradition. The Liturgy is our common prayer. The words that we use have been carefully chosen. They help to create a feeling of holiness. During our worship we use many symbolic rituals which are full of meaning. They help us to worship with all our senses – the beautiful music which sounds like angels, the smell of the incense which reminds us of our prayers going to heaven, and the icons which are like windows into heaven.❞ [Nadya, a Russian Orthodox Christian]

Orthodox Christian worshippers in Uspensky Cathedral, Helsinki, Finland.

Worshippers in a United Reformed church in London.

"We worship because we want to praise God for all his goodness. We do not follow a set form of words but want to be free to sing and dance to God. By music we express our feelings to God. In our prayers we speak out loud and tell God what is in our hearts. In our church we celebrate God's love for us with music and joyful clapping." [Mike, a Baptist]

1 Why did Sunday become the main day for Christian worship?

2 (a) What do you think Kelly means when she says that "when we pray we are standing before God our Maker"? What feelings might she have when she prays?
(b) Christians pray in many ways: for instance, they may kneel, stand, close their eyes, use rosary beads. Choose two of these ways and write down reasons that you think Christians might give for praying in those ways.

3 (a) Which of the photographs in this unit is closest to your idea of worship? Explain why.
(b) Choose one emotion to go with each photograph. Explain your choice.

4 (a) Write down four reasons why Nadya thinks liturgical worship is important. What does she mean by "symbolic rituals"?
(b) Write down four reasons why Mike likes non-liturgical worship.

On holiday at the Othona Community in Dorset, these Christians are sharing Holy Communion, each offering another the bread and the wine.

Holy Communion

Holy Communion is the most important service for many churches. It commemorates the Last Supper that Jesus had with his disciples before he died [Matthew 26: 21-29; Mark 14: 22-25; Luke 22: 14-20]. At that supper Jesus commanded his followers to remember his death by breaking bread and drinking wine. Jesus said that the broken bread was his body that was to be broken on the cross. The wine was his blood that was to be shed.

Roman Catholics, Orthodox Christians, and some Anglicans believe that the bread and wine become the actual body and blood of Jesus when the priest prays over them. Protestant Christians (for example, Methodists, Baptists, United Reformed, and many Anglicans) believe that the bread and wine do not change but are symbols of the body and blood of Jesus. Some Anglicans call the Holy Communion service "Eucharist" (meaning thanksgiving). Roman Catholics call it "Mass". Orthodox Christians call it the "Divine Liturgy". Some Anglicans and many non-conformist churches call it "the Lord's Supper".

5 Explain the importance of Holy Communion for Christians.

UNIT SIX

All you need is love

Jesus taught that people should be able to identify who his followers were by the way that they loved other people. But what did he mean? In this unit you will consider what love is, and learn about the Christian ethic of love.

The ethic of love

“I give you a new commandment: love one another; as I have loved you, so you are to love one another.” [Jesus, John 13: 34]

“If Christianity has to be defined in one word, then this word would be ‘love’.” [Mother Teresa]

THE GREAT COMMANDMENT TO LOVE GOD AND YOUR NEIGHBOUR [Mark 12: 28-34]

Narrator: A teacher of the Law came to him with a question:
Lawyer: Which commandment is the most important of all?
Narrator: Jesus replied:
Jesus: The most important one is this, “Listen, Israel! The Lord our God is the only Lord. Love the Lord your God with all your heart, with all your soul, with all your mind, and with all your strength.” The second most important commandment is this: “Love your neighbour as you love yourself.” There is no other commandment more important than these two.
Lawyer: Well done, Teacher! It is true, as you say, that only the Lord is God and that there is no other god but he.
Narrator: Jesus noticed how wise his answer was, and so he told him:
Jesus: You are not far from the Kingdom of God.

The love relationship between God and people is at the heart of Christian moral thinking. Christians believe that there is nothing people can do to stop God from loving them: God loves unconditionally and is always willing to forgive people for their wrongdoing if they are truly sorry and turn back to Him. Jesus called people to place God at the centre of their lives. He also pointed out that people's love of God would show itself in their love for each other.

Christianity does not demand that people succeed at loving. It does demand that people should passionately try to love and care. Jesus's teachings are challenging, requiring self-sacrifice.

The Salvation Army is a Christian organisation founded in 1865 and devoted to helping the poor and needy. Putting money in a charity box is quickly done, and can be done without much thought. How can someone giving money to a charity make the gift feel more like an act of loving his or her neighbour?

“Love your neighbour as yourself.” [Mark 12: 31]

“Do not judge and you will not be judged.” [Matthew 7: 1]

WHAT DOES IT MEAN TO LOVE YOUR NEIGHBOUR? THE PARABLE OF THE GOOD SAMARITAN [Luke 10: 25-37]

A teacher of the Law came to Jesus and asked: "How do I get eternal life?" Jesus asked him what the scriptures said and the man answered: "Love God with all your heart [Deuteronomy 6: 5] and love your neighbour as you love yourself [Leviticus 19: 18]." Jesus said he was right. But the man asked: "Who is my neighbour?" Jesus told this story:

Bandits attacked a traveller along the desert stretches of the Jerusalem-Jericho road. They stripped him, beat him, and left him for dead.

A Priest saw him and passed by as far away as possible. A Levite saw him and passed by as far away as possible. A Samaritan saw him and stopped.

The Samaritan cleaned and disinfected the man's wounds, put him on his donkey, and brought him to an inn. He gave the owner two denarii [silver coins] and promised to pay the rest when he returned.

Then Jesus asked: "Which of the three men do you think was a neighbour to the man who was attacked?"

1 (a) What answer would you have given to Jesus's question at the end of the Good Samaritan story?
(b) What answer did the teacher of the Law give? Look it up in Luke 10: 37.

Comments on the story

- Because the man's attackers stripped him naked, passers-by would not be able to tell from his clothing whether he was a Jew or a Gentile – so they would not know if he was a neighbour or not.
- The Priest and the Levite were Jewish religious leaders who were expected to keep the Law of God. The Law demanded that they love their neighbours. They believed this to mean only other Jews. A non-Jew was not considered a neighbour.
- The victim probably looked dead, at least from the other side of the road. The Priest, returning to Jericho after duty in the Temple in Jerusalem, would be in a state of ritual purity. Touching a corpse would destroy his purity. He was not allowed to come closer than five feet to a corpse.
- Samaritans had the same code of purity as Jews, so the Samaritan might also have had reason to walk by. However, the Samaritan is moved by compassion to help the man.
- The Samaritans were of mixed race, descended from Jews who were left behind rather than taken into exile after the Assyrian conquest of the land of Israel in 722 BCE. These Jews then intermarried with outsiders who settled among them. When the Jews returned from exile and rebuilt the Temple in Jerusalem, the Samaritans were not allowed to take part and therefore built their own temple on Mount Gerizim. There was bitter hostility between Samaritans and Jews in the time of Jesus.

Taking care of a leprosy patient in the Amazon, Brazil. This picture is of a Christian nun showing love to her neighbour. What do you think "neighbour" means in this context? It is obviously not just referring to next-door neighbours. Are there neighbours you would find difficult to love? Explain why.

Loving your enemies

What about enemies? Do they have to be loved too? In a passage of the Bible known as the Sermon on the Mount Jesus teaches his disciples:

"You have heard that it was said, 'Love your friends, hate your enemies.' But now I tell you: love your enemies and pray for those who persecute you, so that you may become the sons of your Father in heaven. You must be perfect – just as your Father in heaven is perfect." [Matthew 5: 43-48]

2 Is Jesus's teaching about loving your enemies realistic?

ST PAUL'S CONCEPT OF LOVE [1 Corinthians 13]

If I have no love, I am nothing.
Love is patient and kind;
it is not jealous or conceited or proud;
love is not ill-mannered or selfish or irritable;
love does not keep a record of wrongs;
love is not happy with evil, but is happy with the truth.
Love never gives up;
And its faith, hope and patience never fail.
Love is eternal.

3 Many couples choose to have St Paul's description of love read at their marriage. Why do you think this is? How would their relationship be affected if they lived according to these words? Give practical examples.

UNIT SEVEN

To forgive or not to forgive?

What does it mean to forgive somebody? Is it always right to forgive? In this unit you will learn what Jesus taught about forgiveness.

1. Are there things which you would find very difficult to forgive? For example, could you forgive someone who cheated you, or someone who hurt someone you loved?
2. Read the news story about the murder of Philip Lawrence. If you were a member of his family, could you forgive his killer?

Headmaster stabbed to death at his own school gates

Philip Lawrence, head of St George's School in London, died from a single stab wound after rushing to help a 13-year-old pupil who was being bullied outside the school gates.

Mrs Lawrence said that she had no hatred towards her husband's killer. "Learco Chindamo killed my husband and, in doing so, he not only destroyed my family, he also destroyed his own future. My heart goes out to him and his family. People say that some lives are beyond redemption, but I do not believe that. If I did, I think I would just feel like giving up completely." [December 1995]

In October 1996, Frances Lawrence, widow of the murdered headmaster Philip Lawrence, launched a national movement to tackle violence and promote good citizenship.

Consider the following descriptions of what forgiveness means:

"If you forgive someone you are saying 'I will carry on the relationship with them even though they have hurt me'." [Jessie]

"Forgiveness means to bear no grudges." [Andrea]

"To forgive does not mean to forget. You cannot always forget what has happened but you can start again with the person." [Mufid]

"It is important to forgive if you are not to become bitter yourself." [James]

"You have to find a way of hating the sin and loving the sinner." [Michael, whose 6-year-old son was killed by a drunk driver]

"Being forgiven is like being healed." [Craig]

"To forgive oneself – No, that doesn't work: we have to be forgiven. But we can only believe this is possible if we ourselves can forgive." [Dag Hammarskjöld, Secretary-General of the United Nations, 1953-61]

"Once a woman has forgiven her man, she must not reheat his sins for the breakfast table." [Marlene Dietrich]

"If we cannot forgive one another, we have nothing to tell the world." [Rev. Chuck Kopp]

"If you refuse to forgive a person, and you continue to hold grudges, you are binding yourself to that person. You become locked in an emotional prison, and refuse to take the key of forgiveness out of your own pocket to unlock the door." [J. C. Arnold, quoted in *I Tell You A Mystery*, Plough Publishing House, 1996]

JESUS'S TEACHING ON FORGIVENESS

One of the most difficult things that Jesus commanded his followers to do was to forgive one another. Jesus often taught about forgiveness.

- He taught his followers to pray, "Forgive us the wrongs we have done, as we forgive the wrongs that others have done to us." [Matthew 5: 12]
- He said: "Do not take revenge on someone who wrongs you." [Matthew 5: 39]
- He said: "Love your enemies and pray for those who persecute you." [Matthew 5: 44]
- As well as speaking about forgiveness, he showed in his own life what it means to forgive. Of his murderers, he said: "Forgive them, Father! They don't know what they are doing." [Luke 23: 34]

Q

3 (a) In the story of "The Confession", what do you think of the priest's reaction to the Red Army soldier? What personal qualities must the priest have had?
(b) Do you think he has a right to forgive the man?

4 Should a person still be punished even though he has been forgiven?

5 "It is better to forgive and forget than to resent and remember." Do you agree?

THE CONFESSION

This true story took place during the Spanish Civil War (1936-39). It starkly illustrates the challenge of Jesus's teaching that we should love and forgive even our enemies.

Narrator: A troop of National soldiers had just cleared a village of their enemies, the Red Army, when they found, in a corner of a wall, a badly wounded Red. The wounded man feebly raised a hand and stammered:

Red: A priest! Fetch me a priest.

Narrator: The soldiers found and brought a priest to him.

Priest: You want to confess?

Red: Yes, I want to confess. But tell me, are you the priest of this place?

Priest: Yes I am.

Red: My God!

Narrator: It was a long time before the priest left the dying soldier. His hair was soaked with sweat and his face white, as he returned to the waiting patrol.

Priest: Brothers, take the wounded man into the nearby house so that he does not die in the street.

Narrator: When the soldiers approached the man, he raised himself a little and signed to them.

Red: He forgave me!

Soldier: Why shouldn't he forgive? That's his business.

Red: [groaning] You don't know what I have done. On my own I have killed thirty-two priests. In every village I forced my way first to the priest's house. I did it here too. The priest was not in, but I found his father and his two brothers. I asked them where the priest was. They refused to betray him. So I shot all three. Do you understand? The priest who heard my confession: I killed his father and his brothers . . . And yet he forgave me.

[adapted from Lefevre, *Hundred Stories,* St Paul's Publications, 1991]

Government soldiers firing on rebels in the Spanish Civil War (1936-39).

Jesus taught that the gracious God forgives those who do wrong, no matter how bad they have been. All that is necessary is for people to repent and turn back to God, to ask for forgiveness. Jesus taught his disciples to be like God, to forgive others.

THE PARABLE OF THE UNFORGIVING SERVANT [Matthew 18: 21-35]

Narrator: Peter came to Jesus and asked:

Peter: Lord, if my brother keeps on sinning against me, how many times do I have to forgive him? Seven times?

Narrator: Jesus answered:

Jesus: No, not seven times, but seventy times seven, because the Kingdom of Heaven is like this. Once a king had just begun to check on his servants' accounts when one of them was brought in who owed him millions of pounds. The servant could not repay this money, so the king ordered him to be sold as a slave, with his wife and his children and all that he had, in order to pay the debt. The servant fell on his knees before the king. He begged:

Servant 1: Be patient with me and I will pay you everything!

Jesus: The king felt sorry for him, so he forgave him the debt and let him go. Then the man met one of his fellow-servants who owed him a few pounds. He grabbed him and started choking him. He said.

Servant 1: [roughly] Pay back what you owe me!

Jesus: His fellow servant fell down and begged him:

Servant 2: [pleading] Be patient with me, and I will pay you back!

Jesus: But he refused. Instead, he had him thrown into jail until he could pay the debt. When the other servants saw what had happened, they were very upset and went to the king and told him everything. The king called the servant in.

King: You worthless slave! I forgave you the whole amount you owed me, just because you asked me to. You should have had mercy on your fellow-servant, just as I had mercy on you.

Jesus: The king was very angry and sent the servant to jail to be punished until he paid back the whole amount.

Narrator: And Jesus concluded:

Jesus: [looking round] That is how my Father in Heaven will treat every one of you unless you forgive your brother from your heart.

6 When Peter asks Jesus how many times a person should forgive, Jesus replies "seventy times seven" [Matthew 18: 22]. Jesus did not mean a specific number of times: he was telling Peter that he must always forgive. Do you think this is (a) a good ideal to aim at, or (b) an unrealistic goal? Give your reasons.

Comments on the story

- Two Christian themes are present in this parable. (1) God is just and will see that justice is done. The servant who does not show mercy is punished, in order to educate him. (2) God is forgiving and merciful and is willing to accept anyone back who admits their wrongdoing and asks for forgiveness.
- The parable repeats a theme which is elsewhere in Jesus's teaching: God relates to people in the same way that they relate to each other. This idea is found in the Lord's prayer, which Jesus taught: "Forgive us our sins as we forgive those who sin against us." [Matthew 6: 12]

THE WOMAN CAUGHT IN ADULTERY [John 8: 2-11]

Narrator: Early the next morning Jesus went back to the Temple. All the people gathered round him and he sat down and began to teach them. The teachers of the Law and the Pharisees brought in a woman who had been caught committing adultery, and they made her stand before them all.

Pharisee: Teacher, this woman was caught in the very act of committing adultery.

Lawyer: In our Law, Moses commanded that such a woman must be stoned to death.

Pharisee: [To Jesus] Now, what do you say?

Narrator: They said this to trap Jesus, so that they could accuse him. But he bent over and wrote on the ground with his finger. [Long pause] As they stood there asking him questions, he straightened himself up.

Jesus: Whichever one of you has committed no sin may throw the first stone at her.

Narrator: Then he bent over again and wrote on the ground. When they heard this, they all left, one by one, the older ones first. Jesus was left alone with the woman still standing there. He straightened himself up.

Jesus: [to the woman] Where are they? Is there no one left to condemn you?

Woman: No one, sir.

Jesus: Well, then. I do not condemn you either. Go, but do not sin again.

Comments on the story

- The Jewish Law taught: "If a man commits adultery with the wife of his neighbour, both the adulterer and the adulteress shall be put to death" [Leviticus 20: 10]. There is no record of this punishment being used.
- Jesus taught that all people stand in need of forgiveness and therefore should show mercy and forgiveness to others. He warned his followers: "The measure you give will be the measure you get" [Matthew 7: 2].
- Jesus does not drag up the past. Instead, he calls the woman to a new way of living: "Go, but do not sin again."

Some Christian churches have a ceremony called "Believer's Baptism" for adults (like this woman in Zanzibar) who have decided to follow Jesus. The baptism is a symbol of their old life, without Jesus, being washed away. In the same way as Jesus gives a new start to the people in the stories here, "Believer's Baptism" has the sense of a new beginning.

Jesus sent his disciples out to teach and heal people, in the same way as he did, by faith in the power of God. Some Christian ministers use faith healing. Here Dr Rudy Trigo prays over a woman in Negros, in the Philippines, 1996.

THE POWER OF FORGIVENESS: JESUS HEALS A PARALYSED MAN [Matthew 9: 1-8]

Narrator: Jesus got into the boat and went back across the lake to his own town, where some people brought to him a paralysed man, lying on a bed. When Jesus saw how much faith they had, he said to the paralysed man:

Jesus: Courage, my son! Your sins are forgiven.

Narrator: Some teachers of the Law said to themselves:

Lawyer: This man is speaking blasphemy!

Narrator: Perceiving what they were thinking, Jesus said:

Jesus: Why are you thinking such evil things? Is it easier to say, "Your sins are forgiven" or to say "Get up and walk"? I will prove to you, then, that the Son of Man has authority on earth to forgive sins.

Narrator: So Jesus said to the paralysed man:

Jesus: Get up. Pick up your bed, and go home!

Narrator: The man got up and went home. When the people saw it, they were afraid, and praised God for giving such authority to men.

Comments on the story

- In this story Jesus goes further than the Jewish Law. In the Old Testament only God has the authority to forgive people. However, this account ends with God giving humans authority to forgive each other.
- The passage contains a subtle play on words. The term "Son of Man" can mean two things: (a) a heavenly being, like Jesus; or (b) humanity. When Jesus says the Son of Man has authority to forgive, he is saying that humanity has the authority to forgive.

7 What was Jesus trying to teach people in (a) his meeting with the adulteress, and (b) his healing of the paralysed man?

CHAPTER

Buddhism

UNIT ONE

What makes you feel peaceful and fulfilled? Have you ever wondered why there is so much suffering in the world? How do we escape suffering and find peace? The Buddha asked these questions and discovered some answers. In this unit you will identify the issues at the heart of Buddhism, and consider your own answers.

Where do I find peace?

1 (a) In groups, discuss what you think are the most important things in life.
(b) What is happiness? How long can you stay happy?
(c) What is the difference between happiness and peace?

2 (a) Do you ever wonder why there is so much suffering in the world? In what ways have you yourselves suffered? (Think about different forms of suffering: physical, emotional, mental, spiritual.)
(b) How do you explain why all this suffering happens?
(c) Are all forms of suffering painful?

Just because we are at a party, we don't always feel in a happy, party mood.

Outer and inner worlds

When people think about what makes them happy, they often think of external things such as earning a good wage, or having a large house and a healthy family. However, many people achieve an outer happiness in those ways, and yet feel unsettled and unfulfilled inside. You can probably think of some famous people who appear to have everything – large houses, fast cars, luxury holidays, and fame – but who apparently remain hurt and unfulfilled: their relationships do not last; some resort to using drugs to fill the "empty" feeling.

Happiness is a feeling we like and seek. Notice how it is often connected with getting what we want. Someone says something we like to hear, and we feel happy. The sun shines and we feel happy. Similarly, unhappiness is often associated with not getting what we want. Notice, too, how happiness lasts for a while and then changes. Like nearly all feelings, including unhappiness, it is impermanent.

The worldly values by which happiness is so often measured – including power, beauty, and wealth – are impermanent too. Each has its opposite and exists only in the absence of that opposite. Each depends on things being a certain way. Wealth does not last, and when it finishes there is poverty. Because wealth can change to poverty so quickly, relying on wealth does not bring inner happiness or peace. The same is true of all worldly values.

Inner happiness is something different. People who are happy inside are often called "content" or "at peace". They have found a meaning and purpose to life.

Buddhist nuns listen to the teaching of the Dalai Lama, speaking in 1998 at Bodh Gaya in India, the site of the Buddha's enlightenment. Learning and thinking about Buddhist teachings seems to give these nuns a quiet sense of direction.

The Buddhist remedy

Buddhism places importance on achieving inner contentment or peace. Such contentment or peace does not depend on the outside, material world. This external world, where things do not last, is an unsafe place; it is not peaceful. Real inner peace is only realised by understanding this, by investigating the nature of impermanence. Buddhism offers a lifestyle and a path of mental development for people to achieve inner peace in this way.

The historical Buddha, Siddattha Gotama, is likened to a doctor who examined the state of the patient, the world. He realised that the world is filled with suffering – by which he meant something more than physical suffering. The Pali word he used was "dukkha", which can be translated as "unsatisfactoriness".

Like a doctor, the Buddha went on to prescribe a cure for this suffering and to show people how to reach true peace. The word he used for this peace was "enlightenment". "Buddha" is not a name but a title, meaning "the enlightened (or awakened) one". The Buddha taught that the way to enlightenment is through an inward journey – by taking the medicine of mind training. (See pages 38-39 on meditation.)

“This body of yours is just a temporary shelter. This world is nothing to rely on – it's an endless round of disturbance and trouble, pleasures and pain. There's no real peace to be found in the world. Our real home is inner peace.” [Ajahn Chah, *Our Real Home*, Amaravati Publications, 1989]

A POISONED ARROW

Imagine that you have been shot with a poisoned arrow. You are lying on the ground and becoming weaker and weaker as your life-blood drains from you. What do you do? Do you look at the arrow, examine from where it might have come and who might be trying to kill you? This is the likely response of the philosopher. Or do you pull out the arrow immediately? This is the Buddhist way.

3 Explain why Buddhists would say that happiness does not depend on material success.

4 (a) What does the example of "A poisoned arrow" (which comes from the Buddha's teachings) tell you about Buddhism?
(b) In what ways have all of us been shot with the poisoned arrow of suffering?

UNIT TWO

Three precious jewels

Buddhists say that, to become a Buddhist, the first thing to do is to take refuge in Buddha, Dhamma, Sangha, by reciting and contemplating the formula:
"I go to the Buddha for refuge.
I go to the Dhamma for refuge.
I go to the Sangha for refuge."
In this unit you will learn about these three refuges, which are also known as "precious jewels".

"A refuge is a place of safety. Today many people take refuge in their houses and bank accounts. They try and establish worldly security. But this is taking refuge in something which doesn't last. We take refuge in that which offers security: Buddha, Dhamma, Sangha. By taking the refuges again and again we remind ourselves to seek safety in these things." [Ajahn Chah, *Our Real Home*, Amaravati Publications, 1989]

1 What does it mean to take refuge in something?

2 (a) Do you agree that many people take refuge in their bank accounts and houses? Why do they do this? (b) What else do people take refuge in?

This Tibetan Buddhist tanka (a painting used for teaching and meditation) shows the three refuges or jewels – Buddha, Dhamma, and Sangha. The Buddha is holding the pearl of wisdom, and scenes of his past lives are shown in the outer ring around him.

Refuge in the Buddha

The word "Buddha" is sometimes explained as "the one who knows" or "the one who is awake" to the way things are in the world. When Buddhists take refuge in the Buddha, this does not mean that they are placing their trust in one historical man who lived two and a half thousand years ago. It means that they are taking refuge in wisdom, in that which is wise in the world. Doing so reminds them to be wise, alert, and awake. At the heart of a Buddhist's life is meditation – the means by which people awaken. For Buddhists, it is not learning at university which leads to wisdom. Wisdom is achieved by meditation: reflecting on and learning from life, studying the true nature of this world.

THE REAL BUDDHA

A monk from the West went to Thailand to learn from the Buddhist teacher Ajahn Chah. After a time he asked to leave, since he found monastic life hard and started to find fault with all the other monks, including his teacher. He said to Ajahn Chah, "Even you don't seem so enlightened." Ajahn Chah laughed at this. "It's a good thing I don't appear to be enlightened to you," he said, "because if I fit your model of enlightenment you would be caught looking for Buddha outside yourself. It's not out there – it's in your heart." The monk bowed and returned to his meditation hut to look for the real Buddha.

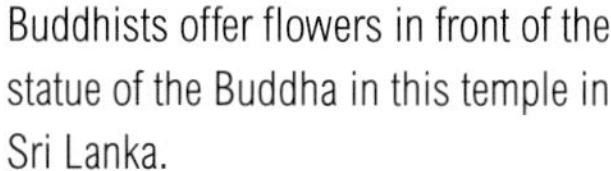
Buddhists offer flowers in front of the statue of the Buddha in this temple in Sri Lanka.

3 (a) What does it mean to take refuge in the Buddha?
(b) What is the story of "The real Buddha" teaching?

Refuge in the Dhamma

The Dhamma is the Buddha's teachings, on how to be free from suffering and how to be loving and wise and filled with compassion. When they take refuge in the Dhamma, Buddhists are not just referring to a ready-made set of ideas or beliefs. They are experiencing those ideas as their own and realising them as the truth, here and now. It encourages them to awaken to the way things are; to live an awakened life.

Refuge in the Sangha

The Sangha means a group or community. In many Buddhist monasteries the community is made up of monks (bhikkhus) and nuns (bhikkhunis). A bhikkhu is someone who seeks the truth. Taking refuge in the Sangha means finding safety in being part of a group which is committed to realising the truth about the way things are, and which practises compassion – doing good and refraining from evil.

4 (a) List different types of knowledge.
(b) Do you know anyone who you think is wise? What makes this person wise? What is the difference between knowing information – the kind of knowledge that you can learn at college – and being wise?
(c) What does taking refuge in the Dhamma mean?

Worship

In their worship, Buddhists show respect for the Three Refuges. They bring offerings of flowers (representing the Sangha), which are fresh today but will soon fade and die, just like ourselves; candles (representing the Dhamma), which give light just as the Buddha's teachings give truth and wisdom; and incense (representing the Buddha), whose sweet-smelling smoke is formless and unbound, like the qualities of the Buddha.

UNIT THREE

Nothing lasts forever

The Buddha's teaching shows people one way of looking at life. It is based on the understanding that there is nothing in this world that lasts forever. Everything – including yourself – is subject to change. This affects the way a Buddhist approaches all aspects of life.

The Three Marks of Existence are a summary of the Buddha's teaching.

Mark 1: Anicca. Everything changes

Everything in the world in which we live changes. Nothing lasts forever. The Buddhist scriptures use a variety of images to illustrate this, as in the Diamond Sutra (below). Buddhism teaches that, since everything changes, it is dangerous to become attached to anything or to count anything as permanent.

This sandcastle, like everything in the world, will not last forever.

“As stars, a fault of vision, as a lamp,
A mockshow, dew drops, or a bubble,
A dream, a lightning flash, or cloud,
So one should view what is conditioned.”
[From the Diamond Sutra, in *Buddhist Wisdom Books*, George Allen & Unwin, 1953]

“The Buddha's teaching is a very simple one. What could be more simple than 'what is born must die'?”
[Ajahn Sumedho, *Now is the Knowing*, Amaravati Publications, 1989]

1 How do you think the teaching about Anicca might affect a Buddhist's attitude towards (a) money and possessions, (b) relationships?

Mark 2: Dukkha. Life is unsatisfactory

Realising that everything changes, one can see that becoming attached to any “thing” will only bring suffering. Understanding this offers a way of ending suffering. The Buddha's teaching on suffering is contained in the Four Noble Truths:

1. *Dukkha (suffering/unsatisfactoriness) is part of everyday life.*
   Everyone knows this. (When a doctor wrote a book starting with the words, “Life is difficult”, it became a number-one bestseller!) The Buddha taught that this obvious truth needs to be understood.

2. *Dukkha has a cause, which is craving.*
   Do you find it difficult to do nothing? Do you always need to be stimulated? What do you chase after – shopping, eating, television, computers? The Buddha taught that following craving fuels dukkha, as wood fuels a fire. The problem is that the fire consumes what it feeds on but is never satisfied. The Buddha spoke of people as being “ablaze with desire”.

3. *The end of dukkha comes as a result of the end of craving.*

4. *There is a way leading to the end of dukkha: it is the Eightfold Path.*

Above the entrance to a Buddhist monastery in Bhutan, an eight-spoked wheel, a symbol of the Eightfold Path, rests on a lotus flower, a symbol of enlightenment.

In the Eightfold Path the Buddha laid out a framework for individual development: themes for contemplation and suggestions for living a good life. Following this path leads to freedom from suffering. The path can be divided into three main elements: wisdom, morality, and mental development (or meditation). The eight steps of the path are:

1. Right Understanding } wisdom
2. Right Attitude
3. Right Speech } morality
4. Right Action
5. Right Livelihood
6. Right Effort } mental development
7. Right Awareness
8. Right Concentration

Mark 3: Anatta. Not self

A lot of people live very much as if they are their habits, thoughts, feelings, and memories. But notice how each of these changes. There is nothing about you that stays the same. Even your so-called personality changes throughout life. This is "anatta": there is no such thing as a permanent self that stays the same.

"Buddhists talk about living skilfully, in a wise way. If you recognise the truth of anatta – that you are not your habits and feelings, that all these things are changing – you do not feel the need to act out of your habits. Instead, you should live skilfully: responding in a mindful way. Being caught in habits and feelings is like being caught up in a fire. The skilful thing to do is to escape the fire. We do this by following the Eightfold Path." [Christine]

The precepts

All Buddhists observe five precepts to help them develop Right Speech, Action, and Livelihood (from the Eightfold Path). These precepts are not "rules from above", but are tools for enlightenment.

1. I will not harm living beings.
2. I will not take what is not given.
3. I will avoid irresponsible and selfish sexual activity.
4. I will avoid using words in incorrect ways.
5. I will not take drugs or drink that confuse the mind.

"We're not being moral because we're afraid of being immoral. We choose to do this and rise up to that which is noble, good, kind and generous." [Ajahn Sumedho, *The Way It Is*, Amaravati Publications]

2 What is a habit? Do you have any habits? What do people mean by "good" and "bad" habits?

3 Which emotions do you feel most often: love, anger, jealousy, greed, kindness? Are you ever caught unaware by an emotion? For example, are you ever surprised at suddenly feeling angry when someone "presses the wrong button" inside you?

4 The Buddha said: "Refrain from what is bad, do good, and purify the heart." Taking into account the five precepts, give examples of what it might mean to (a) refrain from what is bad (for example, not to kill animals for food); (b) do good; and (c) purify the heart.

UNIT FOUR

Calm the heart and investigate the mind

Meditation is very important in Buddhism, for it was while the Buddha was meditating that he experienced enlightenment. He realised his own true nature and the nature of reality. He taught his followers many different techniques of meditation so that they might share this realisation. His teachings always emphasise the "here and now" nature of reality. Meditation is a tool used to become awakened to the present moment.

"Yesterday is a memory.
Tomorrow is the unknown.
Now is the knowing."
[Venerable Ajahn Sumedho, *Now is the Knowing*, Amaravati Publications, 1989]

1 Try sitting very still for five minutes. What does it feel like? What did you notice happening?

Meditation

Buddhists meditate to bring about clarity of mind. Seen through a dirty window, everything looks grey, grimy, and ugly. Meditation is a way of cleaning the window, purifying the mind, allowing things to come up into consciousness, and letting them go. Meditation is about awareness, clear seeing. In meditation Buddhists observe, they become aware and awake – knowing that whatever arises passes away. This kind of meditation is what Buddhists mean when they say that they take refuge in the Buddha.

A statue of the Buddha in Thailand. The statue represents the Buddha meditating. His hand touching the ground is a symbol of his enlightenment.

"In meditation we are training the mind. At first we train our mind to be still – to stop rushing about, being distracted by everything around it. One useful way of doing this is to watch the breath. We don't try and change it by breathing harder. Instead, we just note the gentle rhythm of the breath. At first the mind wanders off. Once we become aware that we have wandered we gently return to the breath. This focussing of the mind, calming and being still is called samatha." [Venerable Ajahn Sumedho, *Now is the Knowing*, Amaravati Publications, 1989]

A laser beam is a good analogy for samatha meditation. Whereas an ordinary beam of light spreads out and is relatively powerless, a laser beam is focused and concentrated and can cut through steel.

IN NEED OF TRAINING

We must train our mind as a farmer trains his cow. The cow is our thinking. The farmer is the meditator. The mind is like the cow who wants to eat the wheat harvest. When you tend a cow you let it go free but you keep watch over it. You put a fence around the field. If it goes too close to the wheat fields you restrain it with the fence. The mind is like this. It needs to be trained.

“Watch over the mind as a parent watches over a child. Protect it from its own foolishness.” [Ajahn Chah, *A Still Forest Pool*, Theosophical Publishing House of Wheaton]

“In meditation we are observing and investigating our mind. We are looking into and seeing the nature of whatever we experience, in order to learn about ourselves. When our mind is calm we can then investigate it. If we watch the mind as though it was a film projected on a screen we see how everything changes. We watch thoughts come into the mind and then slip away. We observe how emotions arise in us – boredom, anger etc., and we watch them go away. Nothing lasts forever. We are not trying to control the mind, just observe it. This observing and investigation is called vipassana.” [Venerable Ajahn Sumedho, *Now is the Knowing*, Amaravati Publications, 1989]

“Learning to meditate is a bit like learning to play a musical instrument: it requires determination, commitment, and daily practice.” [Damien Keown, *Buddhism: A Very Short Introduction*, OUP, 1996]

2 Explain the difference between samatha and vipassana meditation.

3 Meditation has been likened to walking into a raging storm as we observe our heart and mind. What do you think this means?

In London, two and a half thousand years later, people learn to meditate in the way the Buddha taught.

UNIT FIVE

Caught in a fire

The Tibetan Wheel of Life is a summary of Buddhist teaching (the Dhamma). It illustrates how people are locked into an endless cycle of suffering, death, and rebirth. There are two ways of understanding this wheel. First, it describes the six realms into which people are reborn. Second, it acts like a mirror, reflecting back what each person is like inside.

Buddhists believe that all life is locked in a cycle of birth, death, and rebirth, called samsara – which means literally "endless wandering". When someone reaches enlightenment, then he or she escapes from the cycle. The Tibetan Wheel of Life illustrates the Buddhist idea of samsara.

Yama: the Lord of Death

At the top of the Wheel is Yama, the Lord of Impermanence, Change, and Death. He holds the Wheel in his fangs and is actually eating it. This powerfully shows that each person caught in the Wheel is in Yama's trap. Inside the Wheel is a sad place to be. The Buddha taught a way of becoming free from the Wheel.

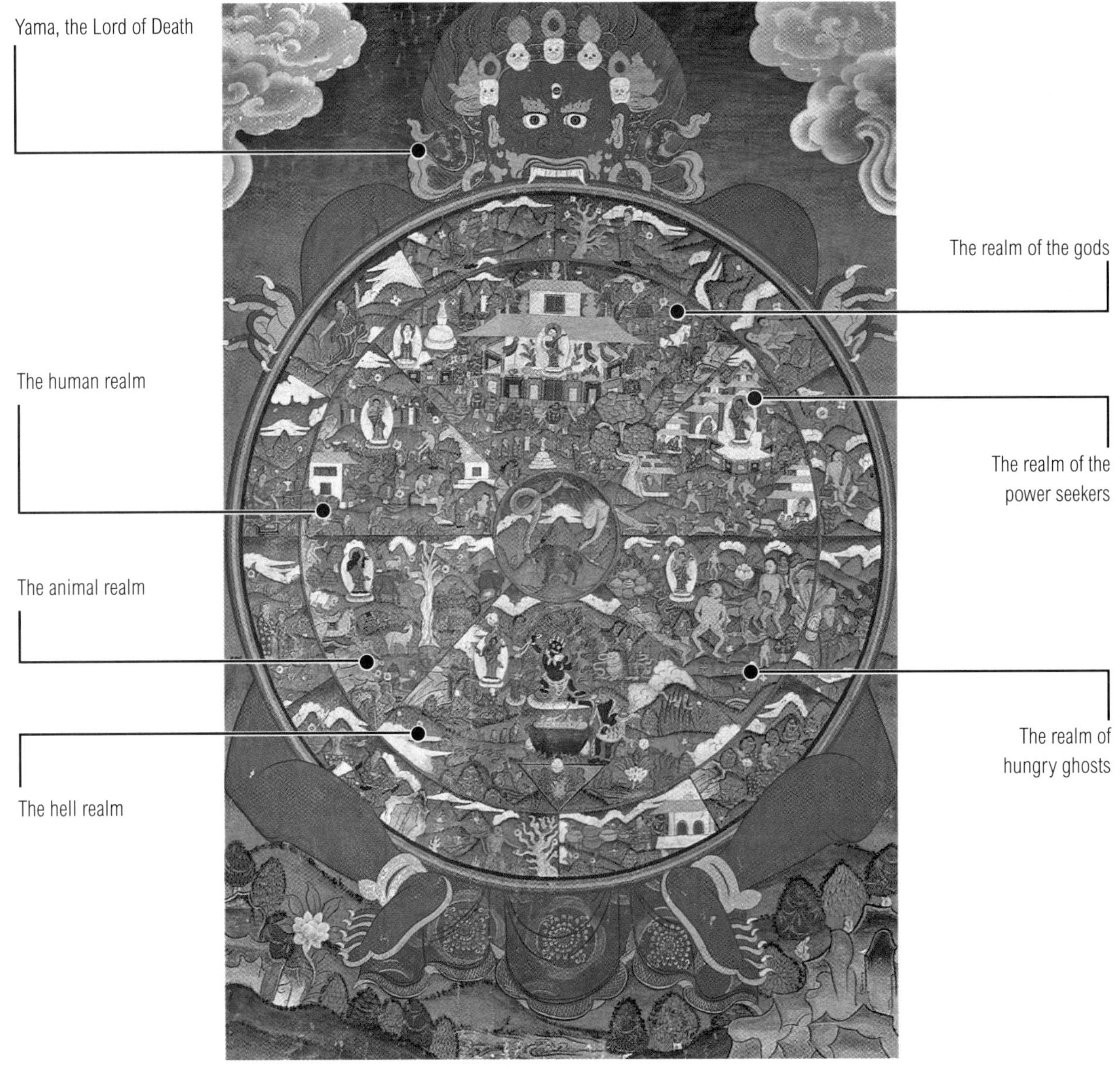

1 Look carefully at each of the twelve pictures in the outer frieze and think about how people's actions, represented in the pictures, have effects. Give two examples.

Twelve stages of life

In the outer frieze are twelve pictures showing stages in human life. This is the human world of birth and death in which people are caught up at the moment. The pictures show people driven along by their feelings, trying to get pleasure where they can. The very nature of such an existence is dukkha. It is imperfect and unsatisfying. People are always seeking new experiences in things which are themselves changing and impermanent.

The six realms of existence

The six sections inside the outer frieze show the various realms into which rebirth is possible. The Buddha is shown teaching in each realm, to help people to reach enlightenment. The realms represent types of existence, not actual places. They can be seen as experiences of life that every individual person knows – sometimes all six within the same day. Do you recognise these six realms?

- The realm of the gods: do you ever feel carefree, living a life of pleasure?
- The realm of the power seekers: do you ever feel at war with others, in a battle for power? What sort of power might you be trying to gain?
- The animal realm: do you ever give in to your appetites and instincts? When was the last time you gave in to your emotions without thinking?
- The hell realm: do you ever feel that life is terrible? What does it mean when someone says s/he is "going through hell"?
- The realm of hungry ghosts: are you ever greedy? How do people show their greed?
- The human realm: at its best, human life is characterised by choice. Each person has the ability to make good and bad choices. How difficult is it to make good choices? What are the important decisions in life?

2 Have you ever heard anybody say, "I can't change; that's the way I was made."? Maybe you have used that excuse yourself. Do you think that you can change the way you are? Do you let your emotions control you, or do you control them?

3 (a) Which animals would you use to represent the three fires or poisons?
(b) For each of the three forces, provide an example of how it can be dangerous and poisonous. For example, hatred can be dangerous because it can lead to fights and revenge.

4 (a) In groups, and concentrating on a different section each, draw a Wheel of Life to represent the Buddhist teaching in your own way.
(b) Write a brief explanation of your own section.

The three forces (fires or poisons) of samsara

At the centre of the Wheel, making it turn, are three forces. These forces or emotions burn within people constantly and threaten to rule them. They stop people from becoming enlightened. The cock represents greed (e.g. lust, craving). The pig represents confusion or ignorance, leading people to see, for example, the valueless as valuable. The snake represents hatred and aggression, causing people to speak and do wrong. Notice how all three animals are attached to each other. It is as if they encourage and feed each other, just as ignorance of the truth can lead to greed which can lead to hatred.

The way out of the Wheel

The world goes on, but there is a way out. In the top right-hand corner of the Wheel stands the Buddha. He is free from the cycle of rebirth. He stands there showing that becoming aware can break the power of ignorance, greed, and hatred. Instead of being controlled by emotions deep inside, people are called by the Buddha to wake up, to be aware – to act rather than just to react.

CHAPTER

Hinduism

UNIT ONE

In this chapter you will learn something about how Hindus "see" the world. Try to work out in what ways the Hindu view is similar to, and in what ways it is different from, your own view. This will help you to understand the Hindu response to the issues that we will be looking at later in the book.

We have been here before

1 Discuss the meaning of these statements:

- Life is like a merry-go-round.
- We seem to be in a downward spiral.
- There is nothing new under the sun.
- I think we have been here before.

Have you heard people say things like this about life? What do the statements have in common? Do you think there is any truth in them? What are the beliefs or assumptions behind the statements?

Hindus believe that all things are involved in an eternal cycle. The universe is created. It runs through four great ages and it is dissolved. Then there is a period when nothing material exists, before the process begins again.

Essential to Hindu thought is the belief that all living creatures are also caught up in a cycle of birth, death, and rebirth, called samsara.

Hindus believe that we make a mistake in thinking that this world, this life, and this body are all-important. This life is only one of many lives, and this world, which people think of as permanent, will pass away and another will take its place. Hinduism teaches people that they should search for the truth that is beyond these never-ending cycles of change.

The river Ganges is sacred to Hindus. There is a belief that it flowed in heaven before coming to earth; in art, it is often shown flowing down from Shiva's hair. Every evening at Hardwar, a town on the Ganges, Hindus assemble by the river for worship.

INDRA AND THE WISE VISITOR

The mighty Indra, king of the gods, was enjoying being in power. He employed Vishvakarma, the architect of the world, to build him a palace. As the building developed, Indra's requirements became increasingly elaborate and ambitious. He demanded more pleasure grounds, lakes, and terraces. Disturbed by Indra's uncontrollable ambition and vanity, Vishvakarma went to Lord Brahma, the Creator. Brahma took the matter to Lord Vishnu, the Supreme Lord, who reassured him that all would be well.

The next day, a boy dressed as a pilgrim called at the palace and Indra invited him in. His guest intrigued him. The youth smiled as if he knew the secrets of eternity, and his voice was soft, sweet, and low. He said he had heard of the mighty palace Indra was building and he asked when the work would be complete. He added that he knew of no Indra before him who had ever managed to accomplish such an extravagant project.

Indra smiled nervously and asked "And have there been so many Indras to your knowledge?" The boy nodded and, in his calm sweet voice, he said: "I have seen many Indras. I knew your father before you and your grandfather. I know Brahma the Creator and Vishnu the Supreme Being. I have seen the universe dissolved into the ocean of eternity and then re-created. Many have been the universes that have come and gone, each with its Brahma, Vishnu, and Indra ... and who can count the worlds that have been created and destroyed?"

As he spoke, a procession of ants began to cross the hall, each column followed by another and each four metres wide. The stranger laughed. "Why are you laughing?" asked Indra. "I do not know who you are but you appear to be Wisdom itself. Please, I beg of you, disclose the secret of your laughter."

The youth told the king of the gods that each of the ants had been an Indra in a previous existence and in another age and another universe. He went on to unfold the mystery of the never-ending cycle of the universe. He explained how every creature lives and dies and then returns in another body and another life. This life is only one in the countless cycle of many births. This universe is only one in an endless cycle of creation and dissolution. At the end of the boy's teaching Indra was humbled, and all that had seemed important to him moments earlier became unimportant. He gave up his extravagant ambitions and prepared to live the life of a hermit.

[This story is from the Brahmavaivarta Purana.]

2 What does the story of Indra tell us about:
(a) the Hindu view of the universe and the world;
(b) the Hindu deities;
(c) the Hindu view of time and eternity?

3 (a) What was Indra's mistake in building his palace? What did Indra learn from his visitor? What do you think is the teaching of this story for Hindus today?
(b) What do you think are the most common mistakes people make in their hopes, concerns, and plans for the future? Why do they make these mistakes? Discuss these questions and write your answers to (b) in the form of a "thought for the day", as if for a radio broadcast.

UNIT TWO

Ultimate Reality

In this unit you will consider the way in which Hindus understand "Ultimate Reality". You will have an opportunity to compare the Hindu view of God with those of other religions.

We live in an age of toys and games that allow us in to "virtual reality" – a world that seems as real as the "real world". But is the real world real? What if I see it differently from you? Which is the real world – yours or mine? Things change and die, and everything is fluid – so where is the solid ground? The world will not last forever: it will eventually pass away. And so what, if anything, has lasting reality? What is ultimate reality?

Brahman

Hindus believe that there is one reality – Brahman, the universal supreme spirit which is eternal and unchanging. Brahman is described in several ways. It is called the Supreme Spirit, Ultimate Reality, or even the Absolute. Sometimes Brahman is simply described as God.

In Hindu thought there are two ways in which Brahman has been understood. Some Hindus say that Brahman is without form, neither male nor female, and that it is only the human imagination that needs to see God in personal terms. Other Hindus say that Brahman can be known as the Supreme Lord and that people can have a personal relationship with God.

According to the teachings of the Hindu scriptures, Brahman is present everywhere and in everything. All things depend on Brahman for their existence. Without Brahman there would be nothing. Brahman is Being itself – Ultimate Reality.

1 Break down the description of Brahman into separate statements. How do these descriptors of a supreme universal spirit compare with other views about God that are known to you? In what ways are they similar to your own views? Discuss in pairs.

THE PINCH OF SALT

A story in the Upanishads tells of a student who wants to understand the nature of Brahman. His guru, or spiritual teacher, tells him to put a pinch of salt in a bowl of clear water. The next day the student returns and his guru tells him to go and look for the salt. Of course it has dissolved and there is nothing to see. "Take a sip from one side of the bowl. What can you taste?" asks the teacher. "Salt," the student replies. "Take a sip from the other side and tell me what you taste," the guru instructs. "Salt," comes the reply. "So it is with Brahman," says the guru. "Brahman is everywhere – you cannot see Brahman but it pervades all that is."

2 (a) In your own words say what the story of "The Pinch of Salt" explains about the nature of Brahman.

(b) Make up a story that illustrates one of the other important teachings about Brahman – for example, that Brahman is neither male nor female.

A scene in the east Indian state of Orissa. Why do you think the cow is protected in Hinduism? Most Hindus do not eat meat at all.

Atman

Hindus believe that Brahman is present in every living creature. The presence of Brahman in each individual creature is called Atman, which is translated as "self" or "soul". Like Brahman, Atman is eternal and is pure spirit.

Hindus say that people make the mistake of identifying the self with the changing body or with passing feelings or desires. The body grows, changes, ages, and dies, but Atman, the eternal soul, does not change or grow old. When the body dies, the atman (individual soul) takes on another body and returns to another life. In the Bhagavad Gita this is explained as the atman moving from one body to another as a person discards worn-out clothes and puts on new ones.

❝The wise one [Atman] is not born, nor dies.
This one has not come from anywhere, has not become anyone.
Unborn, constant, eternal, primeval, this one is not slain when the body is slain.❞ [Katha Upanishad II 18]

In some of the Upanishads, Brahman and Atman are described as identical. Some Hindus believe that there is no difference between Brahman and Atman and that, through yoga and meditation, it is possible to become one with God. Others believe that even when Atman finds union with Brahman, the soul remains a servant of God. In other words, Atman and Brahman are the same in that they are both pure spirit, but God is greater than the individual soul.

Hindus believe that most people fail to recognise the real and eternal (Brahman) behind the temporary forms of the world, and the eternal within themselves. A twelfth-century Hindu poetess and devotee of the god Shiva wrote:

❝Like
treasure hidden in the ground
taste in the fruit
gold in the rock
oil in the seed
the Absolute hidden away in the heart
no one can know the ways of our lord.❞
[A. K. Ramanujan transl., *Speaking of Siva*, Penguin Classics, 1985]

3 What does this poem tell you about the nature of the soul? Write your own poem about the soul and its presence in every human being and living creature.

4 (a) Why do you think that most people fail to recognise the presence of God (Brahman) in themselves and in the world around them?
(b) The poem suggests that the presence of God is like hidden treasure within the heart. What hidden treasure do you think is hidden within a person?

Gods and goddesses

In this unit you will consider how to interpret the stories and images of the various Hindu deities that represent different aspects of God (Brahman). You will be able to identify some of the features and qualities of God which are represented by or through the different deities.

Brahman is described sometimes in impersonal terms, such as the Supreme Spirit or the Ultimate Reality, and sometimes in personal terms, for example, as Lord, or as Friend, or as Lover. Individuals experience the power and presence of God in the world and in their own lives, and this experience is often expressed in a personal way. For example, God's protection may be likened to the loving care and protection of a mother.

1 In the picture of Durga – God as Mother – find symbols that might represent (a) protection from evil, (b) reassurance, (c) power to overcome problems and difficulties, (d) beauty, (e) wisdom. How would you represent these aspects of God in a picture?

"Although it is not possible to describe the qualities of the Lord who is the Absolute without material form and material attributes, unless humans feel his personal form, touch and presence they cannot relate to him. He therefore takes shape in the world, showers his grace on creation and enables devotees to attain Him by seeing, hearing and singing of His glorious deeds." [Gujurat Hindu Society, Preston, 1985]

The many different deities within Hinduism allow for different approaches to God. For some Hindus, Vishnu is the Supreme Being and they may worship him in the form of Krishna or Rama. Others consider Shiva to be the Supreme Lord. Many Hindus worship God as Mother, in the form of the goddess Durga.

Just as a person may be, at the same time, a son, a brother, a student, a member of the football team, the paperboy, and a boyfriend, so God is Creator, Mother, Preserver, and Destroyer all at one and the same time. Hindus are able to say that God is both many and one.

For some Hindus, the gods and goddesses represent different aspects of the impersonal Supreme Spirit. For others, the gods and goddesses are more than just symbols; they actually exist and they represent the various forms and features of a personal God.

Three important functions of God are represented in the Trimurti (the three gods Brahma, Vishnu, and Shiva). Brahma is God's creative power. Vishnu is the Preserver, who comes to earth in different forms to overthrow the powers of evil and to establish righteousness. The two most well-known avatars (descents) of Vishnu are Rama and Krishna. Shiva holds the power to destroy all things, but also the power to recreate.

The goddess Durga represents the energy of Shiva, both creative and destructive. Durga carries weapons to overcome the powers of evil in the world.

Statues of Brahmins (priests) are shown making offerings to this figure of Ganesh. What aspects of an elephant make it an appropriate symbol for God?

Some Hindu deities illustrate aspects of the relationship between the worshipper and God. The elephant-headed god Ganesh is the remover of obstacles. Hindus pray to Ganesh to remove all that stands in the way of spiritual progress. He is worshipped at the beginning of any religious ceremony or ritual.

2 Represent the teaching that "God is one and many" in a story or diagram or symbol. "How many Gods are there?" (below) is a famous story from the Upanishads which may help you think about this task.

3 Prepare a leaflet for non-Hindu visitors to a Hindu temple, to illustrate the way in which the various deities of Hinduism represent different forms and aspects of the same God.

HOW MANY GODS ARE THERE?

The wise and holy man Yajnavalkya is asked: "How many gods are there?" He answers: "As many as are named in the scriptures – namely three hundred and three, and three thousand and three."
"Yes," says the questioner, "but just how many gods are there?"
"Thirty three."
'"Yes, but just how many gods are there?"
"Six."
"Yes, but just how many gods are there?"
"Three."
"Yes, but just how many gods are there?"
"Two."
"Yes, but just how many gods are there?"
"One and a half."
"Yes, but just how many gods are there?"
"One . . . They call him Brahman."
[Brihadaranyaka Upanishad III.ix.I,9]

UNIT FOUR

Key concepts

In this unit you will be able to test your knowledge and understanding of some of the key concepts in Hinduism. You will be able to compare these beliefs and concepts with some of your own beliefs and ideas, and consider the ways in which beliefs shape your approach to life and death.

Dharma

Hindus often call their religion Sanatana Dharma (the Eternal Law). Sanatana means eternal. Dharma can be translated as righteousness, and also as duty, law, path, or religion. Dharma is that which sustains our existence, or that which is in the nature of something: for example, the dharma of fire is to be hot and the dharma of water is to be wet. According to the Hindu scriptures, everyone has particular duties to follow. These duties – the person's dharma – depend on his or her social status and stage in life.

1 Discuss what you would consider the duty or dharma of the following people: student, doctor, father, teacher, soldier, religious leader or priest, political leader, businessperson.

2 (a) Do you feel a sense of duty or responsibility in any aspect of your life? Is having a sense of duty or responsibility a good thing? When is it helpful and when does it get in the way?
(b) What sense of duty or responsibility would you want to pass on to your own children? How would you go about this?

Aims in life

The Hindu scriptures describe four aims in life. Each offers a person opportunities for moral and spiritual development and is to the benefit of society. One of these aims is to do one's duty (dharma). Without righteousness or a sense of morality, no human civilisation can endure for very long.

Three generations of a Hindu family in London. The boy is in the stage of life that Hindus call "brahmacharya" – a stage of learning about the religion and his duties as a Hindu. His parents are in the "grihastha" (householder) stage, in which people concentrate most on the aim of "artha" (making a living). The grandmother is in the "vanaprastha" (retirement) stage, in which there is more time for spiritual practices.

3 Read the quotation from the Mahabharata on the meaning of dharma (righteousness) – page 49. It stresses the importance that Hinduism attaches to not-harming any creature – the concept of "Ahimsa". Make a list of twenty human activities, such as shopping, praying, fighting, studying, etc. Decide which activities on your list promote dharma and which do not. Discuss your lists and your answers with a partner.

"... it is difficult to say what righteousness (dharma) is . . . Righteousness was declared for the advancement and growth of all creatures. Therefore, that which leads to advancement and growth is righteousness. Righteousness was declared for restraining creatures from injuring one another. Therefore, that is righteousness which prevents injury to creatures." [Mahabharata, Santiparva 109: 9-11]

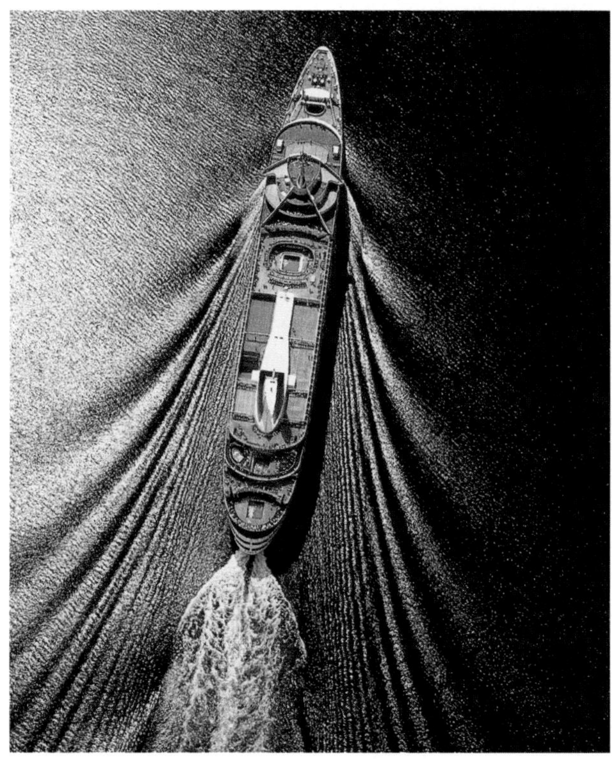

As this ship disturbs the water it passes through, so our actions have effects. Hindus believe that all actions (of the mind and of the body) and their results carry karma. Karma binds them to the cycle of rebirth. However, Krishna's teaching is that the karma of dutiful, selfless actions does not bind them in this way.

Another aim in life for Hindus is "artha": to earn a living, to be successful in one's job, and to contribute to the prosperity of society. Material success and economic development are essential to the survival of any society. However, the rewards of artha do not last.

The third aim is pleasure ("kama"). Pleasure, including the enjoyment of the senses and sexual pleasure, is an important aspect of a healthy and fulfilled life. So, for example, a wife must look to the physical needs of her husband and the husband must ensure that his wife is materially comfortable. The Hindu scriptures explain that sensual needs and pleasures must be regulated and not given free rein. Physical pleasure is important. However, it cannot bring lasting happiness.

The ultimate aim in life is "moksha", which means liberation from samsara, the cycle of birth, life, death, and rebirth. Achieving moksha is believed to bring peace or lasting happiness. The soul, atman, is reunited with Brahman.

Karma

Hindus believe that, when they die, unless they have achieved moksha, the soul, atman, returns to life in a new body. They believe that their next life depends on their actions in the present one. Good deeds will bring good experiences and bad deeds will lead to suffering. This is the law of karma. Karma means both "actions" and "the results of actions". All actions carry karma and karma fuels the next birth. According to Lord Krishna in the sacred text of the Bhagavad Gita, it is only with God's help that one can find release from the bondage of karma and attain moksha.

4 What are your long-term aims in life? How do they compare with the Hindu aims of dharma, artha, and kama?

5 (a) Do we all have a sense that our actions will come back on us one day? In what ways do you think this idea is true?
(b) Does it help us to see justice in life and in the world? Prepare a classroom debate on the truth of the statement "We reap what we sow!"

UNIT FIVE

Hindu worship

There are several ways to God that Hindus may follow. Some Hindus choose the way of asceticism, meditation, and yoga. Many choose the way of loving devotion. In this unit you will consider different forms of Hindu worship. You will be able to reflect on the value of this diversity within the religion and in the life of the Hindu community.

For most Hindus daily worship or "puja" includes making an offering at a shrine – which may be at a mandir or temple, or on the roadside, or at home. A Hindu shrine contains an image of a god or goddess, and the offerings may include a lamp or a flame, flowers, water, food, and incense.

One of the Hindu scriptures, the Bhagavad Gita, tells how the god Krishna teaches people to live and to try to reach moksha. Some Hindus believe that Krishna is Brahman (God) in human form. Krishna tells his followers: "If one offers Me with love and devotion a leaf, a flower, fruit or water, I will accept it."

The word "love" in that quotation is a translation of "bhakti", which means loving devotion or devotional service. Following the path of loving devotion – bhakti yoga – is one way that Krishna teaches which can lead people to moksha and union with him. Many Hindus try to follow the path of bhakti yoga, which means dedicating every action to God and serving only him.

Krishna speaks of two other ways to moksha. One is the path of knowledge – jnana yoga. To follow this, Hindus must leave behind all worldly comforts and desires and discipline their minds and bodies through yoga and meditation. To try to achieve freedom from the effects of karma, they do not work or do anything for material gain. Few Hindus take this path, for it is very hard.

The third path which Krishna describes is karma yoga – the path of unselfish action. Hindus believe that our actions are driven by our desires and emotions. It is these desires that generate good or bad karma. Unselfish desires lead to good actions and good karma. Selfish desires lead to selfish action and bad karma. Taking the path of karma yoga means acting without any desire to enjoy the results. In this way no karma is generated and the chains of samsara fall away to release the soul.

1 What do you understand by Krishna's teaching on worship? Explain the teaching in words and pictures which could be used for a poster for Hindu children.

The mandir or temple

In India the Hindu temple, or mandir, is primarily a home for the deity whose image stands in the central shrine. Worshippers usually come to the temple with a small gift or offering of food, flowers, or money. They may stop to offer respects or prayers or to meditate on the form of the deity. In the UK the mandir offers opportunities for community worship. Most temples hold a service called arti. This is a welcoming ceremony involving an offering of light. The following arti prayer is a welcome to God:

"O Lord of the universe, Supreme Soul, Dispeller of sorrow, praise to thee! May Thy rule of righteousness be established everywhere for it is Thou who banishes the sufferings of thy devotees. May Thy Kingdom of virtue reign supreme. Whoever meditates upon Thee receives Thy grace. The worries of his mind disappear; his home is blessed with peace, happiness and plenty and all his bodily pains will vanish. Thou art my Mother and Father. Who else's protection can I seek? Besides Thee there is no other in whom I can place my hope. Thou art God perfect, the knower of our innermost thought, the Most Exalted Master of all.❞ [Translation of arti prayer by the Gujurat Hindu Society, Preston, 1985]

2 (a) What is the relationship between the worshipper (devotee) and God expressed in this prayer?
(b) What are the hopes and feelings of the devotee?
(c) What does the devotee believe that God can do for the believer?
Write your answers in the form of an interview with a devotee at a Hindu temple.

Meditating by the river Ganges at Varanasi, India.

Meditation and yoga

Many Hindus spend time each day in meditation. They may use a mantra or sacred chant to help them centre their thoughts on God. They may also use a yantra or sacred symbol to help them in their meditation.

Some Hindus practise yoga to help them gain control over their body. Yoga begins with controlling selfishness, greed, envy, and anger. Another aspect of yoga involves learning to control the body and its functions so that it does not get in the way of meditation and so that the mind and heart can be directed towards God.

3 Put aside some time to try to focus and calm your mind – use the steady rhythm of your breathing as a focus or watch a candle flame. Is this kind of concentration hard to do? Why? Discuss your experience with a partner. Write your thoughts on the value of meditation and why it is important to Hindus.

4 The aim of the Hindu life is to reach moksha. However, Hinduism teaches that there are many paths.
(a) Name the three paths described by Krishna.
(b) Describe what is happening in the photographs and say which paths these represent.

Performing the arti ceremony in a Hindu temple in Manchester: a tray of five arti lamps is waved in front of the image of the deity on the shrine.

CHAPTER

Islam

UNIT ONE

About 1,000 million people – one fifth of the world's population – are Muslims, and the number is growing. This unit describes the origins of the Muslim community (the "Ummah") and shows how Islam affects the whole way of life of its followers.

Submitting to Allah

Islam is an Arabic word meaning "submission", "surrender", or "obedience". It comes from the same root as a word meaning "peace". Muslims (the name, from the same root, for followers of Islam) are people who surrender to the will of Allah (God), which is known through reading the Qur'an, the holy book of Islam.

At its most basic, Islam is a vision of a single community, the Ummah, in which everyone comes from the Creator and returns to Him. There is no compulsion to become a Muslim; in fact, the Qur'an specifically says that you cannot force an individual to become a Muslim and commands: "Do not cast aspersions on their [other religions'] idols". Muslims insist that Islam is both inclusive and tolerant. However, at the same time, as a Principal of the Muslim College in London explained:

“Every Muslim is a missionary. He has to spread the word. He's got to set an example. We try to convert the world. Our objective is to have one state, one religion, and one community.” [Quoted in John Bowker, *What Do Muslims Believe?*, BBC World Service, 1989]

This is the cave where the Prophet Muhammad received his first revelation on the 27th of the month of Ramadan in 610 CE. The revelations, written in Arabic exactly as the Prophet received them, form the Qur'an.

1 In groups, think of news stories concerning Islam and Muslims that you have heard or seen in the media. What impression of Islam have you received from them?

Islam is more than a religion: it is an entire way of life. In all areas of their lives, Muslims must follow a code of behaviour based on the Qur'an, known as Shari'ah (Islamic law). This law is unchangeable. It affects each individual's morality and lifestyle and, in countries where Islam has a large influence, the law of the state is based on the Shari'ah. So Islam affects matters such as the content of the education system, the role of women, and the inheritance of property. At the moment, no country is meeting all three conditions for being an Islamic state. These conditions are that there must be a caliphate (i.e. caliphs rule); the Shari'ah must be upheld; and the instruments of the Shari'ah must be available to its citizens. But Islam does have a very strong influence in some countries in the Middle East, Asia, and Africa. Many Western governments have come to realise the importance of understanding Islam, in order to understand the politics of these countries.

2 "Religious leaders should not get involved in politics."
(a) How far do you agree with this statement? Give your reasons.
(b) How far would a Muslim agree with this statement? Give reasons.

3 Why do you think Muslim leaders sometimes speak out against the "evils" of (i) atheism and (ii) capitalism?
(b) Why do you think some Muslims think that many Western governments are corrupt?

Muhammad: the seal of the prophets

Muslims say that the Prophet Muhammad did not start Islam, which they believe is as old as humanity, but he started the Islamic community, the Ummah, in Arabia in 622 CE. They say that the Prophet completed the religion. Many prophets are mentioned in the Qur'an, including Adam, Ibrahim (Abraham), Musa (Moses), Dawud (David), and Isa (Jesus), but Muslims regard the Prophet Muhammad as the last of the prophets. He is called the "Seal of the Prophets".

“Today I have perfected your religion for you, completed My favour upon you, and have chosen for you Islam as the way of your life.” [Qur'an, 5: 4, the last revelation given to the Prophet Muhammad]

Today, Muslims all over the world – like these girls at school in Sudan – learn to read the Arabic of the Qur'an.

The Prophet Muhammad was born in Makkah, in 570 CE. Orphaned when he was six, he was brought up by his grandfather and then by his uncle. He did not attend school and did not learn to read or write, but as a camel driver delivering merchandise he earned the name of "the Trustworthy One". When he was 25 he married his employer, Khadijah. He liked to spend time alone in prayer in the cool caves near Makkah. He was a thoughtful man who searched for God's guidance.

In 610 CE, at the age of 40, Muhammad had an experience that would change his life. He had gone to pray in a cave on Mount Hira. Suddenly he heard the voice of the angel Jibril (Gabriel), which called his name and commanded him to "Recite!" (read aloud). The Prophet Muhammad opened his mouth and recited:

“Proclaim! In the name of your Lord and Sustainer who created Man from a clot of congealed blood, speak these words aloud! Your Lord is the Most Generous One – He who has taught the Pen, who reveals directly things from beyond human knowledge.” [Qur'an, 96: 1-5]

The night this happened became known as Laylat-ul-Qadr, "the Night of Power". Muhammad rushed home, shivering with fright. Khadijah became the first person to believe that he was receiving Allah's (God's) message, but for the next two years the Prophet did not spread the message. Then Jibril appeared again and Muhammad was ordered to preach the revelations that Allah gave him. The Prophet Muhammad received these revelations over a period of 23 years. His friends wrote down his words, which form the Qur'an. Muslims believe that the Qur'an is the exact word of Allah.

THE MAIN POINTS OF ALLAH'S MESSAGE SPOKEN TO THE PROPHET MUHAMMAD

- There is only one God (Allah), to whom all people should submit.
- Life after death is real.
- There will be a time for judgement when people will be rewarded or punished according to how they have lived.
- Allah is merciful and will forgive, but Allah is also perfect justice.
- Allah requires dignity for all people (including women and slaves – people who had few rights in the days of the Prophet Muhammad).

The people of Makkah opposed the Prophet Muhammad when he challenged them to give up cheating, drinking, fighting, and worshipping idols. During this time of ridicule and persecution the Prophet had another amazing experience. In 620 CE he made a miraculous journey by night to Jerusalem, "the farthest place of worship" [Qur'an,17: 1], on the back of a winged horse-like creature named al-Buraq ("Lightning"). He was then taken through the seven heavens, where he spoke with the earlier prophets, and finally reached the throne of Allah and experienced Allah's presence. On this "Night Journey" the Prophet was told that people should pray five times each day. This has become Muslim practice.

❝For Muslims, the real meaning of this night was not the making of a journey from Makkah to Jerusalem, but the inward and mystical experience of the Prophet's spiritual ascension from earth to heaven – the soul's journey to God.❞ [Ruqaiyyah Waris Maqsood, *Islam*, Heinemann, 1995]

4 Explain the importance to Muslims of (a) the Night of Power, and (b) the Night Journey.

Soon the people of Yathrib invited the Prophet Muhammad to live with them. They hoped he would be able to settle the disputes between the three Arab and two Jewish tribes in their community. In 622 CE he left Makkah and went to Yathrib, which was renamed Madinah. He built a house there, which still exists as the first mosque, and, for the next ten years, he worked to unite the tribes into one community under the rule of Allah. In this new Islamic community of Madinah, all people belonged to Allah and had equal rights.

❝The most noble among you in the sight of Allah is the one who is most virtuous.❞ [Qur'an, 49: 13]

❝You shall not enter Paradise until you have faith, and you cannot have faith until you love one another. Have compassion on those on earth, and Allah will have compassion on you.❞ [Hadith]

5 The Prophet Muhammad taught that Muslims should put loyalty to Allah before any other loyalty – for instance, to family, tribe, or nation. How do you think this binds Muslims together?

A view of Makkah today. In the centre of the Grand Mosque with its tall minarets is the Ka'bah, the shrine to which all Muslims turn when they pray. Muslims believe that the sacred Ka'bah was first built by Adam and rebuilt by Ibrahim. In one corner of the building, about 1.5 metres from the ground, there is a black stone. It is said that this stone was given to Ibrahim's son, Ismail, by the angel Jibril. Muslims kiss the black stone if they get near enough to it, or raise their arms towards it if the crowds are too great.

The Prophet Muhammad's journey from Makkah to Madinah is known as the Hijrah ("migration"). The Islamic calendar is dated from this event – dates are AH (after Hijrah) – which also marks the beginning of the Ummah.

The Makkans, who were particularly angered by the Prophet Muhammad's denunciation of their idols and his insistence that there was only one God, still tried to harm him. Eventually, in 630 CE, the Prophet returned to Makkah with a force of 10,000 men and conquered the city in the name of Allah. Soon everyone in Makkah became Muslim, and Makkah became the holy city dedicated to Allah. To this day only Muslims may enter it.

Tradition says that the Prophet Muhammad died on 8 June 632 CE, at the age of 63. His life is an example to Muslims of what it means to submit to Allah. Muslims attempt to follow his example and live out the will of Allah in every situation in which they find themselves.

Why do you think Makkah is off-limits to non-Muslims?

“People, no prophet or messenger will come after me; and no new faith will emerge. All those who listen to me will pass on my words to others, and those to others again.” [Hadith]

6 Submission to the will of Allah involves obedience, surrender, discipline, and trust. How did the Prophet Muhammad show his surrendering to Allah?

UNIT TWO

The one and only God

At the heart of Islam is belief in one God. In this unit you will explore what belief in God (Allah) means to Muslims.

Tawhid – the oneness of God

The most important belief in Islam is that there is only one God. The oneness, or unity, of God is called tawhid. The first of five basic practices, known as the Pillars of Islam, is to make the declaration called the Shahadah: "There is no God but Allah and Muhammad is the Prophet of Allah."

Muslims believe that Allah has no equal. Allah is the Creator and Sustainer of the universe, and therefore owns everything. Allah lends people the world and even their own bodies; only He owns them. This belief affects Muslims' attitudes towards their own bodies and the created world, which they are to look after as responsible stewards.

Allah knows all, and can do everything. Allah is above human knowledge, and is transcendent. Even if the existence of suffering seems mysterious, Muslims believe that Allah is in control and that people suffer and die for a reason and at the time Allah appoints. Muslims are taught to be constantly aware of Allah, and to submit to him in everything they do. The feeling of love and fear that a Muslim has for Allah is called "taqwa". A person with taqwa wants to behave in ways which will please Allah and tries hard to stay away from things that would displease Him.

To suggest that anyone or anything is in any way equal to Allah is to commit the sin of "shirk", which Muslims regard as the worst of all sins. Statues or pictures of Allah are forbidden, as it is impossible to represent Allah. Also, if there were such statues or pictures, people might begin to treat them as idols. Worshipping idols is forbidden in Islam. Instead the mosque may be made beautiful and colourful through the use of decorative patterns. Often calligraphy is used as an art form.

Studying the Qur'an in the mosque at Isfahan, Iran. Many Muslims can recite the whole Qur'an. They are known as Hafiz. It is read with respect and used as a guide to the whole of life.

"He is Allah, the One, Allah is Eternal and Absolute. None is born of Him, He is unborn. There is none like unto Him." [Qur'an, 112]

1 (a) Use the section on tawhid to write a paragraph explaining what Muslims believe about Allah.
(b) Why do Muslims believe it is impossible for people to describe God in human terms?

Muslims pray at the Badshahi Mosque, Lahore, Pakistan. Beautiful calligraphy and geometric or flowery, leafy patterns are used in the building and decoration of mosques.

What's in a name?

Muslims believe that Allah is so great that it is impossible to describe His total nature. The Qur'an reveals 99 names for Allah, each describing an aspect of His nature, qualities, and greatness, and thus helping to explain why He should be worshipped. But Allah is not limited by only these 99 names. In Islam, 100 is regarded as a perfect number, and the fact that people do not know Allah's 100th name symbolises human imperfection. The opening surah (chapter) of the Qur'an gives some of Allah's names:

“In the name of Allah, the Compassionate, the Merciful. Praise be to Allah, Lord of the Universe, the Compassionate, the Merciful, Sovereign of the Day of Judgement! You alone we worship, and to You alone we turn for help.”

“Some non-Muslims allege that God in Islam is a stern and cruel God who demands to be obeyed. He is not loving and kind. Nothing can be farther from the truth than this allegation . . . With the exception of one, each of the 114 chapters of the Qur'an begins with the verse: 'In the name of God, the Merciful, the Compassionate . . .' But God is also Just. Hence evil doers and sinners must have their share of punishment and the virtuous His bounties and favours.” [*Concept of God in Islam*, World Assembly of Muslim Youth]

2 What does the opening surah of the Qur'an tell you about the nature of God?

UNIT THREE

The Five Pillars of Islam

The five essential practices or duties of Islam are known as the Five Pillars. This unit shows how the Five Pillars shape the entire way of life of each Muslim. Their importance is sometimes explained by referring to the "House of Islam": the Qur'an is its foundation, the Five Pillars are the uprights or supports, and the Shari'ah (the holy law) is the roof.

"The Five Pillars are the framework for every Muslim's life." [Cameron Azeem]

The Pillars of Islam are so basic to Islam that an attack on them is taken very seriously. On 14 February 1989, the author Salman Rushdie had a "fatwa" (a religious decree) issued against him by the Muslim leader of Iran, Ayatollah Ruhollah Khomeini. The decree stated that Muslims had a duty to kill Salman Rushdie for alleged blasphemy against Islam in his novel *The Satanic Verses*. The novel was seen as a deliberate attempt by a Muslim to use his experience of the religion to hurt the house of Islam. Such an action is completely forbidden in Islamic law. In September 1998, the death threat over Salman Rushdie was removed, but it was impossible to remove the fatwa because this can only be done by the religious leader who has declared it. Ayatollah Khomeini died in 1989.

Rushdie joy at "freedom" from fatwa

By Christopher Lockwood, Diplomatic Editor, at the United Nations

The author Salman Rushdie last night celebrated the end of 10 years under Muslim death threat when the Iranian government pledged that it would not assist or encourage his assassination.

Mr Rushdie, condemned to death by the former Iranian leader Ayatollah Khomeini, in 1989, for writing *The Satanic Verses*, was emotional as he left the Foreign Office.

Mr Rushdie was condemned by edict or fatwa for what was seen by Muslims as blasphemy in his book. The fatwa was not lifted as part of last night's agreement. Iran claims – and the British government accepts – that it could have been reversed only by the late Ayatollah.

Mr Rushdie has had to live under heavy protection as a virtual prisoner since the death sentence. His marriage collapsed as a result of the strain. There have also been attacks on his publishers and translators abroad.

[*The Times*, Friday, 25 September 1998]

1 (a) What does blashpemy mean?
(b) Should there be limits to free speech – especially if a person uses free speech to cause offence to others?
(c) Salman Rushdie wrote as a Muslim. Do you think there is a conflict between his being a Muslim and his fight for free speech?

"The reason we have ... kept the issue alive is not just because somebody's life was in danger but because some incredibly important things are being fought for: the art of the novel, the freedom of the imagination and the overarching freedom of speech ... It is a source of great satisfaction that one of the great principles of free societies has been defended." [Salman Rushdie, quoted in *The Times*, Saturday, 26 September 1998]

The Shahadah – the first Pillar of Islam

The first Pillar of Islam is saying the Shahadah, the Islamic declaration of faith. It is a summary of belief: "I believe there is no other God but Allah, and Muhammad is the Messenger of Allah." All a person must do to become a Muslim is to say the Shahadah and believe it with all his or her heart.

A longer statement of belief, known as the "seven articles of belief", is:

Q

2 (a) What are the two main beliefs that make up the Shahadah?
(b) What are the main beliefs in the "articles of belief"?

"I believe in Allah,
in His angels,
in His revealed Books,
in all of His prophets,
in the Day of Judgement,
in that everything – both good and bad –
comes from Him, and
in life after death."

"The first of the five pillars is Shahadah, which means 'witness' . . . This witness must result in action and the first process of this action must be prayer. In Islam, prayer is meant to help the individual to develop his/her consciousness of the creator, Allah. The next important pillar is that of fasting so that I am able to come to terms with what it must be like for those who have to go without food for the best part of their lives. And the next pillar would therefore result in me contributing financially to the needs of people who are suffering in the world. This is done through zakat . . . These three important pillars set me on the road of sacrifice, perseverance and patience. And these kind of virtues are encapsulated for me in the Hajj, where the Hajj becomes the ultimate sacrifice that I am prepared to make in a pilgrimage not only to Mecca but . . . toward God." [Dr Mashuq Ibn Ally, Director of the Centre for Islamic Studies, Federal University of Wales, quoted in *Pillars of Faith*, BBC World Service, 12 November 1989]

Evening prayers on the beach in Jeddah, Saudi Arabia.

Salah – praying five times a day

During his Night Journey (page 54), the Prophet Muhammad was told that Muslims should constantly remember and submit to God by praying five times each day. Wherever they are, at home, at work, at school, on holiday, Muslims stop five times each day to say their prayers in the same way.

Praying together confirms the Ummah (community of Islam) and so, when possible, Muslims go to pray in the mosque, which means "place of prostration". But prayer can take place in any clean place. Many Muslims carry a prayer mat with them, so that they always have a suitable place for prayer.

Prayer is preceded by the ritual wash called wudu. Then, wherever they are in the world, Muslims face towards the Ka'bah (a cube-shaped building in the centre of the Grand Mosque in Makkah – see page 55) to say their prayers. The direction of the Ka'bah is called qiblah and, in every mosque, a qiblah wall with an alcove called the mihrab shows the direction. When not

3 (a) What do you think is the purpose of the physical movements which accompany the saying of prayers in Islam? How can these movements help a Muslim?
(b) What do you think are the differences for a Muslim between praying alone and praying with others? Why do you think it is important for Muslims to meet together for communal prayer at least once a week, on Friday?

4 "You don't need a special place for worship." How far do you think this statement is true in Islam? Show that you have thought about different points of view, giving reasons to support your answer.

at the mosque, Muslims may use a special compass showing the direction of the Ka'bah. The prayer routine follows a distinct ritual. A series of rak'ahs (movements) are performed to go with the words.

In addition to salah, a Muslim may devote time to personal prayer. Some Muslims use prayer beads as an aid. A collection of 33 or 99 strung beads are used when reciting the names of Allah. The beads are called tashib or subhah.

Zakah – almsgiving

As well as "giving to charity", zakah means "purity". So the word conveys the idea that giving to people in need helps to purify one's heart from greed and selfishness. This Pillar of Islam is that each year Muslims must work out what money they have, after paying for essentials such as food, clothing, and accommodation, and then give two and a half per cent of this money as zakah. The money may be used for helping the poor, the disabled, and debtors, and for religious purposes. Each person's honesty is relied upon, and the money is usually paid in secret. Muslims believe that not to pay zakah would be cheating Allah. They believe that all wealth and property belong to Allah and that people act as trustees.

As well as the annual zakah, which is looked on as compulsory, Muslims may give other money to charity (called sadaqah).

❝Be steadfast in prayer, and regular in giving. Whatever good you send forth from your souls before you, you will find it (again) with God; for God sees well all that you do.❞ [Qur'an, 2: 110]

5 Do you find it easy to give things away? Do you give to charity? How does it make you feel? Why do you think religions think it is important to give to people in need?

6 (a) Why do Muslims pay zakah? Do you think that 2.5 per cent is a reasonable amount?
(b) Do you think that the money you own is yours to do what you like with? Why might you think this? What is the Islamic attitude to money? Does it differ from your attitude and, if so, how?
(c) Who do you think is the richer: the person who is able to give money away, or the person who keeps it?

Sawm – fasting during the month of Ramadan

❝O believers, you must fast so that you may learn self-restraint. Fasting is prescribed for you during a fixed number of days.❞ [Qur'an, 2: 183-4]

Ramadan is the ninth month of the Islamic calendar, and the month in which the Prophet Muhammad always received the revelations in the Qur'an. Between sunrise and sunset every day for the whole of Ramadan, Muslims fast: eating, drinking, smoking, and sexual intercourse are not allowed. All Muslims over the age of puberty are expected to fast unless they are sick, old, pregnant women, or mothers who are breast-feeding. Children younger than 12 may take part in a partial fast.

In Ramadan, Muslims get up early to have a meal before sunrise and then fast until after sunset, when they can eat and drink again. During this month

7 (a) What is the purpose of fasting?
(b) Why do Muslims observe Ramadan so strictly? What effect do you think it has on the Muslim community?

especially, they focus on the teachings of the Qur'an. A conscious effort must be made that no evil deed or thought is committed. At the end of the month, when the new moon can be seen, the festival of Eid-ul-Fitr begins, marking the end of the fast.

Hajj – pilgrimage to Makkah

At least once in their lives, in the twelfth month (Dhul Hijjah) of the Islamic calendar, Muslims who can afford to do so must go on pilgrimage (Hajj) to the "House of Allah" in Makkah. Nowadays over two million believers each year make the pilgrimage. For many, it is a very special, once-in-a-lifetime experience.

As they approach Makkah, pilgrims call out "Labbaika!" ("I am here, Allah, at your service!"). At the Grand Mosque they circle the Ka'bah seven times; this is known as completing the tawaf. Next they run seven times between two hills, Safa and Marwah, reenacting and remembering the story of Hagar, who searched desperately for water for her son Ishmael. The story tells that, returning to where she had left Ishmael, Hagar found that he had kicked the sand and discovered water. The place where this happened is now known as the Zamzam Well.

Thousands of pilgrims meditate at Mount Arafat. Male Muslims on Hajj wear two pieces of white cloth to show that they are in a consecrated state (ihram) of submission to God and that they are all equal. Women also wear a simple all-covering white garment. They must be accompanied by a male relative.

The pilgrims travel 21 km to Mount Arafat (the Mount of Mercy) to meditate from noon to sunset. They then go to Mina, collecting 49 stones en route to throw at three pillars which represent the devil. The pilgrims are reminded of how Ibrahim and Ismail refused to listen to the devil. A sheep or goat is sacrificed (representing Ibrahim's willingness to sacrifice his son if it was Allah's will) and the meat is given to the poor. The feast of Eid-ul-Adha (Great Festival of Sacrifice) is the climax of the Hajj pilgrimage and lasts for four days.

Back in Makkah the pilgrims again walk seven times around the Ka'bah. This is the end of the official pilgrimage, but many pilgrims then travel on to see the tomb of the Prophet Muhammad in Madinah.

8 (a) What is a pilgrimage?
(b) What is the Ka'bah?

9 Imagine the once-in-a-lifetime experience of the Hajj. Write a diary of what happens or a letter describing the events, atmosphere, and importance of pilgrimage.

CHAPTER

Judaism

UNIT ONE

In this unit you will explore how belief in God affects the way of life of Jews. You will learn why Jews are called God's "chosen people". You will also consider the question, "Where can God be found?"

A covenant God

A chosen people

Traditionally, Jews trace their beginnings to Abraham (about 18 centuries BCE), who is called the father of the Jewish people. Abraham is, incidentally, also the ancestor of the Arab people. In their daily prayers Jewish people call to mind the patriarchs (fathers) of their faith, Abraham, Isaac, and Jacob.

The Hebrew Bible, the Tenakh, relates how God called Abraham, who was living in Ur in Babylonia, and made promises to him: "Leave your country, your relatives, and your father's home, and go to a land that I am going to show you." [Genesis 12]. Although both Abraham and his wife were old, God promised them "many descendants and they will become a great nation. I will bless you and make your name famous, so that you will be a blessing." [Genesis 12]. God's promises to Abraham are called a covenant. This means a promise that demands commitment on both sides.

Some people argue that Judaism (the religion of Jewish people) started when Moses received the Torah (God's "teaching") at Mount Sinai, about six hundred years after the time of Abraham. It was at this stage that God spelt out the conditions of his covenant with the Jewish people.

One of the most important events in Jewish history, known as the Exodus – the Jews' escape from slavery in Egypt – took place under the leadership of Moses. Jews celebrate this each year in the Passover festival (Pesach). After their escape, the Jews wandered in the desert for 40 years, before they reached the "Promised Land" of Israel. It was in the desert that they received the Torah through Moses.

1 (a) When did Judaism begin?
(b) Who is regarded as the father of the Jewish nation?
(c) What is a covenant? What promises did God make to Abraham?

The Jewish people have understood their existence as being governed by the covenant relationship between God and themselves. God promised Abraham land and descendants. The Jewish people's side of the covenant was to keep God's commandments, given in the Torah.

The Torah and the Talmud

Torah means teaching – all the things that God has "told" the Jewish people. The Torah is the name of the first five books of the Tenakh. It contains stories about the Jews' early history, mitzvot (commandments), poems, and sayings.

The Torah contains 613 commandments that God gave to Moses. Jews believe that in this way God set His absolute standards which His people should live up to. The Jewish religion has therefore been said by some Jews to be a task, or an activity. Being Jewish is a matter of doing the commandments. However, Jewish morality is not simply a matter of keeping rules. The commandments were given to make people morally sensitive, to bring holiness into the world.

THE TEN SAYINGS

The Ten Sayings (also known as the Ten Commandments) act as a summary of the commandments that God gave to the Jews. Tradition says that they were written on two stones of the covenant which Moses brought down from Mount Sinai, according to the Torah. There are two accounts of the Ten Sayings: one in Exodus 20 and the other in Deuteronomy 5. The sayings describe people's duty towards God and towards each other.

1. I am the Lord your God who brought you out of slavery in Egypt. You should have no other gods but Me.
2. Do not make for yourselves images of anything in heaven or on earth.
3. Do not use my name in untrue ways.
4. Observe the Sabbath and keep it holy. On the Sabbath you must not do any work.
5. Respect your father and your mother.
6. Do not commit murder.
7. Do not commit adultery.
8. Do not steal.
9. Do not testify against someone falsely.
10. Do not covet.

2 Are the Ten Sayings relevant to today's world?

In addition to the teachings that were revealed to them, Jewish people have many commentaries on how the commandments should be followed in everyday life. The Talmud is a collection of writings by Jewish teachers (rabbis) from about 200-500 CE, who discussed and worked out how to live as a Jew. The Mishnah (compiled at the end of the 2nd century CE) records how the rabbis debated the essence of the law. For example:

“Rabbi Simlai taught:
613 commandments were given to Moses.
Then David reduced them to 11 in Psalm 15, beginning: 'He who follows integrity, who does what is right and speaks the truth in his heart.'
Micah reduced them to 3 [Micah 6: 8]: 'Act justly, love mercy and walk humbly with your God.'
Then came Isaiah and reduced them to 2 [Isaiah 56: 1]: 'Keep justice and act with integrity.'
Amos reduced them to 1 [Amos 5: 4]: 'Seek Me and live.'
Habakkuk also contained them in 1 [Habakkuk 2: 4]: 'But the righteous shall live by his faith.'

Akiba taught: The great principle of the Torah is expressed in the commandment: 'Love your neighbour as you love yourself; I am the Lord.' [Leviticus 19: 18].

But Ben Azai taught a greater principle [Genesis 5:1]: 'This is the book of the generations of man. When God created man, He made him in the likeness of God.'” [Mishnah: Makkot]

Members of a Jewish congregation in Manchester parade a new Torah scroll from the office of the Hebrew scribes to their synagogue.

The rabbis' interpretation of how the laws applied to everyday life became known as the Halakhah (Hebrew for "path" or "way"). First written down in the Talmud, the Halakhah has continued to develop over the centuries, to meet new situations. In the past, Jews everywhere had a common system of belief and practice: they lived in closed societies and administered their own courts and social life. Now many Jews live amongst people of all different faiths and none.

❝If 'law' is a central element in Judaism, it is because it is the basis of our constitution as a people, regulating our behaviour towards each other, to others and to God. The essential term in this regard is Halakhah, from the root h-l-kh, meaning 'to walk'. Halakhah, translated usually as 'Jewish law', is actually 'conduct': how the individual and community are to conduct themselves.❞ [J. Magonet, *The Explorer's Guide to Judaism*, Hodder & Stoughton, 1998]

3 (a) What are Torah and Halakkah?
(b) Why are laws important in life? What would happen without them?
(c) Why does Rabbi Magonet think the Law is important?
(d) How is the importance of Jewish Law changing today?

A mezuzah and the written prayer, the Shema ("Hear, O Israel . . ."), which goes inside it.

Belief in One God (monotheism)

People in the time of Abraham and the early Jews believed in many gods. The most important teaching of the new religion was that the God of Abraham was the one and only God, and that people should worship only Him. Moses told the people ("Israel"):

❝Hear, O Israel, the Lord our God, the Lord is One! and you shall love the Lord your God with all your heart and with all your soul and with all your might.❞ [Deuteronomy 6: 4-5]

These words are the beginning of a Jewish prayer that is said in the evening and in the morning, to this day. The prayer is also what is written on the tiny scroll kept inside every mezuzah – the box that many Jews have fixed to their doorposts.

HIDE AND SEEK

The grandchild of Rabbi Baruch was playing hide-and-seek with another boy. He hid and stayed in his hiding-place for a long time, assuming that his friend would look for him. But finally he went out and saw that his friend had gone, apparently not having looked for him at all, and that his own hiding had been in vain. He ran into his grandfather's study, crying and complaining about his friend. On hearing the story Rabbi Baruch broke into tears and said: "God too says: 'I hide, but there is no one to look for me.'" [A. J. Heschel, *Man Is Not Alone*, Harper & Row, 1951]

What kind of God?

The Jewish Bible (the Tenakh) opens with an account of God creating the world. However, Jews do not believe that God created the world and then retired. They believe that God intervenes in the world to sustain it. But where is God to be found? "Hunting for God" and "Hide and Seek" are two stories which explore this question.

HUNTING FOR GOD

A man was going from village to village, asking "Where can I find God?" He journeyed from rabbi to rabbi, and nowhere was he satisfied with the answers he received. One day he arrived wearily at a very small village in the middle of a forest. He sought out the rabbi. "Rabbi, how do I find God?" The rabbi simply said, "You have come to the right place, my child. God is in this village. Why don't you stay a few days? You might meet him."

The man was puzzled. He did not understand what the rabbi could mean. But the answer was unusual, and so he stayed. For two or three days, he strode around, asking all the villagers where God was, but they would only smile and ask him to have a meal with them. Gradually, he got to know them. Every now and then he would see the rabbi by chance, and the rabbi would ask, "'Have you met God yet, my son?" And the man would smile, and sometimes he understood and sometimes he did not. He stayed in the village for months and then for years. He became part of the village and shared in all its life. He went with the men to the synagogue on Fridays and prayed with them, and sometimes he knew why he prayed and sometimes he didn't. And then he would go home with one of the men for a Friday night meal, and when they talked about God, he was always assured that God was in the village, though he wasn't quite sure where. He knew, however, that sometimes he had met Him.

One day the rabbi came to him and said, "You have met God now, haven't you?" And the man said, "Thank you, rabbi, I think that I have. But I am not sure why I met Him, or how or when. And why is He in this village only?" The rabbi replied, "God is not a person, my child, nor a thing. You cannot meet Him in that way. When you came to our village, you were so worried by your question that you could not recognise an answer when you heard it. Nor could you recognise God when you met Him, because you were not really looking for Him. Now that you have stopped persecuting God, you have found Him, and now you can return to your town if you wish."

4 (a) What does monotheism mean?
(b) Which Jewish prayer begins with the words "Hear, O Israel"?

5 (a) In "Hunting for God", how did the man's idea of God change as he lived in the forest village?
(b) Where, according to the rabbi, can people find God?

6 What do you learn about a Jewish understanding of God from the story of "Hide and Seek"?

Return to God

Teshuva (penitence) is an important concept in Judaism. It means a "return" to God. In this unit you will see how returning to God is the central theme of two Jewish festivals.

1 (a) Do you make New Year resolutions? For how long do you keep them?
(b) Why do people make resolutions when they know they are probably going to break them?

The Hebrew Bible gives an account of the covenant relationship between God and the Jewish people. It is a relationship marked by God's faithfulness and the Jewish people's unfaithfulness towards God. Over and over again the Jewish people neglect God and need to return to Him in penitence (teshuva). Turning back to God is the central theme of two Jewish festivals: New Year (Rosh Hashanah) and the Day of Atonement (Yom Kippur).

Rosh Hashanah

Rosh Hashanah means "head of the year" or "first of the year". The New Year is a time to plan a better life, to make resolutions. In the Bible this holiday is called Yom Ha-Zikkaron (the day of remembrance). During synagogue services to celebrate the New Year, prayers are recited which concentrate on the image of God as creator, king, and judge. God will show forgiveness and compassion towards those who remember their sins, return to Him, repent of their wrongdoing, and seek His mercy.

The shofar (ram's horn) is blown every day in the month before Rosh Hashanah (these are called the Days of Awe), on Rosh Hashanah itself, and when Yom Kippur is over. The piercing sound of the horn calls people to prayer and penitence. Just as trumpets sometimes announce the arrival of a king or queen, so the shofar announces the arrival of God, the king of the universe, who comes to judge.

Another symbolic action during this festival is tashlikh ("casting off"). Jews walk to flowing water, such as a river, and empty their pockets into it, symbolically casting away their sins.

TURN TO GOD

Rabbi Eliezer said: "Turn to God the day before you die."
And his disciples asked him: "Does a man know on which day he will die?"
And he answered them, saying: "Just because of this, let him turn to God on this very day, for perhaps he must die on the morrow, and thus it will come about that all his days will be days of turning to God." [L. Blue with J. Magonet, *The Blue Guide to the Here and Hereafter*, Collins, 1988]

"On Rosh Hashanah man is judged. We must examine ourselves ... How will we answer when we stand alone before God, and He asks: 'Who are you?' The shofar heralds judgement and thereby frightens us. Yet it is we who summon ourselves to judgement by blowing the shofar. In doing so, we demonstrate that we accept the need for judgement, the need for having our attention riveted on the quest for our essential selves. We show God that we recognise the need for change, for re-creation of ourselves. And by so doing we arouse His mercy; we cause Him to move, as the Midrash says, from the throne of strict judgement to the throne of mercy." [Jonathan Rosenblum, in *The Jerusalem Post*, Sunday, 20 September 1998]

2 (a) How do Jews turn back to God at Rosh Hashanah? What symbols do they use to help them do this?
(b) What does Jonathan Rosenblum mean when he writes "we accept the need for judgement"?

Yom Kippur

The theme of Yom Kippur is atonement. Atoning for something you have done wrong means doing something to show that you are sorry for it. On Yom Kippur Jewish people confess their wrongdoings and ask for forgiveness from God and from people they have hurt.

"Before Yom Kippur starts we approach people we have hurt during the year. It's an opportunity to visit friends and say we're sorry for anything we may have done to hurt them. It's difficult to admit to someone that you took something from him, or acted rudely, or gossiped about him. And sometimes, when you hurt someone, it's so hard to fix afterwards." [Jacob]

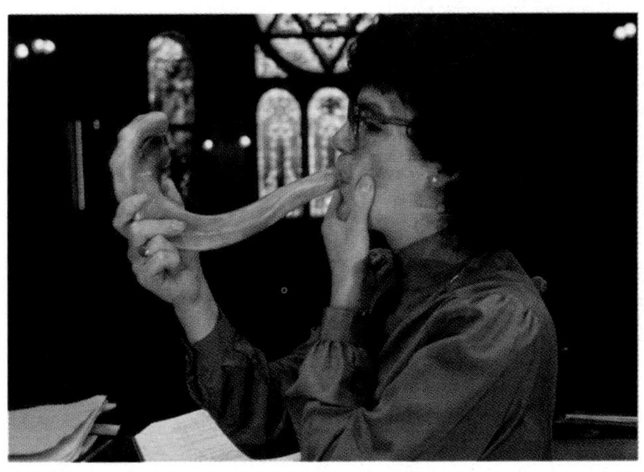

A rabbi blows the shofar for Yom Kippur in the synagogue in Greenburg, Mississippi, USA.

It is a most serious day. Even Jews who do not act religiously in the rest of their lives observe Yom Kippur. Most people spend long periods in the synagogue. In Jerusalem, for example, all streets are empty of cars. On this festival not only is work forbidden, as on the Sabbath, but also there is no eating or drinking, no using of oils, no sexual relations, and no washing for pleasure.

Most of Yom Kippur is spent in the synagogue. It is customary to wear white, symbolising purity and calling to mind the promise that sins will be made as white as snow [Isaiah 1: 18]. The central aspect of the synagogue service is public confession. All sins are confessed in the plural (we have done or not done this or that), emphasising the communal responsibility for sins, and the majority of sins confessed involve mistreatment of other people. But the services only atone for sins between people and God; Jews do not believe that prayer takes away the need to work for justice and make good relationships between people.

The final service of Yom Kippur is Ne'ilah (the "closing of the gates"). Worshippers are encouraged to make the most of this last hour during which the gates of heaven are said to remain wide open, before they are closed at the end of the fast. Yom Kippur ends on an emotional high with the singing of "Avinu Malkenu" ("Our father, our king") and a final blast of the shofar.

3 Why do Jews fast and wear white clothes on Yom Kippur? How do they show their sincerity in turning back to God in repentance on Yom Kippur?

4 (a) Why is it hard to say sorry to people you have hurt? Is it important to say sorry? What happens if you don't?
(b) Why do you think Jewish people think it is important to say sorry to God?

Keeping kashrut

Judaism has more to do with being than believing. Jews believe that God is revealed in people's relationships and actions. In this and the next unit we try to discover how Jews come to know God through what they do – through keeping kashrut and observing the Shabbat.

The importance of food

Do you eat food in order to live, or is food important in itself? It is certainly the case that many people love eating, and people often have special meals to celebrate special occasions. But what makes certain foods special?

Food plays an important role in Judaism, and one can easily understand why. The tastes and smells of the foods that have always been eaten at different festivals help to create the particular moods of those festivals, and become associated with them in people's memories. In addition, all food that Jews eat has to be kosher. This means that certain laws govern the buying, preparation, and eating of food.

Cholent is a dish that was designed for Shabbat; it could be prepared and cooked the day before and kept hot, without spoiling, for 24 hours. The basic ingredients are meat, potatoes, and fat.

1 How is food important in Judaism?

Kashrut regulations

Rule 1: Certain foods are kosher (allowed) and certain foods are treif (not allowed).

Rule 2: Do not mix milk and meat products – for in the Tenakh it says: "You shall not boil a kid in its mother's milk". This gives a glimpse of how compassionate the Jewish food laws are.

Rule 3: Food must be prepared in the correct manner. Animals should be killed by the "shechitah" method: this involves killing the animal by a short, quick slit in the carotid artery so that it dies instantaneously, and then draining the blood, which stands for the life-force given by God.

The kashrut laws fulfil a number of purposes:

“Some modern Jews think that our dietary laws are out-of-date health regulations. Many of the health benefits from kashrut were made obsolete when the refrigerator was invented. The main reason we observe kashrut is because the Torah says so. For a Torah-observant traditional Jew, there is no need for any other reason. By keeping kashrut we show our obedience to God – following the laws even though there is no clear reason.” [Mical, Israel]

“The modern world is a powerful thing, and ... we decided that we would not observe kashrut outside the home but we would retain our sanctuary at home ... It works for me! I may have a chicken burrito for lunch at work, but if I use the wrong utensil at home by accident, I'll rush outside to bury it in the ground for three days! If, when making an egg, I almost put a pat of butter in a meat pan, stop, and switch to dairy, it is in this act of correcting my almost error that I realise my connection to God.” [Rick, England]

Buying traditional cakes for the festival of Purim, in Jerusalem. The festival remembers the story of Ester, the Jewish wife of the King of Persia, who saved her people from a tyrant, Haman. The three-cornered cakes are said to be like Haman's ears or like his purse, which he intended to fill with Jewish gold.

Q

2. When buying and cooking meat, Jews observe the laws of kashrut. What are the rules that govern their food?
3. Use the quotations on these two pages to explain why Jews keep these food laws.

"Paying attention to what we eat, and acting on the central concept that not everything in nature is subject to the whim and desires of humankind, is elevating and raises our consciousness . . . It can help us to not take food for granted . . . we are, in eating, engaging in a life-sustaining, spiritual, and miraculous process. Anything that helps us to remember that can only be beneficial." [Eric, Vienna]

A kosher butcher's shop in Paris. What signs are there that this is a Jewish butcher's?

UNIT FOUR

Observing the Shabbat

Judaism is centred on the family and the local community. The weekly celebration of Shabbat helps to maintain the strong sense of Jewish identity.

1 (a) Do you have a special day of the week? If so, what makes it special?
(b) Does your family sit down for a meal together? Why do you think some families think this is important?

"More than Israel kept the Sabbath, the Sabbath kept Israel."
[Asher Ginzberg]

"Six days a week, we wrestle with the world, wringing profit from the earth. On the Sabbath, we especially care for the seed of eternity planted in the soul. Six days a week, we seek to dominate the world. On the seventh day, we try to dominate the self. The world may have our hands, but our soul belongs to Someone Else."
[Abraham Joshua Heschel, an American Conservative rabbi, 1907-72]

"Observe the Sabbath and keep it holy. You have six days in which to do your work, but the seventh day is a day of rest dedicated to me. On that day no one is to work ... In six days I, the Lord, made the earth, the sky, the sea, and everything in them, but on the seventh day I rested. That is why I, the Lord, blessed the Sabbath and made it holy."
[Exodus 20]

"It has been said that whereas Christians build cathedrals in space, Jews build them in time. The Shabbat with all its complex structure is precisely that." [Jonathan Magonet, *The Explorer's Guide to Judaism*, Hodder & Stoughton, 1998]

2 What do the four quotations above tell you about the reasons for observing Shabbat?

The best of days

For Jews, days start and end at sunset. Shabbat lasts from Friday evening to Saturday evening. The name Shabbat is derived from the Hebrew verb "to rest" or "to cease". The other days of the week don't have names – just numbers. But Shabbat has a name because it is a special, holy day.

Friday night has become a great Jewish institution. Each week people attend prayers in the synagogue and sing joyful songs. They then return to a brightly lit home and a festive table to share a Shabbat meal. Family, friends, and strangers are invited to the table and an evening of relaxation begins.

Shabbat recalls two events: the creation of the world and the freeing of the Hebrews from slavery in Egypt. One blessing recited during Shabbat is:

"Blessed are You, Eternal our God, Sovereign of the universe, whose commands make us holy, and who delights in us. Willingly and with love You give us Your holy Shabbat to inherit, for it recalls the act of creation. This is the first day of holy gatherings, a reminder of the exodus from Egypt." [from the Shabbat kiddush]

❝What the Shabbat does is to highlight two perspectives on the world that we need constantly to understand and 'remember' if we are to exist and function within it. First that the world is God's creation which sets the boundaries upon our ambitions, personal and collective, and our freedom to exploit the world . . . Second, by reference to the exodus from Egypt, a boundary is set upon our right to exploit and 'enslave' one another.❞ [Jonathan Magonet, *The Explorer's Guide to Judaism*, Hodder & Stoughton, 1998]

Children at a school in Berlin, Germany, learn to light the candles for Shabbat.

The Shabbat is a central pillar of Jewish experience. It is a special day, set apart, made holy. It is an island created in time. Solomon Goldman describes the unique quality of the Sabbath:

A ceremony called Havdalah marks the end of Shabbat. It includes the lighting of a plaited candle, as is happening in this picture of a family in Maryland, USA. The fire of the candle flame symbolises work, so the ceremony marks the start of the working week after the Shabbat rest.

❝First it was to constitute a day of physical relaxation, of complete rest, when all manners of work are prohibited. Second it was to teach man to be kind to the beast and more particularly to his fellow man, be they slaves or aliens. Third, it was to be a joyous day spent at home with one's family. Fourth, it was to be a day of intellectual stimulation. Fifth it was to be a day of spiritual delight or ecstasy. Sixth, it was to link the Jewish people to God, to His function as Creator, and to their emergence as a free people. In other words, it was to be a holy day; that is a day by means of which the Jew was to have every week a foretaste of the ideal world order, which it was his responsibility to help bring into existence.❞ [Solomon Goldman, *The Book of Human Destiny: From Slavery to Freedom*, Abelard-Schuman, 1958]

3 (a) Name two teachings from the Tenakh (the Hebrew Bible) that encourage Jews to observe Shabbat.
(b) Which two events does Shabbat celebrate?

4 How do Jews make Shabbat a special occasion?

5 What have you learnt about the reasons for observing the Shabbat?

CHAPTER

Sikhism

UNIT ONE

In this unit you will learn about the way Sikhs look at life and the world, and you will discover the way in which the Sikh scriptures shape and influence the Sikh approach to life. You will be able to reflect on the things that shape and influence your world view.

Becoming close to God

What are we here for?
Where did we come from? Where did life come from?
Where are we going? Are we going anywhere?
What is the purpose of life?

1 (a) Give your answers to these questions.
(b) Where did you get the answers?
(c) Have your views changed over time – since you were a young child? Who or what is influencing your views today?

Sikhs find their answers to these questions in the teachings of their scriptures, the Guru Granth Sahib. According to Sikh belief, the Guru Granth Sahib is the word of God revealed to the Sikh Gurus.

Sikhs believe that we are all here for a purpose: to become reunited with God. They believe that God is the source of all things and is in all things. Everyone has the presence of God within him or her. This divine inner light or soul is eternal and does not die when the body dies. According to Sikh belief we have lived many lives before this one. We have passed through different births and taken many different forms. Through a cycle of birth, life, death, and rebirth we have come up through the animal kingdom to be born as human beings. We now have a purpose and that is to find God and to be united with him.

“Now, being possessed of his ‘spark’ we have finally been given the opportunity, in this life, to rejoin that source from which all things come. Even as sparks rising up from a fire tend to rejoin it and as all water at some time becomes reunited in the sea, it is here and now, in this life, that we have finally been given the opportunity to rejoin that creator who made us.” [Quoted from Lou Singh Khalsa Angrez, “Is Sikhism the way for me?” in *The Sikh Bulletin*, No. 4, 1987]

2 According to the Sikh scriptures, human life is the highest life form on earth. In words and pictures explain Sikh beliefs about life and its purpose.

Sikhs believe that men and women fill their lives with concerns for things that do not last, and seek happiness in pleasures that are only temporary. They forget that their true nature is eternal and that they can only find peace and true happiness when they become close to God.

The Guru Granth Sahib shows Sikhs how to develop their awareness of God's presence in all aspects of their lives. By singing God's praises, and meditating on and chanting God's holy name, Sikh worshippers become close to God. Ultimately, this will lead to union with God and freedom from the cycle of rebirth.

“He who nurtures the Name within will find the Lord ever present there. Gone forever the pain of rebirth, his precious soul in an instant freed. Noble his actions, gracious his speech; his spirit merged in the blessed Name. All suffering ended, all doubts, all fears; renowned for his faith and his virtuous deeds. Raised to honour, wondrous his fame; Priceless the pearl, God's glorious Name!” [Guru Granth Sahib]

A Sikh woman bows in front of the platform (the “palki”) from which the Guru Granth Sahib is read. The book rests on cushions, and a “chauri” (fan) is waved over it.

The Guru Granth Sahib

The Guru Granth Sahib is shown the reverence and respect that would be due to a living Guru. The holy book is read at all acts of community worship. It is lavishly enthroned on a raised platform in the prayer hall at the gurdwara, the Sikh place of worship. The Guru Granth Sahib is the centre of focus on ritual occasions such as marriage and the naming of children. The hymns and prayers sung at the gurdwara are taken from the Guru Granth Sahib and worshippers find inspiration, comfort, and strength in its teachings.

The Guru Granth Sahib is a unique scripture because it contains the words of teachers from more than one religious tradition. It includes hymns that are by Muslims and some that are by Hindus. This reflects the nature of the religion itself.

“It is inclusive rather than exclusive. What I mean is that a devout Sikh respects the adherents of all other faiths as did Guru Nanak, the founder of Sikhism.” [G. S. Sidhu, *Introduction to Sikhism*, The Sikh Missionary Society, UK, 1987]

3 (a) What evidence is there in the photograph that the Guru Granth Sahib is a holy book?
(b) Write an interview with a Sikh in which he or she explains the importance of the Guru Granth Sahib and the guidance it offers.

4 The Guru Granth Sahib is not only treated as a living guru. Its words live in the hearts and minds of the members of the Sikh community. What songs, words, mottoes, and teachings do you keep in your heart and mind? What influence do they have on your life?

UNIT TWO

One God, one humanity

In this unit you will begin to understand what Sikhs believe about God and you will be able to reflect on ways in which this teaching influences the Sikh way of life.

1 (a) Think of the ideas about God you have discovered in your religious studies and write down as many words, titles, and terms as you can that you have heard associated with the idea of, or belief in, God.
(b) Underline those words that describe God as like a person. Put a circle around the terms that are more abstract.
(c) Which of these two kinds of descriptions do you think is the more helpful for believers in understanding and expressing their relationship with God?

The Sikh concept of God is clearly set out in the Mool Mantra, which is the basic belief statement of the Sikh faith. It is from the opening verses of the Japji, the prayer of Guru Nanak which Sikhs recite each morning.

“There is one God,
Eternal Truth is his name,
Creator of all things and the all pervading spirit.
Fearless and without hatred,
Timeless and formless.
Beyond birth and death.
Self enlightened.
By the grace of the Guru he is known.”
[Guru Granth Sahib 1]

According to the teachings of Sikhism, God is present everywhere:

“Around us lies God’s dwelling place, his joyous presence on every side. Self existent and supremely beautiful, he dwells as a presence immanent in all creation. Birth and death are abolished by his power, by the grace made manifest in his being. Eternally present within all humanity he reigns in glory for ever.” [From translation of the Jap by W. H. McLeod, *Textual Sources for the Study of Sikhism*, Manchester, 1984]

Sikhs believe that God is the Creator and the Eternal Truth. God is also a personal God who can be loved and worshipped. The relationship between the worshipper and God is often described in personal terms in Sikh tradition:

“Thou art the Master, to thee I pray.
My body and soul are thy gifts to start life with.
Thou art the Father, Thou art the Mother, and we Thy children.”
[Guru Granth Sahib]

Sikhs believe that everything has been created by God. The natural world is in his command and runs according to his law. It is wrong to question the wisdom of God or to try to interfere with his will. This is a difficult lesson, as the story of Bibi Jeevai suggests.

2 What does the story of Bibi Jeevai tell you about:
(a) the relationship between God and the natural world;
(b) the correct relationship between the believer and God; and
(c) the role of the Guru in the Sikh community?
Answer the questions in the form of a conversation in which a Sikh parent explains the story to his or her child.

GURU ANGAD AND BIBI JEEVAI

Guru Angad, the second Sikh Guru, lived in the village of Khadur Sahib in the Punjab. The Guru set up a community kitchen (langar) in the village, where men, women, and children, rich and poor, and from any social class, could eat. The food was free. Many people offered their food and their time to help at the langar.

One such person was a woman called Bibi Jeevai. Every day she took fresh sweet yogurt to the langar. One day a storm broke just as she was setting out with her gift of yogurt. Afraid that the storm would make her late, she wished in her heart that the storm would stop. As it happened, the rain did stop and she reached the langar in time. However, Guru Angad would not accept the yogurt she brought that day. When she asked why, he said, "Dear Jeevai, you have argued with the will of God. We are not supposed to grumble or try to interfere with God's will." Bibi Jeevai was deeply sorry and she realised how important it was to accept and obey God's will.
[adapted from *The Guru's Way*, the Sikh Missionary Society, UK]

Oneness

The symbol "Ik Onkar", found for instance above the Guru Granth Sahib in the gurdwara, means "there is one God". Sikhs believe that the oneness of God is mirrored in the oneness of humankind. Fundamental to Sikhism is the belief that people everywhere – regardless of race, religion, social status, or sex – make up one single human race created by God; all are equal in his sight. It is therefore the duty of every Sikh to serve others as brothers and sisters and to stand up for their rights as equals.

For Sikhs, believing in God is not enough; belief must be expressed in action. The important thing for Sikhs is to declare God as one in their speech, their thoughts, and their actions, and to trust God more than money, relatives, and all other worldly possessions. Through becoming close to God through prayer, and by expressing love for God through service to others, the true worshipper becomes one with God.

A large blue Ik Onkar symbol identifies the gurdwara in Hounslow, Middlesex. All gurdwaras also fly the Sikh flag, called the "Nishan Sahib".

3 Write an introduction to Sikh beliefs. Write under the following three headings: God is One, God and the World, God and Humankind.

UNIT THREE

The ten Gurus

In this unit you will learn about the Sikh Gurus and understand something of their importance in the faith. You will consider the men and women we look to today for leadership and example.

1 Most communities and societies look to a leader who will guide them. What are the qualities of a good leader? What kind of leader do you think we need in the world today? Are the qualities needed in a time of peace different from those needed in a time of war?

Guru Nanak

The first of the ten Sikh Gurus was Guru Nanak. He was born in 1469 into a Hindu family in the Punjab, and grew up in a community where Muslims and Hindus lived alongside one another. Every day Guru Nanak would rise early to bathe in the river before spending time in prayer and meditation. One morning he went to bathe but did not return. Friends and family searched for him and feared he had drowned. Three days later Guru Nanak reappeared. The first words he spoke were: "There is neither Hindu nor Muslim. So whose path shall I follow? I shall follow God's path." From then on Guru Nanak devoted his life to taking God's love to people. He challenged the religious leaders of his time who made it difficult for ordinary people to feel close to God, and he rejected meaningless religious rules and rituals that got in the way of true worship. In his teaching he proclaimed a way of life based on the belief in the unity of God and the equality of all people.

An artist's impression of Guru Nanak and the nine other Sikh Gurus who followed him.

2 What qualities and experiences prepared Guru Nanak for becoming a religious leader? Look at the picture of Guru Nanak. What is the artist trying to tell us about the Guru? Look again at the text about Guru Nanak. Prepare a news article on Guru Nanak and his teaching.

The Gurus and the Sikh community

Guru Nanak spent many years teaching and travelling with his companion Mardana, who was a Muslim. When Guru Nanak was about fifty, he set up a community at Kartarpur which lived according to the teachings of the Guru. Before he died, Guru Nanak appointed his faithful follower Angad as Guru in his place. Guru Angad continued the work of his master and collected together his hymns and teachings so that they would not be lost.

Guru Amar Das became the next Guru to lead the Sikh community. The Emperor Akbar, who visited the Guru's langar (community kitchen) in the village of Goindwal, knew of his work. The Guru's followers had wanted to organise a special reception for the Emperor, but the Guru insisted that Akbar should sit and eat with the others at the gurdwara. In this way he was putting into practice the belief in the unity and equality of all humankind.

Each of the ten Sikh Gurus made a contribution to the life and development of the community. For example, the fourth, Guru Ram Das, founded the city of Amritsar. The fifth, Guru Arjan, built the Harimandir or Golden Temple and established it as a place of pilgrimage. Guru Arjan also put together the first full compilation of hymns and teachings – the Adi Granth ("first collection").

Later Gurus had to lead the Sikh community through difficult times, as the years of tolerance enjoyed under the Emperor Akbar were replaced with a period of religious persecution. The tenth Guru was Guru Gobind Singh. He saw his mission as preserving truth and justice in the face of evil and tyranny:

> "The divine Guru sent me for righteousness' sake
> On this account I have come into the world to
> Extend the faith everywhere and to
> Seize and destroy the evil and the sinful."
> [Guru Granth Sahib]

When the Sikhs assembled on Baisakhi Day in 1699, Guru Gobind Singh called for volunteers who would be willing to give up their lives for the faith. There was silence. Eventually one Sikh stepped forward. The Guru took him into his tent, and came out again, his sword dripping with blood. One by one, four more Sikhs offered themselves and were taken into the Guru's tent. Each time, Guru Gobind Singh came out with blood on his sword. Finally the Guru brought the five volunteers out of the tent, all alive. He called them the "Panj Piare" (the "beloved five"). They were given nectar made from sugar and water, and this became the ceremony for initiation into the Sikh community, the Khalsa. By creating the Khalsa, the Guru ensured that the Sikhs were united and ready to stand firm in the face of persecution.

Guru Gobind Singh saw that there would be no further human Guru after him. He declared that the next Guru would be the Guru Granth Sahib, providing guidance, strength, and inspiration for the community. The Guru Granth Sahib remains the "living Guru" for Sikhs today, as the words of a prayer called the Ardas say: "The light which shone from each of the Ten Masters shines now from the sacred pages of the Guru Granth Sahib."

3 Make a spider diagram illustrating the roles and functions of the ten Sikh Gurus. Underline the roles which the Guru Granth Sahib can perform in the Sikh community. In a few sentences underneath your diagram, explain why certain roles are underlined and give your ideas on how the other roles can be performed in the Sikh community today.

UNIT FOUR

The Five Ks and the Prohibitions

In this unit you will find out about the connection between the Sikh Five Ks and the Sikh code for living. You will be able to reflect on the ways in which people need help and support in following a moral code.

1 In a small group, think of five occasions when you would find it hard to do what is right. Talk about what might help you to do the right thing in these circumstances: what would give you courage, support, or encouragement? Write the results of your discussion in a feedback report for the class.

The Five Ks

When Guru Gobind Singh started the Khalsa, he introduced the wearing of the Five Ks. The Five Ks are symbols worn by Sikhs who are members of the community. Outward signs like this can give support to the wearer in his or her "inner", moral life. The Five Ks are a reminder to Sikhs that they are committed to following a certain moral and religious code. It is harder for someone to act out of line with the teachings of the religion if he or she is always reminded of them.

The first of the Five Ks is well-groomed, uncut hair – kes. It is a symbol of commitment. Hair is a gift from God and it is therefore important to keep it intact and not to cut it. Wearing uncut hair shows readiness to accept God's will. It is a way of developing humility and obedience. Well-kept, clean, uncut hair also represents the importance of purity and orderliness in life.

The second of the five Ks is a small wooden comb to keep the hair in place. This is called the kangha. It is a symbol of cleanliness. Combing the hair removes tangles and dirt, so the symbol reminds Sikhs of the need to untangle themselves from evil and remove impure thoughts.

The third of the five Ks is a steel bracelet – kara, which literally means "link" or "bond". Usually it is worn on the right wrist. It stands for the link or bond between the Sikh and his or her fellow believers and, of course, between the Sikh and God. The unbroken circle of the bracelet is a symbol of the unity and eternity of God. Sikhs wearing the bracelet are constantly reminded of God's presence and that their actions must be according to the teachings of the Gurus.

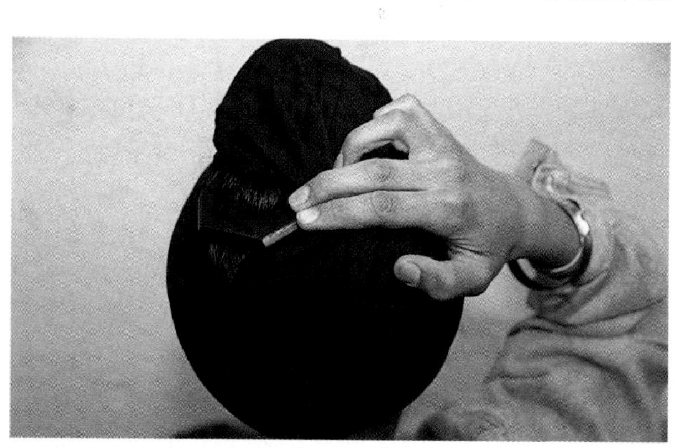

Kes and kangha, two of the Five Ks.

The fourth of the Five Ks is the kachera or shorts. The shorts were given to Sikhs at a time when the usual dress for most people living in India was a long cloth worn around the waist. This could get in the way of a life of action. Shorts were much easier to move in. All Sikhs are called to a life of action. They are to earn an honest living, serve others, and be active in the community. The shorts are also a symbol of purity and self-discipline. Sikhs must avoid sexual relations outside marriage.

The kirpan is the last of the Five Ks. This is the sword. The name kirpan comes from two words: "kirpa", which means an act of kindness, and "aan", meaning self-respect and honour. The kirpan represents fearlessness in the struggle against evil and readiness to defend the weak and fight against injustice. It also stands for moral strength and freedom of spirit.

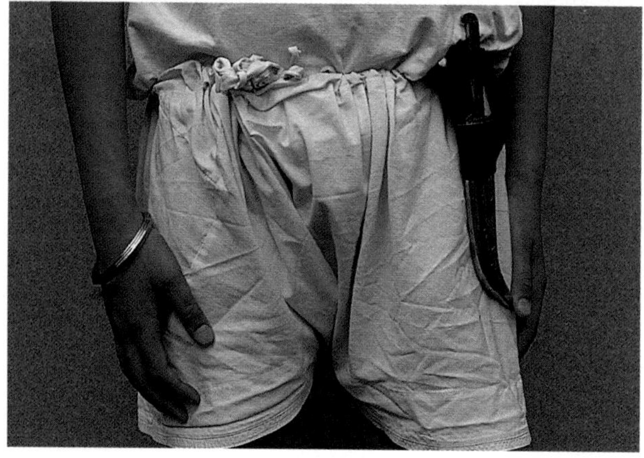

Kirpan, kachera, and kara.

2 Important moral teachings are represented by the Five Ks. Write a discussion between a Sikh and a non-believer in which the Sikh argues the case for wearing these important symbols of the faith and explains the moral teachings behind them.

The Prohibitions

Four things are prohibited to Sikhs who belong to the Khalsa. They are set out in the Rahit Maryada, guidelines drawn up by the Sikh authorities in 1945:

“There are four sins which are particularly serious and which must be scrupulously avoided: 1. Cutting one's hair. 2. Eating meat that has been slaughtered according to the Muslim rite. 3. Sexual intercourse with any person other than one's spouse. 4. Using tobacco.”

However, most of the moral teaching of Sikhism is expressed in positive terms – that is, in terms of things that Sikhs must do: earn their living, give to the poor and needy, and treat all others as brothers and sisters – as equals.

Sikhism rejects meaningless ritual and religious hierarchies. The emphasis is on personal responsibility and the importance of this life and how we live it. The Guru's message in the story of Duni Chand's Needle contains three key teachings that all Sikhs must follow: first, they must remember God and worship him (Nam Simran); second, they should earn their living by honest means (Kirat Karna); and third, they must share what they have with others (Van Cchakna).

DUNI CHAND'S NEEDLE

Once a very rich man named Duni Chand invited Guru Nanak to a feast he had prepared for the priests. Duni Chand's religion had taught him that by feeding the priests he could ensure that they would look after the dead in the next world. He wanted them to look after his father who had died. Guru Nanak turned down the invitation, but afterwards asked Duni Chand if the feast had been a success. Duni Chand remarked on how much the priests had eaten and said he felt reassured that his father would now be well cared for.

The Guru gave Duni Chand a needle and said: “Keep it and use it, but please give it back to me when we meet in the next world.” Duni Chand looked puzzled. “How can I carry this with me when I die?” The Guru replied: “How can the priests carry the food and riches you have given them to your dead father? In the next world we can expect to receive only that which we have earned by honest work and through the service and charity we have given to the needy. Give your riches to the poor. Work alongside your farm hands and share the earnings equally among all the workers. From your own share give away as much as you can to charity. Look upon your workers as brothers and sisters. Love everyone and sing God's praises. Then you will find you are rewarded in the next world.” Duni Chand felt humbled. He and his wife did as the Guru had said and their house became a temple.

3 Write an article for a magazine discussing the teachings of the story of Duni Chand's Needle and its meaning for Sikhs today.

Sikh worship

In this unit you will gain insight into the nature of Sikh worship and think about the way in which being part of a community helps nurture the social, moral, cultural, and spiritual development of the individual.

A Sikh is expected to rise early every morning, before dawn, and, after taking a bath, to meditate on the Name of God. Of the many names for God, the most well-known is "Waheguru" or "Wonderful Lord". Meditating and reflecting on the name of God is a way of putting God at the centre of life and thought. Most Sikhs begin the day by reciting the Japji of Guru Nanak. It begins with the Mool Mantra and continues as a song of praise to God:

“Let every tongue become a hundred thousand; let each be multiplied twice ten times more. Let this multitude of tongues then join together, each repeating a hundred thousand times the name of creation's Lord. This path is a stairway leading to the Master, an ascent to the bliss of mystical union. All may follow it, even the lowliest, if they but heed the word from above.” [Japji 34]

Sikhs pray in the evening after work and again last thing before going to bed. This is the pattern of prayer laid down for all Sikhs in the "Rahit" or Sikh code of conduct. The same code of conduct stresses the importance of worshipping within a community ("sangat") of Sikhs:

“The influence of the Guru's words is best experienced in a religious assembly (sangat). Each Sikh should therefore join in sangat worship, visiting gurdwaras and drawing inspiration from the sacred scripture in the sangat's presence.” [Sikh Rahit Maryada 9]

1 Has belonging to a school community enabled you to develop and grow in ways that would not have been possible if you had grown up on your own, with private tuition? Discuss this question with a partner.

Worship at the gurdwara

The gurdwara is open for daily worship. In some gurdwaras in the UK, a special service is held once a week when the whole community comes together for worship.

Before entering the prayer hall, worshippers take off their shoes, as a sign of respect. When they enter the hall, they bow before the Guru Granth Sahib and make an offering of money or food. This will later be taken for contribution to the langar (community kitchen). Worshippers sit on the floor. The congregation joins in singing kirtan (hymns), which are taken from the scriptures. At most gurdwaras the harmonium and tabla (drums) accompany the hymns. Some gurdwaras have their own professional musicians.

The most important part of worship at the gurdwara is the reading from the Guru Granth Sahib. It may be read by the granthi, who is someone chosen by the community to lead its worship, or by any member of the sangat. To decide the reading for the day, the granthi or reader carefully

2 Prayers at a gurdwara relate to the needs of the particular community. What sorts of things do you think a Sikh community in an inner city in the UK might ask for? Discuss this with a partner and then share your ideas in class, to put together a whole prayer.

holds the pages of the book together before letting them fall open. He or she then reads from the page at which the book has opened. This reading at random from the Guru Granth Sahib is called the "hukam".

There may be a sermon given by the granthi or a visiting speaker and prayers are recited from the Guru Granth Sahib. The service ends with a prayer called the Ardas, which reminds believers of the work of the Sikh Gurus and the importance of the Khalsa. The prayer also asks God for help and support, and finally asks for God's blessing for the whole of humanity.

All are equal

At the end of a Sikh service everyone receives karah parshad or "blessed food". This sweet pudding represents the sweetness of God's grace. Also, sharing karah parshad is a way of saying that all are equal in the eyes of God.

After leaving the prayer hall, worshippers gather for langar, the community meal prepared in the community kitchen. (Both the meal and the kitchen are called langar.) The meal is free to anyone who arrives. Members of the sangat contribute to the cost. A family may take full responsibility for the cost and preparation of the langar one week. This is one way of performing "sewa" (service). In Sikhism, service to others is a way of serving God. It is, in effect, an act of worship. The langar is a demonstration of faith in action. By worshipping together and eating together, the Sikh community demonstrates the two central beliefs of Sikhism – in the unity of God and the equality of all people.

Worshippers share langar after a service in a gurdwara at Amritsar, in Punjab.

3 (a) Just as the body needs exercise, so the spirit needs attention to help it grow fit and strong. What would be the equivalent of exercise or fitness training for the spirit?
(b) Design a poster for a new gurdwara, advertising how it will serve the needs of the community.

A community centre

The gurdwara is not only a place of worship but also a community centre. Many gurdwaras in India have not only a community kitchen but also a school or hospital attached. In the UK, gurdwaras may offer language lessons so that young people can learn to read and write Punjabi, the mother tongue of many families and the language of the Sikh scriptures. They may run lunch clubs for senior citizens, or mother and toddler groups. In this way the sangat looks after both young and old and serves the needs of the wider community.

PART B: QUESTIONING

Questions about life

Does God exist?

Why is there so much suffering in the world?

What will happen when I die?

Is abortion right or wrong?

Should euthanasia be allowed?

"The Thinker" by the great French sculptor Auguste Rodin (1840-1917). The distinguishing feature of humanity is that humans are "thinking animals"; they are able to ask questions about the meaning of life.

Since the beginning of the human race, people have asked questions about meaning and value. In Part B of this book we look at some of these key questions. You will be introduced to some of the ways in which Buddhists, Christians, Hindus, Jews, Muslims, and Sikhs answer these questions.

The "Religion Files" at the end of each chapter provide summaries of the major religious teachings about the issue concerned. You will find the Religion Files useful as sources of information when constructing your arguments for essays. Please note that the first chapter of this section, "Does God exist?" does not contain Religion Files, although it does include many religious arguments. You will see that the six world religions we are studying agree on many issues. You will also learn how they differ in their responses.

Searching for a meaning in life

Sometimes life can feel very meaningless – especially at times of great suffering and tragedy. At such times people ask how they can make life meaningful. The text headed "Attitudes to life" is an extract from a book called *Man's Search for Meaning*, written after the Second World War by Viktor Frankl. During the war, Frankl, a psychiatrist, was imprisoned for three years in Auschwitz and other concentration camps. He noticed that some people became bitter and angry, finding no meaning in their experience, whilst others were not only able to survive the horrifying conditions but also found meaning within them.

1 (a) From Viktor Frankl's description (page 83), how did people respond to the horrors of the concentration camps? Why did some lose hope and others find a meaning in their experience?
(b) What qualities did the two groups of people have?

2 What do you think Frankl means when he says "What was really needed was a fundamental change in our attitude toward life"? In what ways may his words be useful for people today?

ATTITUDES TO LIFE

"The experiences of camp life show that man does have a choice of action. We who lived in concentration camps can remember the men who walked through the huts comforting others, giving away their last piece of bread. They may have been few in number, but they offer sufficient proof that everything can be taken from a man but one thing: the last of the human freedoms to choose one's attitude in any given set of circumstances.

If there is a meaning in life at all, then there must be a meaning in suffering. The way in which a man accepts his fate, and all the suffering it entails, gives him ample opportunity to add a deeper meaning to his life. He may remain brave, dignified and unselfish. Or in the bitter fight for self-preservation he may forget his human dignity and become no more than an animal.

What was really needed was a fundamental change in our attitude toward life. We had to learn ourselves and, furthermore, we had to teach the despairing men, that it did not really matter what we expected from life, but rather what life expected from us. We needed to stop asking about the meaning of life, and instead to think of ourselves as those who were being questioned by life – daily and hourly." [Frankl, *Man's Search for Meaning*, Beacon Press, Boston, 1959]

Men liberated from a Nazi concentration camp in Ebensee, Austria, on 7 May 1945.

The important things in life

The story of "The Bus Journey" illustrates the idea that it is easy to be distracted from the really important things in life.

THE BUS JOURNEY

A group of tourists sits in a bus that is passing through gorgeously beautiful country; lakes and mountains and green fields and rivers. But the shades of the bus are pulled down. They do not have the slightest idea of what lies beyond the windows of the bus. And all the time of their journey is spent in squabbling over who will be applauded, who will be considered. And so they remain till the journey's end. [Anthony de Mello, *The Way To Love*, Doubleday, 1995]

3 What does the bus journey stand for? Why couldn't the tourists see out of the windows? What do the shades of the bus stand for?

4 In what sense do people "squabble over who will be applauded" in today's society?

CHAPTER 7

Does God exist?

UNIT ONE

Who is God?

Language has its limitations. It is good when it talks about objects such as bats and balls; it stammers when it tries to communicate deep feelings, such as love; and it is inadequate when it tries to talk about God. The danger of trying to describe God is that our descriptions are bound to limit Him. God is, by nature, unlimitable. In this unit you will be thinking about key words and ideas used to describe God.

1 If God exists, why do you think many people find it difficult to find him?

2 What is the story in "Escape" trying to say? Do you agree with the message?

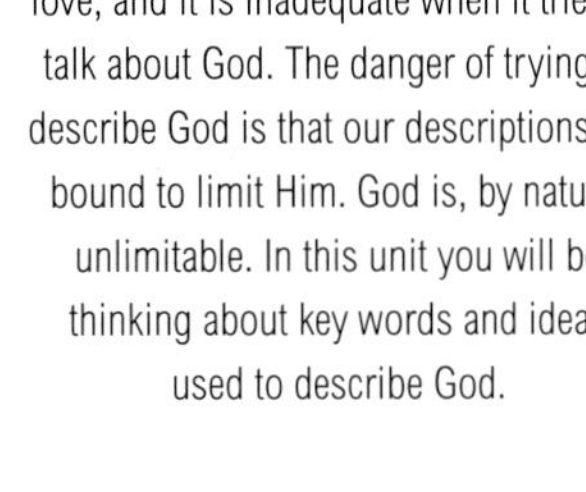

ESCAPE

The Master became a legend in his lifetime. It was said that God once sought his advice: "I want to play a game of hide-and-seek with humankind. I've asked my angels what the best place is to hide in. Some say the depth of the ocean. Others the top of the highest mountain. Others still the far side of the moon or a distant star. What do you suggest?"

Said the Master, "Hide in the human heart. That's the last place they will think of!" [Anthony de Mello, *One Minute Wisdom*, Doubleday, 1983]

Trying to describe God is like trying to describe the indescribable. Therefore, people sometimes use opposites together. They talk of God as both personal and impersonal, both immanent (dwelling in everything) and transcendent (beyond everything we know). Sometimes God is described as a personal being who intervenes in history to help and guide people. At other times God is described in impersonal ways – distant from people, beyond their understanding, and outside their material world. Each religion has particular ways of describing God.

Traditionally, when people write about God, they use capital letters (He, Him, His). Using capitals helps to underline the fact that it is difficult to use everyday language to describe God. By using "He", religions are not saying that God is masculine. In recent years, religious publications have also used "She" and "Her" to describe God.

The religions of the world have different names for God. For example, Muslims use the Arabic "Allah".

Buddhism does not use the word "God" to describe ultimate reality. The starting point of the Buddha's teaching was not "Who created the world?" or "What is God like?" The Buddha was concerned with practical questions such as "How do we end suffering?" and "How do we find contentment?" A monk once asked the Buddha, "Are you a god?" He replied, "No. I am awake [that is, enlightened]." Buddhists do not worship Buddha as a god. Sometimes you might read about Buddhist "gods" or the heavenly realm which is inhabited by gods. These gods are like angels in Christianity, Islam, and Judaism.

Hinduism uses images to help people understand what God is like. Although Hindus believe that there is only one God, Hindu temples contain

3 How would you describe God? What images would you use? What characteristics do you think God has?

4 Look at the seven quotations from different religions on page 85 and find phrases which suggest that God is (a) immanent and (b) transcendent.

Hindus may hang paintings of their gods in their homes, like this one expressing the "universal nature of Vishnu".

pictures and statues of many deities, showing the countless sides of God's nature. God is shown as male, female, creator, and destroyer. Some other religions (for example, Judaism and Islam) do not allow people to make images of God. They believe that there is a danger that people will start to worship the images and not God Himself or Herself. Christians believe that Jesus was God, who came to live with people and share their lives. When they look at Jesus, they believe that they are seeing what God is like – not physically, but spiritually.

“The Lord lives in the heart of every creature. Take refuge utterly in Him.” [Hinduism: Bhagavad Gita 18: 61-62]

“The Infinite is the source of joy. There is no joy in the finite. Ask to know the Infinite.” [Hinduism: Chandogya Upanishad 7: 23]

“We [God] indeed created man; and We know what his soul whispers within him, and We are nearer to him than the jugular vein.” [Islam: Qur'an, 50: 16]

“No vision can grasp Him, but His grasp is over all vision; He is above all comprehension, yet is acquainted with all things.” [Islam: Qur'an, 6: 103]

“I am the Lord your God who brought you out of Egypt, where you were slaves. Worship no God but me. Do not make for yourselves images of anything in heaven or on earth . . . Do not bow down to any idol or worship it, because I am the Lord your God and I tolerate no rivals.” [Judaism: Exodus 20]

“He is not far from each one of us, for in Him we live and move and have our being.” [Christianity: Acts 17: 28-29]

““In all creation is the Lord pervasive.”” [Sikhism: Guru Granth Sahib 376]

Q

5 Why do some religions have images of God? How helpful do you think images of God are? What are the possible dangers of making images of God?

6 Explain what the following words mean: personal; impersonal; immanent; transcendent; omnipotent; omniscient. What do they tell you about the nature of God?

7 In what ways are God and humanity different? What makes God god-like? What is special about God's character?

Information File: Words used to describe God

- God is all-powerful – **omnipotent**.
- God is all-knowing – **omniscient**.
- God is **infinite** and **eternal** – as one writer puts it: "God exists outside of time. God created time as an artist chooses a medium to work with, and is unbound by it."
- God is the **creator**.
- God is **all-loving**.
- God is ever present – **omnipresent**.

UNIT TWO

Arguments for the existence of God

Do you believe in the existence of God? What reasons might someone who does believe in God give for his or her belief? In this unit you will consider two main arguments for the existence of God: the argument from design, and the argument from religious experience.

THE ASTRONAUT AND THE BRAIN SURGEON

A Russian astronaut and a brain surgeon were discussing religion. The brain surgeon was a religious believer but the astronaut was not. The astronaut said, "I've been out in space many times and have never seen God." The brain surgeon replied, "And I've operated on many clever brains but I've never seen a single thought."

Many people find it difficult to believe in God. Here are some reasons why:

"Religious people are not good adverts for God – look how they judge people all the time." [Ron]

"How could God create a world which contains so much suffering?" [Sam]

"I don't need God. I have everything I want." [Marc]

1 Sam, Marc, and Ron give some reasons for not believing in God. Are any of the reasons convincing? Give reasons for your answer.

The argument from design

"Who put the colours in the rainbow?
Who put the salt into the sea?
Who put the cold into the snowflake?
Who made you and me? . . .

Who put the scent into the roses?
Who taught the honeybee to dance?
Who put the tree inside the acorn?
It surely can't be chance . . . "

A tropical swallowtail butterfly.

This popular children's song, which ends "God made all of these!", clearly expresses the "design argument" for the existence of God: nature is full of beauty and intricate design; the ecosystem fits together in such a carefully ordered way that the world is a self-sustaining whole; such design in nature – in its beauty and detail – points to the existence of a great designer, God.

Information File: Believers and non-believers

A person who believes in God is called a **theist**.
A person who does not believe in the existence of God is called an **atheist**.
An **agnostic** believes that it is impossible to know if God exists.
A **humanist** is an agnostic or atheist who believes that it is possible to achieve happiness and fulfilment without religion.

The first time the design argument was recorded was in 390 BCE, when Xenophon quoted Socrates as saying: "With such signs of forethought in the design of living creatures, can you doubt they are the work of choice or design?" William Paley (1743-1805 CE) developed the argument. He said that someone walking in the countryside who suddenly came across a watch hidden in the grass, having never seen one before, would immediately be impressed by its detailed mechanism. A watch surely is not made by chance, but instead points to the existence of an intelligent watchmaker who designed it. Paley drew a parallel between the watch and the world, and said that the intricate detail of the world pointed to the existence of an intelligent designer God who created it.

“I do not feel like an alien in this universe. The more I study the details of its architecture the more evidence I find that the universe in some sense must have known we were coming.” [Physicist, Freeman Dyson, 12 December 1979, quoted in R. Holloway, *Dancing on the Edge*, Fount, 1997]

“According to current thinking, there was a Big Bang some twelve thousand million years ago . . . As a result of the Big Bang, matter moved apart at nearly the speed of light [186,000 miles a second]. But gravity tried to pull it together again. According to Professor Paul Davies, if the explosion had differed in strength at the outset by only one part in 10^{60} [one followed by sixty noughts!], the universe we now perceive would not exist. To give some meaning to these numbers, suppose you wanted to fire a bullet at a one-inch target on the other side of the observable universe, twenty billion light years away. Your aim would have to be accurate to that same one part in 10^{60}. There are many other examples of this 'fine-tuning' and cosmic coincidences.” [Dr Michael Poole, in *RE Today*, Summer 1998]

Objections to the design argument

The design argument was attacked from the start by philosophers such as David Hume (1711-76) and John Stuart Mill (1806-73). Here are some of their reasons:

- If creation is the work of an intelligent designer, who created the designer? Why should we stop at God when seeking explanations?
- The world contains much suffering and evil. What sort of God would create such imperfection and evil?
- Why believe in the existence of only one God? After all, many things in the world (e.g. cars) are designed and made by several people.
- The design argument makes God little more than a superman – a designer on a big scale.

2 (a) Do you think Paley is right to compare the workings of the universe to the mechanism of a watch?
(b) Write a short paragraph explaining the main objections to the design argument. Write a second paragraph saying how valid you think these objections are.

What is this person doing? Prayer has been described as "wasting time with God" and "talking with God". What does it mean to "talk with God"? How does God speak?

3 What exactly is a religious experience? Use the examples in this unit to help you write a definition.

4 (a) Why did Sir Alistair Hardy start collecting examples of religious experience?
(b) Why do you think he felt such experiences had played an important role in the survival of humanity?
(c) Many of Hardy's respondents said that they had these experiences in their early years. Have you had an experience that would fit Hardy's advert in the newspapers? If so, write an account of it.

The argument from religious experience and revelation

Many religious people believe that God reveals himself to human beings. God does this in a variety of ways, including through prayer, sacred books, nature, worship, and everyday experience. All religious traditions have examples of such "revelations": sometimes people see visions, hear voices, or sense the presence of something "other than", "over", or "beyond" the normal.

Religious experiences may be dramatic. The Prophet Muhammad was visited by the Angel Jibril, who ordered him to "Recite!" Muslims believe that the words that the Prophet received were revelations from Allah, which now form the Qur'an, the Muslim holy book (see pages 52-55). The founder of Sikhism, Guru Nanak, experienced being taken into God's presence and receiving a message or revelation from God for all people (see page 76).

On the other hand, some people would say that they have been aware of the presence of God throughout their lives. This is a different type of direct experience of God's presence from the single, dramatic revelation.

Researching religious experience

In 1969 Sir Alistair Hardy, a distinguished evolutionary biologist and Professor of Zoology at Oxford University, set out to collect, analyse, and categorise examples of people's religious experiences. He wanted to build up a natural history of the human experience of the sacred or divine. In his autobiography he explains that his interest in a "biology of the spirit" developed from his own experience, on country walks in his youth, of feeling the presence of something beyond and yet part of nature.

Hardy believed that some awareness of the sacred spreads across the whole of humanity, and that the sense of being in touch with a reality beyond the self is as biologically real as being in love. Although religious experience is as difficult to measure as being in love, his Religious Experience Research Unit would collect and observe specimens, just as biologists do. He placed an advert in major newspapers inviting "all who had been conscious of, and perhaps influenced by, some such power, whether they call it the power of God or not, to write a simple and brief account of these feelings and their effects." Over the next 20 years he collected over 5,000 accounts and these experiences became the basis for the Alistair Hardy Research Centre in Oxford.

In the 1970s and 1980s, David Hay carried out nationwide polls asking "Have you ever been conscious of a presence or power other than your everyday self?" In one of these surveys, 62 per cent of those who replied answered "yes". Research in the USA produced similar results. Many people said that their experiences had had a life-changing effect. Many reported that they had become more tolerant, or more humble and sensitive to others' needs. Several people described their experience as a conversion, which caused them to completely change their attitude and outlook on life.

In his book *The Existence of God*, published in 1979, Richard Swinburne organises people's religious experiences into five groups:

In 1995, Hindu statues around the world appeared to be drinking the milk that was offered to them. Was it a miracle or was there a scientific explanation, to do with surface tension and the dry stone of the statues? Opinions differed.

1. God is seen to be at work in the everyday world. For example, a religious believer looks at the beauty of a snowflake and sees God's hand at work. A non-believer might just see a beautiful snowflake.
2. God is felt to be responsible for a very unusual event, seen as a miracle, involving a break in the natural law – for example, someone walking on water.
3. God is felt to be involved in a particular experience of the believer's life, which the person can describe using ordinary language. Non-believers may look for psychological explanations for such experiences.
4. God is felt to be involved in a particular experience that the believer cannot describe in ordinary language – for example the mystical experience Alistair Hardy had when walking in the country.
5. God is felt to be acting on and guiding the believer's life, in a general sense.

5 In pairs discuss how a believer and a non-believer would explain the following:
(a) My mother was dying of cancer. We prayed with her and she was completely healed.
(b) The other day when I prayed to God I felt His love surround me.

6 Debate the motion: "This house believes that humans have invented God."

Objections to the argument from religious experience and revelation

- Religious experiences are the result of psychological states.
- It is all a matter of personal interpretation. For example, how do you distinguish between "God spoke to me last night" and "It seemed to me that God spoke to me last night"? What one person counts as a religious experience would be explained by another by means of natural phenomena.
- Many people in the world report strange experiences – they experience God, UFOs, witches, demons, devils, ghosts, spirits, aliens. Whom do you believe? How do you distinguish true experiences from imaginary ones?
- Religious experiences can be explained away by the fact that people only have experiences from within their own culture. For example, Hindus have experiences of Hindu gods, while Catholics have visions of the Virgin Mary.

Sample Examination Questions

"God made himself known to people in the past but He does not seem to be making himself known today." [a teenager]

(a) One of the ways in which "God made himself known to people in the past" is by religious writings. Give one example of a religious writing from each of two religious traditions. [2 marks]

(b) Explain two other ways in which "God made himself known". You should refer to two religious traditions in your answer. [4 marks]

(c) How might a religious believer reply to the claim that "God does not seem to be making himself known today"? [4 marks]

(d) Is revelation by itself enough for a person to know God? Give reasons for your answer. [3 marks]

[NEAB Syllabus D Paper 1, June 1998]

CHAPTER

What about suffering?

UNIT ONE

In this unit we will consider whether all suffering is pointless or whether people can give suffering a meaning. In the Religion Files at the end of the chapter, you will discover the answers given by different religious traditions to the question of why there is suffering.

Why is there suffering?

Why there is suffering is one of the most difficult questions to answer fully. Take a few moments to reflect on situations in which people have endured terrible suffering. The examples you think of may be personal to you, your family, or friends, or they may be from situations in other parts of the world. What has caused the suffering?

Types of suffering

Thinkers often divide suffering into two kinds: (a) that which is caused by people and the way they behave towards each other and (b) that which has a natural cause, such as an earthquake or a volcano erupting. Sometimes the causes of the first type – such as war, murder, rape, and child abuse – are referred to as "moral evil", whilst the causes of the second type are called "natural evil".

1 Make two columns – one for natural causes of suffering and one for human causes of suffering. Write the following in the correct column: volcanoes, floods, viruses, starvation, physical handicaps, AIDS. Do any of these examples belong in both columns? Explain why. Add your own examples to the columns.

2 Do you think there is any purpose or value in suffering?

3 (a) Choose one of the quotations from page 91 that you agree with and develop the argument, providing examples.
(b) Choose one of the quotations that you disagree with and say why, giving evidence if possible to back up your arguments.

This mother and her children in Honduras lost their home and their belongings in the floods which followed Hurricane Mitch, November 1998.

In April 1999, two teenagers walked in to Columbine High School in Littleton, Colorado, USA, and shot dead a teacher and 12 students before killing themselves. Here three fellow students share their grief at a prayer vigil.

Q

4 Sometimes you will hear it said that "Through suffering we learn." How far do you agree with this statement? In your answer, try to give examples from your own experience or from stories in books and films to both support and contradict the statement.

Is there any purpose in suffering?

“Pain can be useful – think of toothache. Pain warns us of infection and illness in our body which we need to treat.” [Paul, 14]

“A man may perform astonishing feats and comprehend a vast amount of knowledge, and yet have no understanding of himself. But suffering directs a man to look within. If it succeeds, then there, within him, is the beginning of learning.” [S. Kierkegaard, Danish philosopher, 1813–55]

“There are times when it seems that suffering serves no purpose at all. When young children suffer it is very difficult to understand if there is any purpose behind it.” [Erin, 16]

“Suffering is a punishment from God for something someone has done in this or a previous life.” [Rana, 16]

“Suffering refines us.” [Dereje, 16]

“God might be testing people through their suffering. It is easy to believe in God when you are prosperous because there is no reason to doubt his love. As soon as that wonderful world is invaded by suffering it becomes more difficult for people to believe.” [Bethany, 15]

“Suffering produces depth in our character. We can use our experience of suffering to understand, relate to, and reach out to others who are suffering. Because we have suffered we can understand their suffering.” [Ivan, 16]

“Suffering can make us stronger – emotionally, mentally, and spiritually.” [Pascal, 17]

“I do know that it is my hardest times which have helped me tremendously.” [Susan, 16]

UNIT TWO

Where is God?

In this unit you will be considering why the existence of suffering presents specific problems for religions centred on belief in God.

1 What do you think the Master in "Giving Suffering a Meaning" means?

2 What do you think of each of the "range of viewpoints" listed below?

3 (a) Make a list of the different types of suffering referred to in the poem "Where is He?"
(b) If you could meet God, what would you like to (i) tell God, (ii) ask God?

For someone who does not believe in God, suffering is not necessarily a problem but an unhappy fact of life. However, for the religious believer, the existence of suffering poses difficult questions. It is important to be clear about the differences between religions that started in the Middle East (Judaism, Christianity, and Islam) and religions that started in India (Hinduism, Buddhism, and Sikhism).

Jews, Christians, and Muslims discuss the issue of suffering in terms of what it says about the nature of God. For them, the existence of suffering poses the difficult questions: Why does God allow suffering? and What sort of God allows suffering?

For Hindus, Buddhists, and Sikhs, the existence of suffering is explained by the law of karma – the idea that what people sow they will reap, be it in this life or the next. Suffering is part of being born. It is accepted more as a fact of life (although some Hindus and Sikhs believe that God can override karma). For Hindus, Buddhists, and Sikhs, the religious problem is not so much how to avoid suffering as how to make personal pain, loss, or worldly defeat meaningful.

GIVING SUFFERING A MEANING

A woman in great distress over the death of her son came to the Master for comfort. He listened to her patiently while she poured out her tale of woe. Then he said softly, "I cannot wipe away your tears, my dear. I can only teach you how to make them holy." [Anthony de Mello, *One Minute Wisdom*, Doubleday, 1995]

After an earthquake in Colombia in March 1999, armed looters roamed the streets and even the army found the situation impossible to control.

A range of viewpoints

There seem to be only a few possible viewpoints in answering the question "Where is God in a world full of suffering?"

- The world is immoral, since the innocent suffer and the wicked often succeed.
- The world is amoral and meaningless, ruled by nobody or by chance.
- The world is moral and ruled by a just judge. If you were able to see the whole picture you would see that, although the innocent do sometimes suffer now and the wicked succeed, it will not always be so. Later on, in the future or in heaven, the innocent will receive a just reward and the wicked their just punishment.
- Suffering serves a purpose. The world is moral and is ruled by a mysteriously just judge who sometimes requires human suffering to achieve his ends.
- The world is moral and works according to the law of karma – cause and effect. Suffering is caused by wrong actions.

“God does exist, but is often silent through people's suffering.” [Cassie, 16]

“I have found that it is the times in which I am in some form of pain that God seems to be so close to me. It is then that I see my weakness and his strength the clearest.” [Leah, 16]

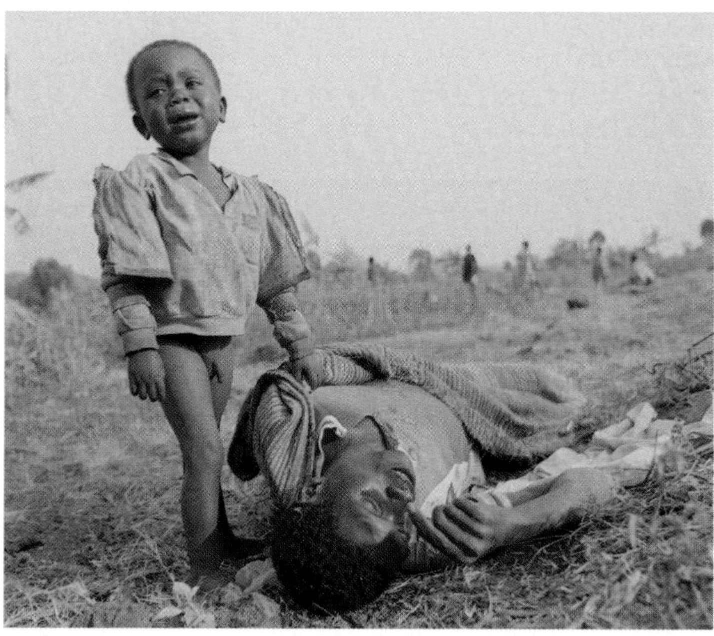

A Rwandan boy stands by his father, who has died from cholera. They had fled the atrocities taking place in Rwanda and just reached the neighbouring country of Zaire.

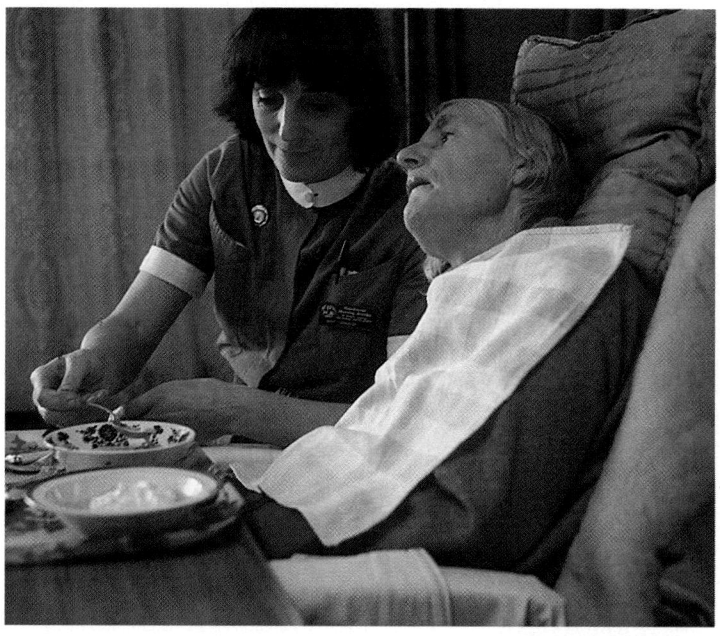

Some old people become dependent in a similar way to when they were very young.

WHERE IS HE?

I'd like to see God.
I'd like to tell him a few things.
I'd like to say:
“God, why do you create people
and make them suffer and fight in vain,
and live brief unhappy lives like pigs,
and make them die disgustingly,
and rot?

God, why do
the beautiful girls you create
become whores, grow old and toothless,
die and have their corpses rot
so that they are a stench
to human nostrils?

God, why do you permit
thousands and millions of your creatures,
made in your image and likeness,
to live like crowded dogs
in slums and tenements,
while an exploiting few
profit from the sweat of their toil,
produce nothing,
and live in kingly mansions?

God, why do you permit people
to starve, hunger, die, from syphilis,
cancer, consumption?
God, why do you not raise
one little finger to save mankind
from all the suffering
on this human planet?”

That's what I'd say to God
if I could find him hiding behind a tree.
But God's a wise guy.
He keeps in hiding!

Religious responses to the problem of suffering

RELIGION FILE

BUDDHISM

- The question of suffering is central to Buddhism. The Buddha taught that suffering is part of the way things are in life. The Buddha is often compared to a doctor who diagnoses the suffering of the world and offers a cure. His diagnosis and cure are summed up in the Four Noble Truths. Study these on page 36 and apply them to the story of Kisa Gotami, whose baby had just died.

Q

1 Which of the Buddha's Noble Truths did Kisa Gotami learn in this practical lesson?

2 (a) When the Buddha first said that he could help Kisa Gotami, what sort of help did she expect? What sort of help did she receive? Explain carefully how the help expected and the help received differ.
(b) What was the cause of Kisa Gotami's suffering? How did she stop her own suffering?

KISA GOTAMI AND THE MUSTARD SEED

One day a woman called Kisa Gotami came to the Buddha holding her dead baby. "Please bring him back to life for me." The Buddha told her that he could help her, but that first she must go in search of a mustard seed from a house where no one had experienced suffering. Wherever Gotami went she heard a similar reply: my father died last year; my baby has fallen ill, and so on. At the end of the day she returned to the Buddha no longer holding her baby. "What have you found?" said the Buddha. "O Buddha, today I have discovered that I am not the only one who has lost a loved one. Everywhere people have died. I see how foolish I was to think I could have my son back. I have accepted his death and this afternoon I cremated him. Now I have returned to you to hear your teachings. I am ready to listen."

RELIGION FILE

CHRISTIANITY

- The Christian Bible tells that God created a world which was good. So where did suffering come from? Ideas differ. Genesis 1-2: 4 tells that people were created "in the image of God". They are spiritual beings who can make moral choices. Life is where people grow spiritually, and suffering serves an important purpose in this process. Some Christians believe that the world is still evolving, and in this process natural disasters do happen. The second account of creation [Genesis 1: 4b-25] describes how the first people, Adam and Eve, misused the free will with which they were created, to choose evil. Suffering is regarded by some Christians as a punishment for Adam's sin.

This picture made in Panama shows Adam and Eve expelled from Paradise for disobeying God's command not to eat from the tree of knowledge.

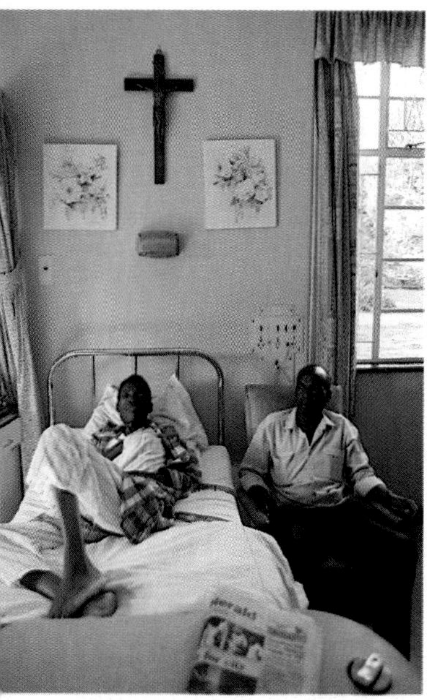

A figure of Jesus on the cross hangs above the bed of this young man at an AIDS clinic in Harare, Zimbabwe.

- The Suffering God. Christians believe in a God who – in the form of His Son, Jesus, who lived a real human life and died on the cross – suffers with and for His people. This belief has given Christians faith that they have not been left alone to suffer – God understands human pain and agony; in fact, God suffers with His creation. Because of the importance of this belief, the cross became the central symbol for Christians.

Frances Young is the mother of a severely brain-damaged and disabled son. She writes: “The only thing that makes it possible to believe in God at all is the cross . . . We do not begin by explaining evil away, justifying God, excusing him for the mess he has made of his creation. We begin by contemplating the story which tells of God entering [the world] himself, taking it upon himself, in all its horror, cruelty, and pain . . . [On the cross] Jesus had experienced even more acutely the abandonment and desolation that I knew . . . It was only because he had that the other side of the story was significant: there, in that utter absence of God, was the presence of God.” [Frances Young, *Face to Face*, T. & T. Clark]

- Suffering is not the end of the story. The story of Jesus did not end with his death: he was raised to life, and returned to be with God in heaven. Christians believe that, when they die, they will also be "raised to life": they can look forward to a continuing relationship with God after death. "There will be no more death, no more grief or crying or pain." [Revelation 21]

- Christians believe that meaning can be found in suffering.

The Christian writer C. S. Lewis wrote the following when his wife was dying of cancer: “Pain is God's megaphone to rouse a deaf world. We are like blocks of stone out of which the sculptor carves the forms of men. The blows of his chisel, which hurt us so much, are what make us perfect. We think our childish toys bring us all the happiness that there is and our nursery is the whole wide world. But something must drive us out of the nursery to the world of others. And that something is suffering.”

- Christians respond to suffering by praying (asking God to help those who suffer), and by serving people who are suffering (working with the poor, in hospitals, etc.)

3 (a) How do Christians explain how suffering came into the world?
(b) Do you think people have free will? Why do you think people sometimes make choices which hurt others?
(c) Some Christians believe in an evil supernatural force (the Devil), which tempted Adam and Eve to disobey God, and tempts people today to do the same. Do you believe that people are tempted to choose the wrong way of behaving by a supernatural power outside themselves?

4 (a) Why do Christians believe it is important that God, in the form of Jesus, suffered?
(b) Why is Jesus's resurrection important to Christians?

5 (a) Can all suffering be explained? Do you think that there is a mystery to suffering?
(b) One Christian wrote: "I cannot endure these people who explain everything . . . I prefer to admit that I don't understand." Why do you think explanations sometimes repel the sufferer?

RELIGION FILE

HINDUISM 

- Hindus believe that every thought and action has consequences. This is the law of karma. Suffering is therefore explained as being the result of paapa (sinful actions) in this and previous lives. The law of karma also leads to the idea that by good actions in this life, people can help reduce suffering in the future. This is called agami karma.

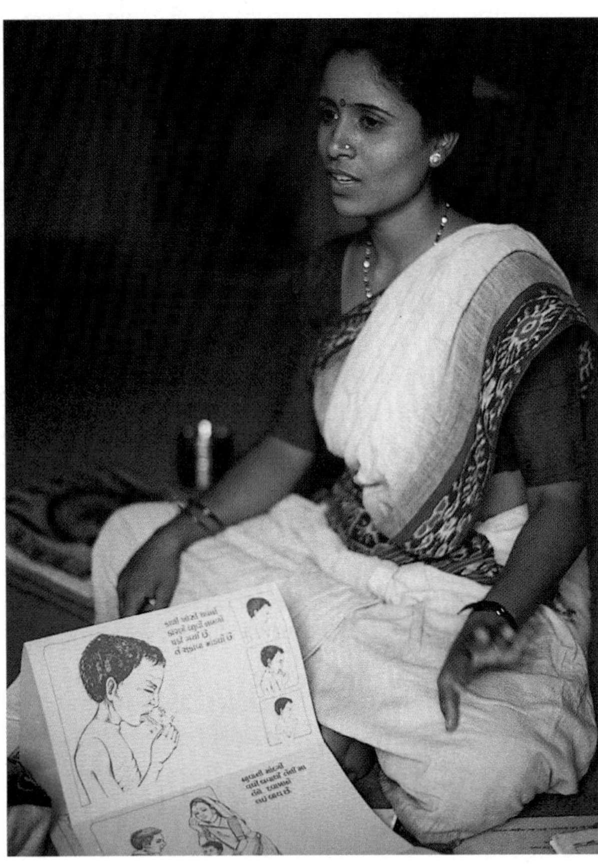

SEWA International is a Hindu charity which works to relieve suffering. Its motto is "Serving Humanity is Serving God". This SEWA health worker is teaching others about re-hydration.

- Suffering is part of samsara: the cycle of birth, death, and rebirth. The goal for Hindus is to achieve moksha: that is, to be free from that cycle, and so from suffering in the material world. "This body is mortal, always gripped by death, but within it dwells the immortal Self. This Self, when associated in our consciousness with the body, is subject to pleasure and pain; and so long as this association continues, freedom from pleasure and pain can no man find." [Chandogya Upanishad 8.12.1]

  To achieve moksha, it is important to follow the right path in life. The right path is called yoga. There are many forms: karma yoga is doing service for humanity; raj yoga is practising self-control and meditation; bhakti yoga is the path of loving devotion; and jnana yoga is the path of knowledge and understanding through study and discipline.

6 (a) What do Hindus say is the cause of suffering?
(b) Provide examples of how good or bad actions have consequences on people's lives.

7 What is the connection between karma and moksha?

8 (a) Do you think the law of karma is fair?
(b) Does it provide a good explanation for the existence of suffering?

RELIGION FILE

ISLAM 

- Muslims believe that all that happens is part of Allah's plan. This belief is called "qadr". Nothing happens without Allah willing it [Qur'an, 81: 29]. Suffering and pain are therefore part of a big plan which people cannot always understand.

- Suffering is a test given by God (Allah). When Allah made the world, He told Adam to look after it as His vice-regent. He made people superior to angels by giving them free will, and He commanded the angels to bow

Well-known British Muslim Yusuf Islam visits an Islamic African Relief Agency project in Sudan.

down to Adam. Because Satan (Ibis) refused to do so, he was thrown out of heaven. Then Allah gave Ibis the kingdom of hell and the job of testing people's faith in Allah. Evil and suffering are therefore the ways in which Ibis tests people's faith.

> ❝Be sure, We shall test you with something of fear and hunger, some loss in goods or lives or the fruits of your toil, but give glad tidings to those who patiently persevere – who say when afflicted with calamity, 'To God we belong and to Him is our return'.❞ [Qur'an, 2: 155-6]

- Muslims believe that they are accountable to Allah for what they do in this life. After death comes judgement. If they act in a cruel and selfish manner, they know that they will be punished by Allah on the Day of Judgement [Qur'an, 74: 39-47]. Those who have followed Allah throughout their life, and have fed the poor, will be rewarded in heaven [Qur'an, 37: 43-38].
- One of the 99 names of Allah given in the Qur'an is "The Compassionate". Muslims believe that they should show compassion to people who are suffering.

Q

9 (a) What would a Muslim say was the purpose of suffering?
(b) If suffering is a test, what are people to learn from it?

10 What is the prize for passing the test? (See also page 108.)

The Ramadan Packet

In 1996, Islamic Relief Worldwide set up the Ramadan Packet project. Packets are made up, each containing essential food items to sustain an average family for approximately one week. Each week during the month of Ramadan the packets are distributed to poor families. In 1997 a total of 22,000 packets were distributed to over 118,000 people all over the world.

RELIGION FILE

JUDAISM

11 Which of the Jewish explanations for suffering do you (a) agree with, and (b) disagree with? Explain why.

- Suffering is the result of free will. As soon as God gave people free will, the potential for human sin and evil was let loose in the world. The biblical account of the giving of free will is found in Genesis 3. In the very next chapter there is an example of the choice of evil – Cain murders Abel. Having granted people free will, God could not control people's use of it.

- The Jewish Bible, the Tenakh, teaches that suffering comes from God and is intended for people's benefit: (a) it is the way God disciplines people [Deuteronomy 8: 5]; (b) it is God's punishment for sin [Deuteronomy 28: 15]; (c) God uses suffering to bring people back to Him [Isaiah 53: 5; Leviticus 26: 41]; (d) it is a test [Genesis 22: 1-2].

- The book of Job in the Tenakh is the story of a truly innocent man who suffers greatly. Why does he have to suffer? What is God trying to tell him? Job calls on God to explain. In chapters 38-39 God answers Job out of a whirlwind: He does not answer Job's accusations directly, but challenges him: Who are you to question my wisdom? Where were you when I made the world? Do you know all the answers? Job recognises that God is in control, even though he himself does not know the reasons.

Sarajevo, Bosnia: touching a name on a memorial to Jews killed in the Second World War is Antonia Slosberg. Herself a Jew, she changed her name to Antonia Babic to hide her origins from the Nazis.

The Holocaust: a case study

From 1933 to 1945, the Nazis carried out a full-scale persecution of the Jewish community in Europe. Jews refer to this persecution, in Hebrew, as the Shoah ("whirlwind"); in English it is called the Holocaust (a burnt offering). Over six million Jews were killed.

More than any other event in history, the Holocaust has caused Jews to revisit the question of undeserved suffering. Many Jews have lost confidence in the belief in a covenant God (see page 62). Others have come to believe that God is limited. There have been two main approaches to the Shoah in the last 50 years:

1. *To offer a response.* There have been different responses: (a) to protest to God, as some of the Psalms do (e.g. Psalm 55); (b) to wrestle with God, demanding some meaning, as Abraham did in Genesis 18: 22-33; (c) to bear witness and make sure that the event is not forgotten, for example, by collecting the testimonies of survivors, by building Holocaust museums, and by commemorating the lives of those who died; (d) to seek justice, hunting down the Nazis responsible for the Holocaust and bringing them to trial.
2. *To attempt to explain the relationship of God to people's suffering.* (a) One modern theologian, E. Berkovits, suggests that God was present in the Holocaust but was in hiding, as He is in Psalm 44: 24. (b) Another theologian, Maza, puts forward the idea that God used the Holocaust to return His people to the study of the Torah, the teachings of their religion. This has echoes in the Bible where we read of God punishing His people in order to bring them back to Himself.

Retired railway worker Andrzel Sawoniuk went on trial at the Old Bailey in London, in February 1999, accused of Nazi war crimes and the murder of two Jewish women during the Second World War. It was Britain's first War Crimes trial.

12 Job heard God's voice and his faith was strengthened. Do you think it is easier to find a meaning in suffering if you believe in God? Do you think Job was right to believe that God had a purpose, even though he himself didn't know what it was?

13 If suffering is a learning process, what lessons do you think are being taught? Could these lessons be learnt without suffering?

14 How have Jewish people responded to the Holocaust? What lessons do you think people should learn from the Holocaust?

RELIGION FILE

SIKHISM

- Sikhs believe that much of the suffering in the world is the result of selfish human action (haumai) and is not God's fault. At the same time, Sikhism teaches that God is the source of everything: "The Creator created both poison and nectar. He attached these two fruits to the world-plant." [Guru Granth Sahib 1172] Everything is in the Creator's hands. We are given to eat as much of them as it pleases God to give us." [Guru Granth Sahib 1172/9]. It is a mystery why some suffering occurs, and also why some people and some parts of the world suffer more than others.

- Sikhism teaches that people should rise above suffering, and develop a trust in God: "Lord, when I am happy I will worship you only; when I suffer, I will not forget you." [Guru Granth Sahib 757]

15 Would the world be a better or worse place without suffering? Discuss.

Sample Examination Questions

"I believe that pain and suffering are never the will of God . . . Some years ago our 21-year-old daughter and the lad to whom some day she would have been married were both drowned in a yachting accident. God did not stop that accident at sea, but He did still the storm in my own heart, so that somehow my wife and I came through that terrible time." [William Barclay, *Testament of Faith*, A. R. Mowbray and Co. Ltd]

(a) Explain one way in which having a religious faith might still the storm of pain and suffering in a person's life. [2 marks]
(b) Explain how pain and suffering can raise doubts about (i) God's love, (ii) God's power. [6 marks]
(c) How might a religious believer explain why God did not stop that accident at sea? [4 marks]
(d) Do you agree that pain and suffering are never the will of God? Give reasons for your opinion. [3 marks]
[NEAB Syllabus D Paper 1, June 1997]

CHAPTER

Is there a life after death?

UNIT ONE

When you're dead, you're dead. Or are you?

"When I die, I rot" said the philosopher Bertrand Russell (1872-1970). And you cannot argue with that. It's obviously true. But is it the whole truth? Does the real "me" disappear? Is death simply the final goodnight and goodbye?

What evidence is there for an afterlife?

What survives death? What are the soul and the personality?

Why do people (want to) believe in an afterlife?

How does belief in an afterlife affect the way people live?

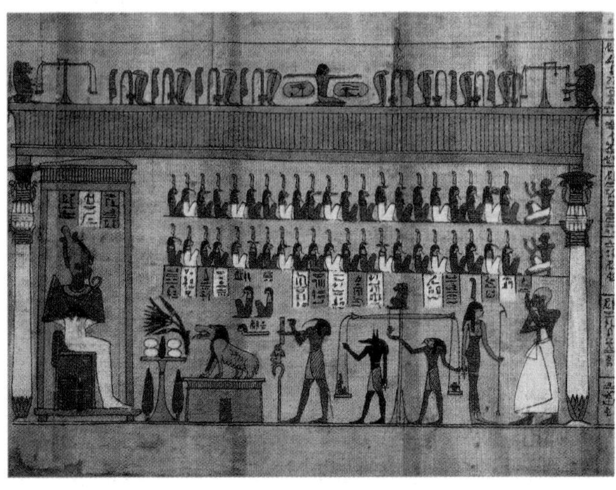

An Egyptian Book of the Dead (a papyrus scroll), from about 1000 BCE, pictures the journeys of a dead person's soul in the underworld – including the moment when the jackal-headed god Anubis weighs the dead person's heart against the feather of truth. If the result was good, one of the person's three spirits would join the immortal spirit world and the other two would return to the person's mummified body in the tomb, and live on there.

These are some of the thousands of terracotta figures of soldiers, horses, and chariots that were buried in his tomb with the Chinese emperor Shih Huang Ti, to guard him in his life after death.

The question of life after death has intrigued men and women since the beginning of the human race. Some of the oldest tombs in existence, from about 5000 BCE, are at Byblos in Lebanon. The skeletons were found with their knees tucked up under their chins, each closed up in an earthenware egg. These people hoped that new life would break out of that egg of death. Archaeologists have found evidence that Neanderthal man, 150,000 years ago, practised ritual burial – which suggests that he believed in a spirit world and a life beyond the grave. China's first emperor, Shih Huang Ti (died c. 210 BCE) was buried with 6,000 terracotta soldiers to guard him on his journey to the next world. The Egyptians went to extravagant lengths to preserve the physical bodies of their dead pharaohs.

Evidence for an afterlife? The presence of the dead

Many societies have a cult of dead ancestors. (For example see the photograph on page 102.) The raw material for such belief systems may be people's awareness of the presence of the dead. According to the researcher David Hay, nearly a fifth of the British population have some experience of a person or people being present in life after they have died.

"It happened either six or seven days after the death of my mother . . . I had just got into bed and lay waiting for my husband to join me: I can't remember what I was thinking of – but I became aware that there was a warm glowing presence and I knew it was my mother. I heard no words spoken but I received a message from her. She told me that all was well with her and that she was very very happy. It was an almost unbelievable experience (because I don't think I really believed in life after death). I remember lying there thinking, 'I must hang on to this experience' and that I must remember it was real and actually happened and I didn't dream it or imagine it." [quoted in David Hay, *Religious Experience Today*, Mowbray, 1990]

"My grandma said she has seen her mother sitting at the bottom of her bed when she was really ill; she even told my aunt to make her a cup of tea. My grandma still believes that her mother came back from the dead to help her get better." [Nikki, 16]

1 In groups, discuss any experiences of "the presence of the dead" which you have either had or heard about. Do you think such experiences prove that there is a life after death?

Evidence for an afterlife? Near-death experiences

A book published in 1977, *Life After Life* by Dr Raymond Moody, included accounts of people who had come near to death and had experiences on the threshold of death, many on the hospital operating table. Some people think that these "near-death experiences" are evidence that there is a life after death. According to Colin Wilson, who studied Dr Moody's book, there were many similarities in people's descriptions of their near-death experiences. They contained a mixture of: "a sense of peace and happiness; the impression of moving through a dark tunnel, usually with a light at the end (sometimes there is a sensation of falling); the person emerges from the tunnel to find themselves looking at their own body from a viewpoint 'outside'; the person becomes aware of inhabiting a 'new body' – shaped like the physical body that had been left behind; people become aware that they cannot communicate with other people surrounding the old body; the physical senses are heightened, so that they can see and hear better than they could in their old body; a meeting with dead relatives or friends; encountering a bright light which seems to radiate a sense of love and warmth; the light might ask probing questions about what the person has done with his life; very often there is a sense of some kind of border or limit; a sense of being directed back to their body on earth; disappointment at having to return; the ability afterwards to recall in detail the experience.

Some people found it difficult to put their experiences into words: they had experienced, what Moody called, 'the vision of knowledge'. One woman said: 'It was like I knew all things'." [Colin Wilson, *Afterlife*, Grafton Books, 1985]

Dr Moody's book was the first of many which have reported thousands of near-death experiences. Kenneth Ring, a Professor of Psychology, carried out his own study. In *Life at Death: A Scientific Investigation of the Near-Death Experience* (Coward, McCann & Geoghegan, New York, 1980) he concludes:

"These experiences clearly imply that there is something more. Something beyond the physical world of the senses. Why do such experiences occur? I have come to believe that the universe ... has many ways of 'getting its message across'. Near-death experiences represent one of its devices for waking us up to the cosmic dimensions of the drama of which we are a part, to this higher reality."

Members of a tribe in Madagascar today "turn the bones" of their ancestors. This custom is known as "famadihana". The dead are laid in a family tomb. About every seven years their bodies are brought out and wrapped in new silk shrouds. It is a time for celebrating and remembering the lives of the dead ancestors. After the celebrations, which may last as long as three days, the bodies are returned to the tomb. It is believed that an ancestor made happy in this way will bring good luck to the family.

On the other hand Dr Peter Fennick, a clinical neurophysiologist, makes the following points in connection with near-death experiences:

- Anaesthetics and drugs such as the opiates can produce mystical experiences. Near-death experiences could perhaps be caused by the release of enkephalin, one of the brain's natural anaesthetics.
  (However, there are difficulties with this explanation. You would expect people under the influence of anaesthetic to be confused, but in near-death experiences they are not. Also you would expect the experiences produced by anaesthetics to be random; but the near-death experience is very specific.)
- The images of the afterlife included in a person's description of the near-death experience are merely the conventional images that the person has grown up with. No new discovery about the nature of the afterlife is made.
- Feelings of ecstasy can be produced when the limbic system in the brain is starved of oxygen.

2 What do you think about near-death experiences? What, if anything, do near-death experiences tell you about the afterlife? Do you think they provide valid knowledge of a World Unseen?

Why is belief in the afterlife important to religious people?

A number of answers keep recurring in the different religions:

1. "Death is not a taker away of meaning but a giver of meaning." [M. Scott Peck, *The Road Less Travelled and Beyond*, Rider, 1997]. Death is like a mirror. It forces us to reflect on our own lives – to find out what is really valuable, what we are living for.
2. Belief in an afterlife provides a reason for people to be moral in this life. This life becomes the cultivating ground where we prepare for the afterlife.
3. There is so much injustice in this world that there needs to be an afterlife for justice to be restored.

Q

1 Why is belief in the afterlife important to people?

2 Why do the religions of the world think it is important to use this life as a preparation for the next?

All the major world religions teach that death is not the end. It has sometimes been described as the "gate of life". Some of the religions teach the importance of using this life as preparation for the afterlife.

"O People! Fear God, and whatever you do, do it anticipating death. Be prepared for a fast passage because here you are destined for a short stay. You must remember to gather from this life such harvest as will be of use and help to you hereafter." [Islam: Nahjul Balagha, Sermon 67]

"This world is like a vestibule before the World to Come; prepare yourself in the vestibule that you may enter the hall." [Judaism: Mishnah: Abot 4: 21]

"O shrewd businessman, do only profitable business: deal only in that commodity which shall accompany you after death." [Sikhism: Guru Granth Sahib]

"Yellow leaves hang on your tree of life. The messengers of death are waiting. You are going to travel far away. Have you any provision for the journey?" [Buddhism: Dhammapada 235]

RELIGION FILE

BUDDHISM 

"It is unsure whether tomorrow or the next life will come first." [The Buddha]

- Buddhists teach the importance of having a right attitude towards death. Death was one of the "four signs" that prompted Siddattha Gotama (who became the Buddha) to leave his palace in search of an explanation for suffering. The Buddha taught that death is not something to be feared. The positive attitude is to accept it.

> "One child plays with his balloon until it catches on a branch or a thorn and bursts, leaving him in tears. Another child, smarter than the first, nows that his balloon can burst easily and is not upset when it does." [Ajahn Chah, *A Still Forest Pool*, Theosophical Publishing House of Wheaton]

- Death is part of a continuous process of changing, decaying, and arising. This process of birth, death, and rebirth is called samsara. A chant sung by monks at funerals is: "All things in samsara [the world of life and death] are impermanent. To be happy there can be no clinging." The body is impermanent: "like foam" and "insubstantial as a mirage" [Dhammapada 46]. Buddhist ceremonies for the dead are occasions for reflecting on the teachings of impermanence. People do not have a permanent soul in terms of a personality that lasts after death.

- Rebirth does not mean that the actual person is reborn. Buddhists believe that the karmic (or kammic) energy of a person sets another life in motion. During his experience of enlightenment the Buddha remembered many of his previous lives. He taught that things are reborn according to their karma. This word, meaning "action", refers to the law of cause and effect.

In Tibetan Buddhism a teacher is called a lama. This photograph shows the present Dalai Lama, the spiritual leader of Tibetan Buddhists. They believe he is the 14th rebirth of the first Dalai Lama.

Belief in rebirth has two consequences for life:
(1) It encourages respect for other beings. If some person or animal is presently annoying you, a way to stop ill-will towards them is to reflect that in a past life they may have been a close relative or friend [Samyutta Nikaya II.186].
(2) It encourages you to use this life to develop spiritually. "Death acts as a reminder to use the spiritual opportunities of human life wisely . . . it produces compassion for others and feelings of solidarity for other living/dying beings." [Dr Peter Harvey, quoted in J. Neuberger and J. A. White, ed., *A Necessary End*, Papermac, 1991]

- Like all Buddhists, Tibetan Buddhists believe in rebirth. The Tibetan Book of the Dead teaches that at death a person will see a brilliant light, a direct vision of ultimate reality. Theravada Buddhism teaches that at the moment of death the karma is reborn straight away. Mahayana Buddhism teaches that there is an "intermediary existence", lasting from seven to 49 days.

- The aim of the Buddhist life is to become free of samsara and to enter Nibbana. Death is just a stepping-stone on the journey to Nibbana. This word means "blown out" – as a flame is blown out. Nibbana is an eternal state beyond suffering and impermanence. It includes qualities of peace and true happiness.

- Buddhists usually, although not always, cremate the body of a dead person. This is a way of recognising the finality of death.

3 (a) What do Buddhists regard as the right attitude towards death?
(b) How do you think this affects the way they live?

4 (a) Explain the Buddhist concept of rebirth.
(b) How does this belief affect the way Buddhists treat other people in this life?

RELIGION FILE

CHRISTIANITY ✝

- Christians believe in a life after death because Jesus was raised from the dead. Therefore, death is not something to be afraid of [1 Corinthians 15: 55-57]. The early Christian communities called the day of death the "heavenly birthday", and it was remembered by an annual party.
- Important Christian beliefs are contained in the Apostle's Creed, which states that: "We believe in the resurrection of the body and the life everlasting". Before Jesus died he promised his disciples that he was going to prepare a place for them [John 14]. Christians believe that eternal life is a gift from God.

Judgement Day, as pictured by the Florentine painter Fra Angelico (c. 1400-55).

- Christians believe that there will be a judgement. The Apostle's Creed states that Jesus "will come again to judge the living and the dead". Jesus taught that there would be a separation into two groups: those who have behaved in a loving way towards others and those who haven't. The former will have eternal life and the latter eternal punishment [Matthew 25: 31-46]. The Christian idea of judgement is not primarily about condemnation. Christians believe in a God who offers salvation to all who wish to take it. There is a cost, and that is for people to accept God as king over their lives – their thoughts, motivations, and actions.
- Christians believe they will be given a spiritual body after death [1 Corinthians 15: 42-44].
- Christians believe that a life that completely ignores God will result in punishment. This punishment takes place in hell. Jesus himself spoke about hell in very vivid language: "Do not be afraid of those who kill the body but cannot kill the soul; rather be afraid of God, who can destroy both body and soul in hell." [Matthew 10: 28]. Christians believe that hell is not simply a punishment: it is something people choose for themselves, day by day. People choose to be separated from God, just as they choose to love God.

- Christians believe that they are going to heaven: it is where God is. Jesus pictured heaven as a party, a banquet that people will share with God [Luke 14: 15-24].

- Belief in the afterlife is important for the Christian belief in justice: "For true justice must include everyone; it must bring the answer to the immense load of suffering borne by all the generations. In fact, without the resurrection of the dead and the Lord's judgement, there is no justice in the full sense of the term. The promise of the resurrection is freely made to meet the desire for true justice dwelling in the human heart." [Vatican document, *Liberatis Conscientia*]

- Many Roman Catholics believe in purgatory – a half-way stop between earth and heaven where people are cleansed of their sin. In *The Road Less Travelled and Beyond* (Rider, 1997), Dr M. Scott Peck likens purgatory to "a very elegant, well-appointed psychiatric hospital with the most modern techniques for as-painless-as-possible learning". He goes on to explain that it is a place in which we must deal with the important issues in our lives. "Whether in an afterlife or on earth, we must do the work of purgatory or remain forever . . . separated from God. Why not get on with it now?"

5 (a) Why do Christians regard death as something that is not to be feared?
(b) Why do you think the early Christian communities called the day of death "the heavenly birthday"?

6 (a) What do Christians believe will happen after death? Provide details in your answer.
(b) What do Christians believe about judgement? How do they understand the concept of Judgement Day?
(c) What is purgatory? What does Dr M. Scott Peck mean by "the work of purgatory"?

7 Why is belief in life after death important for Christians?

RELION FILE

HINDUISM ॐ

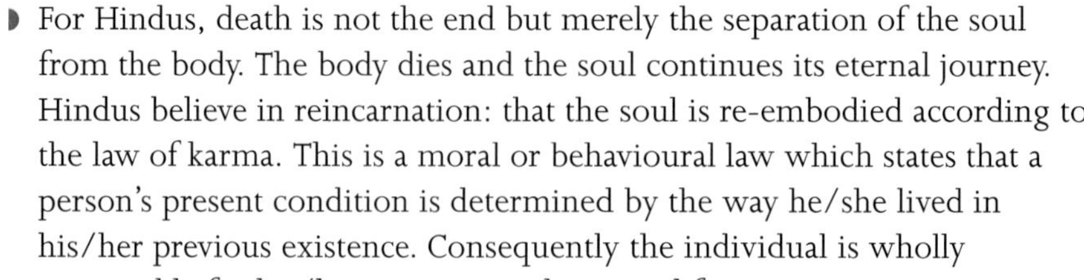

- For Hindus, death is not the end but merely the separation of the soul from the body. The body dies and the soul continues its eternal journey. Hindus believe in reincarnation: that the soul is re-embodied according to the law of karma. This is a moral or behavioural law which states that a person's present condition is determined by the way he/she lived in his/her previous existence. Consequently the individual is wholly responsible for his/her present condition and future.

"As a man acts [karma], as he behaves, so does he become. Whoso does good, becomes good; whoso does evil, becomes evil." [Brihadaranyaka Upanishad]

❝Karma encourages me; when I think that we are going to come back, then I want to do good things, and I want to do my prayers so that God doesn't punish me. He won't punish me if I do good things. I think God is there, and he's always watching us, what we are doing, wrong or right. It's always God who stops me doing that. I'm not scared of my husband or of anyone else. Whenever somebody stops me, it's always God. That may sound like religion born of fear. But in fact it is closer to justice – that our deeds will get their reward.❞ [quoted in J. Bowker, *Worlds of Faith: religious belief and practice in Britain today*, BBC/Ariel, 1983]

- The cycle of death and reincarnation continues many times. The ultimate goal of Hindus is to attain moksha – release from the pattern of death, reincarnation, death.

❝When all desires which shelter in the heart
Detach themselves, then does a mortal man
Become immortal: to Brahman he wins through.❞
[Brihadaranyaka Upanishad]

Family members (with shaved heads) attend to the cremation of a relative. Hindus believe that the soul leaves the body with the flames. Usually the eldest son lights the fire. Prayers are said from the Hindu scriptures. The ashes are scattered on a holy river. Just as the river returns to the sea, the soul journeys on to its new reincarnation.

- Hindus cremate their dead, since they believe that this releases the soul to continue its journey.

❝When a man is dead and his voice enters the fire, his breath the wind, his eye the sun, his mind the moon, his ear the points of the compass, his body the earth, his self space, where then is man?❞ [Brihadaranyaka Upanishad]

8 Explain the Hindu concept of reincarnation.

9 What is the ultimate goal of life for Hindus?

10 Explain why Hindus cremate their dead.

RELIGION FILE

ISLAM 

“Our life on earth is temporary and is meant to be a preparation for Akhirah which is never ending. Life on this earth becomes meaningless if good actions are not rewarded and bad conduct punished.” [from Sarwar Ghulam, *Islam: Beliefs and Teachings*, The Muslim Educational Trust]

- Muslims believe that each person has a soul that lives in the whole body. The soul has been likened to water going through a young plant. It is the invisible element that gives life. Muslims believe that “Allah fixes the time span for all things . . . it is He who causes people to die” [Qur'an, 53: 42-7]. At death the soul leaves the body.

- Life after death, Akhirah, is described in the Qur'an as a physical state and for this reason Muslims do not cremate their dead, but instead bury their bodies as soon as possible after death, before they begin to decay. Muslims believe that when the body is buried two angels, Munkir and Makir, appear to the dead person and ask four questions: Who is your God? What is your religion? Who is your prophet? What is your Guide? If the answers are correct, the tomb will be filled with pleasurable things. If incorrect, the angels bring torture upon the unbelieving dead person.

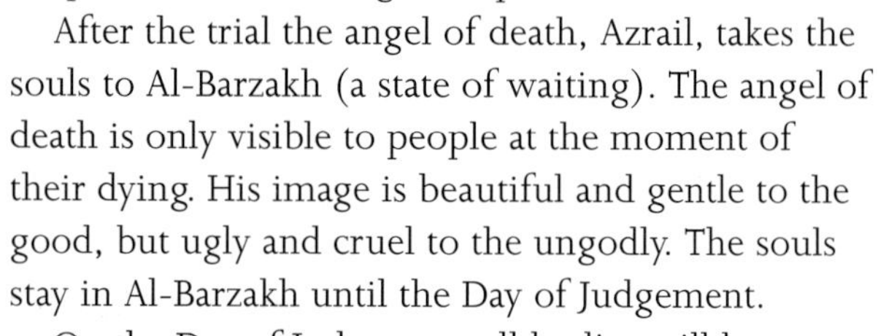

After the trial the angel of death, Azrail, takes the souls to Al-Barzakh (a state of waiting). The angel of death is only visible to people at the moment of their dying. His image is beautiful and gentle to the good, but ugly and cruel to the ungodly. The souls stay in Al-Barzakh until the Day of Judgement.

On the Day of Judgement all bodies will be raised to life again. Everyone will stand before Allah and all souls will be rewarded or punished, depending on how they have lived this life. “On that day, men will appear in droves and be shown their actions and whoever has done an atom's weight of good will see it, while whoever has done an atom's weight of evil will see it.” [Qur'an, 99: 1-8]

Facing in the direction of Makkah, as for all prayers, Muslims say the funeral prayer, “Salatul Janazzah”. The body, either on a stretcher or in a coffin, is then carried to the burial place. Graves are always dug so that the body can be laid in with the head towards Makkah.

The reward for the righteous will be heaven, which is vividly described in the Qur'an as a place of peace and beauty: “You shall enter gardens watered by running streams in which you shall abide forever . . . [The righteous] shall recline on jewelled couches face to face, and there shall wait on them immortal youths.” [Qu'ran, 57: 56]. Not all Muslims take this description literally. The point is that the image of a garden is a powerful one for desert people. Picturing gardens of paradise is a way of describing divine love.

Hell (jahannam) is for unbelievers. It is a place of pain and suffering described again in vivid language: “As for those on the left hand . . . they shall dwell amidst scorching winds and seething water; in the shade of pitch-black smoke, neither cool nor refreshing. Such shall be their fare on the Day of Reckoning." [Qur'an, 56]. As with heaven, not all Muslims believe this literally. The image of burning stands for denial of Allah and being without His love.

"I firmly believe in the Resurrection and the Day of Judgement on two grounds. Firstly, the Revelation in the Qur'an, and secondly, I believe in God's justice. This world is obviously unjust . . . I believe the universe to be the Creation of God, who cannot be unjust. The only way to correct the injustice of this world is through resurrection into another world." [Dr M. A. Zaki Badawi, Principal, The Muslim College, quoted in J. Neuberger and J. A. White, ed., *A Necessary End*, Papermac, 1991]

11 What is your idea of the soul? What is the Muslim concept of the soul?

12 Why do Muslims live life with a constant awareness of death? Is this helpful? How will it affect how they live?

13 (a) Explain what Muslims believe about Judgement Day, heaven, and hell.
(b) Why do you think belief in the afterlife is important to Muslims?

RELIGION FILE

JUDAISM

- The following prayer is said at the approach of death: "I acknowledge before You, O Lord my God and God of my fathers, that my cure and my death are in Your hands . . . May my death be atonement for all the sins, iniquities and transgressions which I have committed before You. Grant me of the great happiness that is stored up for the righteous. Make known to me the path of life; in Your presence is fullness of joy; at Your right hand bliss for evermore." [United Hebrew Congregations, 1990]

  Notice two important points from this prayer: acceptance of the will of God and the hope for forgiveness and for eternal life.

- Within Judaism there are different views about whether there is life after death. On one side, Judaism stresses people's responsibilities in "this world" and pays less attention to belief in an afterlife. One rabbi in the Talmud suggests that we should concentrate on praising God and studying the scripture in this world because there will be no opportunity when we are dead. But other passages in the Talmud affirm belief in life after death. The great philosopher Moses Maimonides (1135-1204) wrote: "I believe with perfect faith that there will be a resurrection of the dead at a time when it will please the Creator." [*Thirteen Principles of Faith*]. On the doorposts of many Jewish cemeteries there is written in Hebrew "The House of Life".

- Judaism teaches that you must live well in this life because each person will have to give an account to God of what he/she has done. Belief in a coming judgement should affect how people live this life: "Plan for this world as if you were to live forever; plan for the world to come as if you were to die tomorrow." [Solomon Ibn Gabirol, 1021-56, quoted in L. Blue with J. Magonet, *The Blue Guide to the Here and Hereafter*, Collins, 1988]

- The "world to come" is a place of beauty, free from pain: "Not like this world is the world to come. In the world to come there is neither eating or drinking; no procreation of children or business transactions; no envy, hatred or rivalry; but the righteous sit enthroned, their crowns on their heads and enjoy the lustre of the Divine Splendour." [Mishnah: Berakot]

- What provisions are possible on a journey to eternity? The rabbis thought our only luggage would be our good deeds. Everything else would have to be left at the frontier post we call death, which separates this world from eternity.

A Jewish cemetery is called "bet hayim" (house of life) or "bet olam" (house of eternity). It is a custom for visitors to a Jewish grave to leave a small stone as a mark of the visit.

14 (a) What does the prayer recited at the approach of death say about the Jewish view of death?
(b) Which of the following words best describe the way in which a Jewish person should approach death: anger, fear, thanksgiving, acceptance, eagerness, dread, hope, despair? (You may choose more than one.)
(c) Write a letter to a friend discussing the different ways in which people approach death. Include a summary of the Jewish approach.

15 (a) Explain what Jews believe about life after death.
(b) What do Jews mean by living well? Why is it important to live well?

RELIGION FILE

SIKHISM

- Sikhs believe that death is not the end. "The dawn of a new day is the message of a sunset. Earth is not the permanent home. Life is like a shadow on a wall." [Guru Granth Sahib 793]. They believe that each person has an immortal soul. "Our soul is the image of the Transcendent God. Neither is this soul old, nor young . . . Neither is it wasted away, nor it dies; since the beginningless time, it is merged in its self." [Guru Granth Sahib 868]

- At death the soul is reincarnated in another body. People are reincarnated according to their karma (the good or bad actions in their previous life).
  The aim is to become free from the cycle of death and rebirth (this is to achieve mukti or liberation) and be joined with God. To achieve mukti people must change the way they live – faith in God must be translated into practice. After death it is too late to change things. (Read the story of Duni Chand's needle on page 79.)

  "For several births was I a worm. For several births an elephant, a fish, a deer. For several births was I a bird, a serpent. For several births yoked as a bull, a horse. After a long period has the human frame come into being. Seek now union with the Lord of the Universe, For now is the time." [Guru Granth Sahib 176]

- Sikhs believe that every person will eventually be united with God. "It is He [God] who sends beings into the world, And it is He who calls them back." [Guru Granth Sahib 1239]

- Sikhs cremate their dead. The funeral service takes place as soon as possible after death.

16 Have you ever thought about whether you would prefer to be cremated or buried? Is there any real difference between the two? How might a Sikh answer this question?

17 How might the Sikh belief in numerous reincarnations affect Sikh attitudes to the natural world?

Sample Examination Questions

(a) What evidence for life after death might religious people give? [6 marks]
(b) How would religious people explain why their belief about life after death is important? [9 marks]
(c) "If you believe in life after death, then you must be religious!" How far do you agree with this statement? Show that you have thought about different points of view, giving reasons to support your answer. [5 marks]
[SEG, Summer 1997]

10 11 12 13 The sanctity of life

It is often said that life is a precious gift that must be protected. But to what extent is it, and should it be, protected? In chapters 10-13 you will be exploring life and death issues, with reference to abortion, euthanasia, war, and animal and plant life. This preparatory section to those chapters introduces some key questions.

1 In groups, choose three of the following questions to discuss. As a group, try to write a statement explaining your beliefs on the issues you have chosen. Present these statements to the class.

(a) What counts as "life"?
(b) Is it always wrong to take human life?
(c) When does human life begin? Is an eight-month foetus already a living being? How about a newly fertilised egg?
(d) When does human life end? Does a person who has irreversibly fallen into a coma count as a living human being?
(e) Do we value life even if it is unconscious or do we value life only as a vehicle for consciousness?
(f) What moral actions would a person object to if he or she held the belief that "taking life is always wrong"? (Consider all forms of life.)
(g) Are there occasions when it is justifiable to take human life? What about in times of war?
(h) Is human life special? If so, what makes it special?
(i) What does it mean to say "people have a right to live"?
(j) When, if ever, is abortion justified?
(k) Is there a difference between ending the life of a grossly abnormal foetus and ending the life of a grossly abnormal baby? If so, where do you draw the line?
(l) Is there a difference between killing someone and intentionally failing to save his/her life? (Consider the case of a terminally ill patient.)
(m) How can you decide whether a person's life is worth living?
(n) Should each person have the ultimate say about whether he or she wants to live or not? Can you think of any exceptions to this?
(o) Is spending money on oneself instead of giving money to a charity to save someone's life a form of killing? If you think it is less bad than killing someone, why?
(p) Can killing sometimes be justified in order to avoid a greater evil (for example in war)?
(q) Is there a difference between a soldier killing in war and the same person killing his neighbour in peacetime? If so, what?
(r) Is animal life less important than human life? If so, why?
(s) Is there a difference between killing a pet dog and swatting a mosquito?
(t) Plants are also living things. Is their life sacred? If so, is weeding the garden wrong?

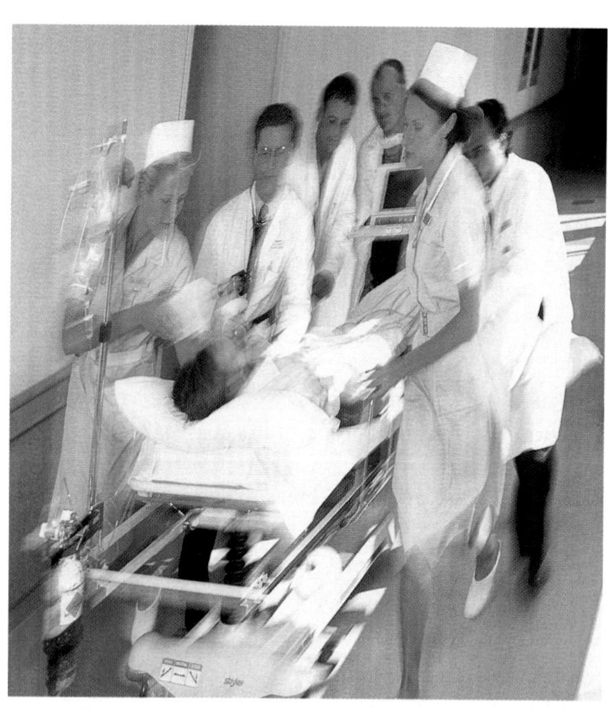

A patient is rushed to the operating theatre.

2 The photographs on these pages show "life forms in danger". Write a dramatic news headline to go with each one. Try to make your headlines express a viewpoint about what is happening.

How valuable? The world's total population is more than five billion people. How much is a person worth? A million pounds or more? Talented footballers might be considered to be worth over twenty million pounds each on the transfer market. On the other hand, when a drought or famine hits a developing country like Sudan or Ethiopia, life appears to be so very cheap.

“I cannot but have reverence for all that is called life. I cannot avoid compassion for all that is called life. That is the beginning and foundation of morality.” [Albert Schweitzer, *Reverence for Life*, London, 1966]

People use the term “sanctity of life”, meaning that life is something sacred. Sometimes people argue that, therefore, all living things have a right to life. They mean this in the sense of an absolute moral right. Other people argue that there are times when it is justifiable to take life, when certain rights have priority over others.

Q

3 (a) Are some human lives more valuable than others?
(b) How can we measure the value of a unique human being?
(c) Is your life more valuable than the next person's? What would you be willing to do to protect it?

Supporters of the Chipko movement in India “hug” trees to stop loggers from cutting down forest.

Orphaned orang-utans are rescued from forest fires in Indonesia.

LIFE MUST BE PROTECTED

All the world religions we are studying teach that life must be protected:

Judaism and Christianity:

“Do not commit murder.” [Exodus 20: 13]

Buddhism:

“Whosoever in this world destroys life . . . interferes with their own progress in this very world.” [Dhammapada, 246-247]

Hinduism:

Belief in the sanctity of all life is expressed in ahimsa: “non-violence”, “non-harming”.

Islam:

“Do not take life – which Allah has made sacred – except for a just cause.” [Qur'an, 17: 33]

Sikhism:

God lives in all beings: “You are immanent in all beings.” [Guru Granth Sahib 1291]. Therefore all life is precious.

CHAPTER

Is abortion right or wrong?

UNIT ONE

Abortion – information and arguments

Each year thousands of pregnancies are terminated by induced abortion. (Nearly 187,000 British women had abortions in 1998.) In this unit you will find out about the legal position concerning abortion – who can have an abortion, and who has the right to decide. You will also consider the issue of when life begins.

Information File: Abortion

Natural abortion brings about the termination of over 50% of human embryos, many of them perfectly formed, though others would have resulted in the birth of a baby with severe disabilities. However, the controversy surrounding abortion is concerned with **induced abortion**: that is, where a woman has an operation to end her pregnancy and remove the embryo or foetus. (The word foetus is often used for the baby in the womb once its parts are distinctly formed.)

When does life begin?

At what point does an embryo become a separate, unique, person? This is a key issue in the debate about abortion. There are also several views on when life begins. Is it:

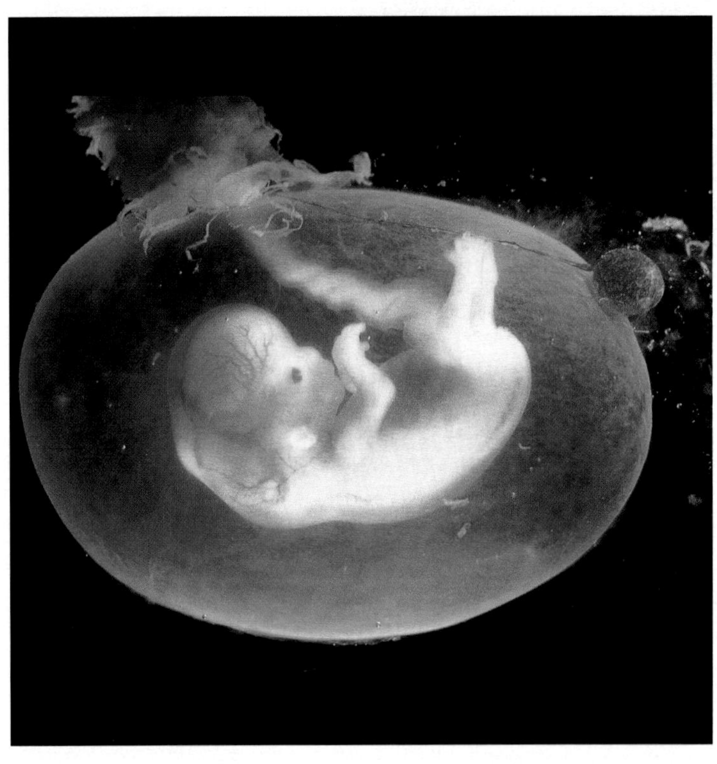

At 7-8 weeks old, a human embryo is about 4 cm long and weighs less than 10 grammes. This picture shows how it is attached to the mother's blood circulation by the umbilical cord.

- at conception, at the moment when the sperm unites with the ovum? At this point all the information to make a unique individual is present; the new being's DNA is fixed.
- at the start of the neurological (nervous) system? The appearance of the "primitive streak", which marks the beginning of the neurological system, after about fourteen days, is obviously an important stage.
- at the first heart beat? Some people regard this as the beginning of real life.
- at viability – that is, when the baby could survive outside the womb if born prematurely?
- at birth? This is when the child has passed down the birth canal and has drawn its first breath independent of its mother.

1 In your opinion, when does life begin? Justify your answer.

Whose choice?

2 Who has the most rights when a choice is to be made about abortion? Think about
(a) the mother – the effect on her of having a baby;
(b) the father – his wishes, values, and needs;
(c) existing children – their desire to have or not to have a brother or sister;
(d) the potential grandparents – their desire for grandchildren;
(e) the doctors and nurses asked to carry out abortions – their conscience;
(f) the unborn child – its right to be protected and to be born.
Get into groups of six and role-play a discussion where each of these people argues his or her point of view.

The legal position in England, Scotland, and Wales

Before 1967 abortion was illegal. There were many back-street abortions (illegal abortions performed by unqualified people), often with tragic results. As a result of the 1967 Abortion Act and the 1990 Human Fertilisation and Embryology Act, a woman is legally allowed to have an abortion under certain conditions. The law says that a woman can have an abortion if:

- continuing the pregnancy would put her life in danger
- there is substantial risk of the child being born with a serious disablity

and also that, up to 24 weeks into a pregnancy, a woman can have an abortion if there is a risk that having the baby would:

- harm her physical or mental health
- harm the health of existing children in the family

For doctors, the law says that:

- no doctor has to carry out abortions
- before an abortion can take place, two doctors must agree to it.

What should I do?

I'm 18 and I was looking forward to starting at university at the end of September. Now I don't know what to do because last week I discovered that I was pregnant. My boyfriend, John, is 19 and we've had a relationship for over a year. Neither of us is ready for this. John says that he will stand by me, but I know he really wants me to have an abortion. I'm worried that if I do I'll not be able to live with myself afterwards.

I'm dreading telling mum. I know that she will be so angry and she has so much to do since dad walked out on us. She has a full-time job and already has to cope with my younger brother and sister in a three-bedroomed terrace house. Please help me. I don't know what to do. I'm willing to consider any sensible advice.

Debbie

3 Brainstorm Debbie's options and consider the arguments. What do you think Debbie should do? Write a reply to Debbie giving your advice.

4 In groups choose what you consider to be (a) the two strongest reasons for allowing abortion, and (b) the two strongest reasons against allowing abortion. Make up your case for each and present to the class in a debate.

Arguments for allowing abortion

- Women have a right to decide what happens to their body. The expectant mother carries the baby in her womb for nine months. She should have the right to end a pregnancy if she wishes.
- Abortion should be allowed, out of compassion, in the case of a pregnancy caused by rape, to spare the rape victim from being constantly reminded of her ordeal during the pregnancy and afterwards as she cares for the child.
- Why bring more unwanted children into an already over-populated world?
- Every child has the right to be loved. It would be better for a child not to be born to parents unwilling or unable to care for it. There are already enough problems created by parents who have neglected or abused their offspring.
- In the case of an under-age pregnancy, it is unreasonable to expect the girl, who has made one mistake, to ruin her education and career by insisting that she goes through the pregnancy and becomes an unmarried mother.
- Where the father has deserted the mother-to-be, she might be unable to cope on her own emotionally, mentally, or financially.
- Where the family is already large, the parents may not be able to cope with more children.
- A family may be too poor to cope with another child.
- Pregnancy may come at the "wrong time", affecting the career of the expectant mother. A woman has a right to a career.
- The quality of life for a severely disabled child might be so low that it would be kinder for that child not to be born.
- Life doesn't really start until birth or, at the earliest, until the foetus is viable.

Why do you think these men in New York dressed in women's clothes to protest for the right to choose abortion?

An anti-abortion demonstration in Cape Town, South Africa. Sometimes the abortion debate becomes much more violent than this. Why do you think this is?

Arguments against allowing abortion

- Each person is unique, and the information that makes the person unique is all there from conception.
- Abortion is murder because life starts at conception.
- Children are a blessing from God, to be cherished. God knows us even before we are born. Abortion is like throwing God's gift of a child back in His face.
- Modern science has proved that the unborn child is a separate human being from conception and that the foetus has feelings and intelligence.
- Unwanted babies could be adopted. There are many couples who would love to adopt a child, because they are unable to have children of their own.
- Abortions often result in depression and guilt. An abortion can leave mental and physical scars on a woman.
- Disabled children and adults can enjoy a fulfilled life. They would undoubtedly choose life rather than termination.
- Abortion is unjust, as it is a denial of human rights for the unborn child. The United Nations Convention on the Rights of the Child states that children need protection both before and after birth.
- The need for abortions could be greatly reduced if more help were provided in the form of sex education (including the use of contraceptives), counselling, and support for single mothers, etc.
- The present law is only one step away from allowing abortion as a form of contraception. It encourages people to use abortion as an "easy way out", instead of facing up to their responsibilities.
- By having an abortion you may deprive the world of a genius – for example, a scientist who would have discovered a cure for aids or cancer, or developed a food source with the potential to abolish hunger in the developing world.

Abortion pressure groups

Several groups, including the following, have formed to promote their views about abortion.

The **National Abortion Campaign** was set up in 1973, to protect the 1967 Act, as its members support the idea of abortion. Indeed, many members want the law to be changed to allow abortion on demand.

The **Society for the Protection of Unborn Children** (SPUC) argues against abortion. It believes that the law should be changed so that abortions would only be allowed on the rare occasions when the mother's life is at risk. SPUC calls for more support for pregnant mothers and increased welfare benefits for single mothers; and it encourages the offering of children for adoption as an alternative to abortion. SPUC believes that a disabled child can live a fulfilled life and so argues that it is not necessary to have an abortion because there is a risk of disability.

Life was established in 1970. It argues against abortion and seeks to provide practical assistance and counselling for pregnant mothers.

5 Why do you think people sometimes become very passionate about the subject of abortion, whether they are fighting for or against it?

6 Is abortion a feminist issue (based on the right of a woman to do what she wishes with her body) or a human rights issue (based on the rights of the mother, the child, or the foetus)?

Religious responses to the abortion debate

The principal religions of the world all teach that human life is of great value and that each individual should be respected. However, religious traditions differ on when they think human life begins. They have different teachings on abortion.

RELIGION FILE

BUDDHISM 

Tibetan Buddhists emphasise their belief in the value of human life by using the following analogy. "Being reborn as a human is as likely as a blind turtle which is swimming in a large ocean and surfaces once every one hundred years, putting its head through a small golden ring which is floating on the surface of the water."

- Buddhism teaches that all living things are caught in samsara (the cycle of birth, death, and rebirth). Being born in human form is rare and very precious. Also, life has already begun before conception in the present form, so abortion at any stage is the taking of life.
- Buddhism teaches that the motives for every action are very important. If a person has an abortion for selfish motives, this will result in bad karma (kamma). But if, for example, the mother's life is put at risk by the pregnancy, she may have good reason to be selfish. Each case should be considered on its merits and wise behaviour should be followed, as it is difficult to think in terms of moral absolutes. In Japan, some Buddhists make offerings and dedicate statues to the bodhisattva Jizosana to lessen their feelings of guilt in cases of abortion.

“Buddhism holds that consciousness penetrates a being at the very moment of conception, and that consequently the embryo is already a living being. This is why we consider abortion to be the same as taking the life of a living being and as such as not a just action. However, there can be exceptional situations. I am thinking, for example, of a case where it is certain that the child will be born with abnormalities or where the mother's life is in danger. Basically, it will all depend upon the intention and motivation behind the action.” [The Dalai Lama, *Beyond Dogma: the challenge of the modern world*, Souvenir Press, 1994]

1 Why do Buddhists believe that human life is precious?

2 (a) How might having or suggesting an abortion affect a person's karma?
(b) What might be a selfish reason for having an abortion?

3 In what situations do you think a Buddhist might consider abortion? What would count as a selfless reason?

4 Explain the meaning of the analogy of the blind turtle.

RELIGION FILE

CHRISTIANITY 

Abortion is treated as a very serious moral matter and is widely debated among Christians. Opinions differ as to whether it can ever be justified, and, if so, under what circumstances. The Bible contains a number of relevant teachings:

- Humans are sacred as they are created in God's image [Genesis 1: 27]. Humans are so valuable to God that He knows them even before their birth [Psalm 139: 13 and 15]. All children are precious to God and are never rejected by Him [Matthew 18: 10]. Children are God's gift to parents [Psalm 127: 3]. They are to be cared for and protected.
- Even before birth God has given every person a purpose in life [Isaiah 49: 5 and Galatians 1: 15]. Many Christians believe that aborting a foetus is therefore murder. One of the earliest Christian documents, *The Didache*, a manual of instruction probably written in Syria in the first century CE, contains the statement "You shall not kill an unborn child or murder a newborn infant."

Speaking in St Louis, USA, in January 1999, Pope John Paul II gave a clear message to Americans that they should oppose abortion.

- Christianity is all about having compassion. Jesus, repeating Jewish teaching, emphasised "Love your neighbour as you love yourself." [Mark 12: 33]

"We affirm that every human life, created in the divine image, is unique . . . We therefore believe that abortion is an evil . . . and that abortion on demand would be a very great evil. But we also believe that to withdraw compassion is evil, and in circumstances of extreme distress or need, a very great evil . . . In an imperfect world the 'right' choice is sometimes the lesser of two evils." [Church of England, 1988]

"Abortion is always an evil, to be avoided if at all possible. However, in an imperfect world there will be circumstances where the termination of pregnancy may be the lesser of evils. Some embryos are grievously handicapped. If born alive, their only prospect is of immense suffering and usually early death. Where the pregnancy is the result of rape, an abortion may be necessary for the recovery of the victim . . . Termination of pregnancy may be the right course because of the social circumstances of the existing family, or the mental or physical health of the mother." [The Methodist Church, quoted in *What the Churches Say*, CEM, 1995]

"Life must be protected with the utmost care from the moment of conception; abortion and infanticide are abominable crimes." [The Roman Catholic Church, Second Vatican Council, Encyclical *Gaudium et Spes*]

"The unborn human being's right to live is one of the inalienable human rights." [Pope John Paul II, September 1985]

Q

5 (a) Why do Christians regard children as a valuable and precious gift?
(b) If children are so treasured, why do some Christians support abortion as an option?

6 Explain how different churches differ in their attitude to abortion.

7 What does it mean to say that abortion may be "the lesser of two evils"?

8 How would some Christians argue that abortion is an issue of absolute morality and others argue that it is an issue of relative morality?

RELIGION FILE

HINDUISM 

- Brahman, the Supreme Spirit, is in every creature, and therefore Hindus consider that all life is valuable and should be respected.
- The soul is believed to enter the embryo at the time of conception, and the baby is considered to be an individual from that time on. Therefore abortion is clearly killing and is against ahimsa (non-violence).
- A main duty for Hindus in the householder stage of life is to have children. The scriptures consider abortion a serious crime and sin. Some texts make distinctions between different forms of abortion and indicate different punishments for such actions. However, an abortion would be allowed in the case of the mother's life being at risk.

Abortion in India

Most Hindus disapprove of abortion. Yet about 5 million abortions occur annually in India. Abortion was legalised there in 1971. In Indian society, it is important for a family to have sons to continue the family name, but at the same time people want to have smaller families. For poor parents, bringing up many children is difficult to afford. Also, there is pressure on parents of girls to provide dowries for them when they marry. For these reasons, since it has become possible to have a test to find out the sex of a child before it is born, some foetuses are being aborted simply because they are female. Some Indian states have passed laws prohibiting sex testing, in order to prevent people from deciding on abortion for that reason.

9 If Hindus believe that life is sacred, why are there so many abortions in India?

10 What might a Hindu say to someone who believes that abortion is just a form of birth control?

11 What advice might a Hindu give to someone who is considering an abortion?

RELIGION FILE

ISLAM 

- Islam teaches that all human life is a gift from Allah and is precious and sacred [Qur'an, 17: 33 and 40: 70].
- There is a potential life from the moment of conception, but it is after 120 days, when the foetus receives a soul, that human life really begins. Up to 4 months, the mother has more rights than the foetus, but after this the child has equal rights with the mother.
- Islam teaches that abortions should never be carried out for social and economic reasons: "You shall not kill your children for fear of want. We will provide for them and for you. To kill them is a grievous sin." [Qur'an, 17: 31]. The Qur'an states that on Judgement Day the aborted children will ask why they were killed [Qur'an, 81: 7-9,11,14]. According to the Hadith, anyone carrying out abortions will not enter paradise.

There are differing views within Islam. In Iran a woman can face the death penalty for having an abortion. On the other hand, some Muslim leaders in other countries have said that an abortion may be performed up until the foetus achieves human form, after 120 days. After that point, abortion is only allowed if the mother's life is in danger. Abortion is performed only as the lesser of two evils.

Muslims celebrate the arrival of a baby as a gift from Allah. Here a Muslim boy carries out the custom of whispering the adhan, the Muslim call to prayer, into the right ear of a new member of the family.

12 Why do Muslims believe that all life is valuable?

13 When do Muslims believe that human life begins? Why do you think they believe this? Find out what happens at this time.

14 How do Muslims who (i) totally oppose abortion, and (ii) allow abortion up to 120 days of pregnancy, justify their positions?

15 What might a Muslim say to someone who believes that "every woman has the right to choose if she wants an abortion"?

RELIGION FILE

JUDAISM

- Some texts in the Hebrew Bible refer to God's knowledge of the unborn child [Psalm 139: 13]. On a number of occasions children are described as having taken some action in the womb: for example, Jacob and Esau struggle against each other [Genesis 25: 22]. On the other hand, in the Midrashic commentary on Genesis, when someone asks Judah, "From when is the soul endowed in man; from the time he leaves his mother's womb or before that time?", he replies: "From the time he leaves his mother's womb." [Genesis Rabbah 34: 10]

“In the Jewish tradition, it has always been clear that abortion is not murder . . . but once the birth has begun and its head has emerged, the child becomes a separate person.” [Julia Neuberger, *On Being Jewish*, Mandarin, 1996]

- Abortion may occur right up to the moment of the birth. Possible reasons for an abortion include that the pregnancy is a result of rape; that the child would have a disability; or that the mother's mental or physical health is at risk.

Judaism has had a variety of views about abortion. Today there is lively debate about the issue, arising from conflict between the religious tradition and trends in modern society:

How do trends in modern society conflict with traditional ideas about having children?

"According to Jewish tradition the first law given to human beings is in Genesis 1: 28: 'be fruitful and multiply'. [However] is the command to be fruitful and multiply without any limiting factor still operative in today's society? The women's movement has forced us all to re-examine the roles played by women . . . Such issues are dramatised by the question 'Whose body is it anyway?!' and the debate about the respective rights of the pregnant woman and her as yet unborn child, given the ready availability of safe medical abortions ... At what stage does quality of life replace quantity of life as an imperative?" [Jonathan Magonet, *The Explorer's Guide to Judaism*, Hodder & Stoughton, 1998]

16 When does life begin, according to Jewish beliefs? How does Judaism justify abortion?

17 For what reasons might a Jew agree with the option of an abortion?

18 In what ways is Judaism having to take on board modern trends in society?

RELIGION FILE

19 How might a Sikh respond to the idea that the foetus is not really a person and so has no real rights or value?

20 What do Sikhs mean by there being a "divine spark" in each individual?

21 In what circumstances is abortion seen as possibly permissible in Sikhism?

SIKHISM

- Life is a gift from God [Guru Granth Sahib 1239]. Human life is the highest form of life on earth and begins at conception. Therefore abortion should not take place. "Abortion is morally wrong as it is interference in the creative work of God." [Mansukhani 1986b: 183]. "The newly baptised Sikhs are told not to associate with those who practise infanticide." [Rahit Maryada]. Possible exceptions are in the case of a pregnancy resulting from rape, and when the health of the mother is in danger.
- There is a "divine spark" (the soul) in each individual. The soul is part of God and will be reabsorbed into God after liberation from the cycle of birth, death, and rebirth (mukti).

Sample Examination Questions

A pregnant woman has been told that she will have a severely handicapped child. She is advised to consider an abortion.

(a) i. Explain why believers in one religious tradition are against abortion in the situation outlined above. [5 marks]

ii. Explain why believers in a different religious tradition think that abortion may be justified in the same situation. [4 marks]

(b) State and explain two circumstances, other than the example above, when abortion is regarded by some religious believers as acceptable. [6 marks]

(c) "If a baby is not wanted by its mother there are many people who would adopt it. It should not be killed." Do you agree? Give reasons for your answer, showing that you have thought about more than one point of view. [5 marks]

[NEAB Syllabus D Paper 2, June 1998]

CHAPTER

Should euthanasia be allowed?

UNIT ONE

Dying well? Or a slippery slope?

Is it ever right to medically end a life? Does quality of life ever become more important than quantity? In this unit you will consider the arguments for and against euthanasia.

Information File: What euthanasia means

Euthanasia comes from two Greek words meaning "gentle" (or "good") "death". In today's debate, the meaning of the word also includes the way that the "good death" is brought about – that is, by drugs or other medical means which bring a peaceful end to the dying process. Sometimes euthanasia is called mercy killing.

Voluntary euthanasia is actively aiding someone to die when that person has asked for this in order to avoid more suffering. It is not the same as suicide, the act of killing oneself.

Non-voluntary euthanasia means ending the life of a person who does not take part in the decision that this should happen: for example, someone on a life-support machine who is considered "brain-dead".

Passive euthanasia is allowing someone to die. Examples include not resuscitating a person after a heart attack, and withholding or withdrawing mechanical life support. One form of passive euthanasia involves giving pain relief treatment in such high doses that, as well as relieving pain, it also quickens death. This is called the **doctrine of double effect.**

1 (a) What is meant by euthanasia?
(b) What is the difference between euthanasia and suicide?

2 Analyse the information below on attitudes to euthanasia. What does it tell you?

“In Britain at any one time there are about two thousand people who have spent more than six months in a persistent vegetative state from which they will never recover.” [British Social Attitudes Survey, 1997]

ATTITUDES TO EUTHANASIA

In the British Social Attitudes Survey, 1997, people were asked if they thought that euthanasia should be legalised (allowed by law) for a number of types of patient. These figures show the percentages of people questioned who thought that euthanasia should "definitely" or "probably" be allowed for patients who were:

Incurable, on life-support machine, never expected to regain consciousness	86
Dying from incurable and painful illness	80
In coma, never expected to regain consciousness	58
Not in much pain or danger of death but dependent for all physical needs	51
Dying from incurable but not very painful illness	44
Suffering incurable and painful illness, but not going to die from it	42
Not ill or close to death, simply tired of living and wishing to die	12

THE WHEELBARROW – A CHINESE STORY

A son became tired of providing for his aged father. The father, worn out by old age, could no longer bring an income into the family. He relied entirely on them to supply him with food and clothing and to look after him. One day the son lost his patience. He fetched the wheelbarrow, put his father in it, and set out for the river. On the way he was stopped by a passer-by who demanded to know what he was doing with his father. "I'm going to dump him in the river. He's a total drain on my resources. I can't be bothered with the burden of caring for him any longer," replied the son. "That's understandable," said the stranger, "but don't forget to bring the wheelbarrow back for your son to use when you too get old."

3 (a) What is the message of the story of "The Wheelbarrow"?
(b) The financial cost of maintaining the incurably ill is a growing concern, to the extent that some groups have moved beyond the concept of someone having a "right to die" to the idea that a person has a "duty to die". What do you think? Do you think it is ever justifiable to practise euthanasia on people who are dying anyway and are a drain on their society's resources? What about when people are taking up needed hospital beds?

Dr Jack Kevorkian (right) is an American doctor who believes he has been right to practise euthanasia. In March 1999 a jury found him guilty of the murder of Thomas Youk, one of the patients he had helped to die. At the trial, the dead man's brother Terry (left) showed his support for the doctor's actions.

Euthanasia and the law

In some countries (for example, Holland) euthanasia is legal, but in Britain it is illegal. It also used to be a criminal offence to take one's own life, until the 1961 Suicide Act changed the law. Today it is an offence "to aid, abet, or counsel" the taking of a person's life. This means it is illegal, for example, for a doctor to help a patient to take his or her own life.

In some cases passive euthanasia may be allowed: permission must first be obtained from a court of law. Tony Bland, a football fan injured in the tragic events at Hillsborough (Sheffield Wednesday's) football ground in 1989, lay in a coma for months. As there was no sign and no hope that he would recover, the court gave permission for his life-support machine to be turned off.

The medical profession has generally been against legalising euthanasia. In order to become a doctor it is necessary to take the Hippocratic oath, which says:

> "I will use treatment to help the sick according to my ability and judgement, but never with a view to injury and wrongdoing. Neither will I administer a poison to anybody when asked to do so, nor will I suggest such a course . . . But I will keep pure and holy both my life and art."

Some people refer to the "doctrine of double effect". Taking an action that will be helpful, knowing that it will also have "bad" consequences, may be permissible:

"The use of medicaments with the intention of relieving pain is good, and if by repeated pain relief the patient's resistance is lowered and he dies earlier than he would otherwise have done, this is a side-effect which may well be acceptable . . . On the other hand, to give an overdose with the intention that the patient should never wake up is morally wrong. It is killing." [Jonathan Gould and others, *Your Death Warrant? The Implications of Euthanasia*, London, 1971]

This is a very "grey area" in British law. When does providing drugs to relieve pain cross over into providing drugs which will bring death closer?

The Voluntary Euthanasia Society (EXIT)

EXIT campaigns for voluntary euthanasia to be made legal in Britain. The society believes that if a patient with an incurable disease has signed a declaration like the following at least one month in advance, then doctors should be allowed to help that person to die peacefully.

LIVING WILL DECLARATION

I __________________________ hereby wilfully and voluntarily make known my wish that my dying shall not be artificially prolonged. I request that, if my condition is deemed terminal, by terminal I mean that I am in the final stage of an incurable or irreversible medical condition, or if I am determined to be permanently unconscious, then I be allowed to die and not be kept alive through life support systems, excluding the provision of nutrition and hydration.

Q

4 (a) What is the law concerning euthanasia in Britain?
(b) What is the Hippocratic oath? How does it apply to euthanasia?

5 Who do you think should have the most rights in deciding whether a very ill person should live or die?

6 (a) For what does the Voluntary Euthanasia Society (EXIT) campaign?
(b) In which circumstances does a person making the "Living Will Declaration" allow death? Do the terms constitute euthanasia?

Arguments for legalising euthanasia

- Euthanasia allows people to die with dignity.
- It can end the suffering of someone who has no hope of recovery.
- Relations and friends suffer when they see a loved one in pain, or unable to take part in life in any real way. Death is then a "happy release".
- Shouldn't everyone have the right to decide how he or she should die?
- We "put down" animals rather than let them suffer. Why not humans?
- Doctors know when a patient is really suffering and if there is no hope of recovery.
- With an ageing population we may not be able to afford to take care of all the really old and decrepit in the future.
- Doesn't everyone have the right to a good quality of life?

Arguments against legalising euthanasia

- The patient has the right to life.
- People may feel pressurised into euthanasia.
- Doctors may make an incorrect diagnosis.
- With modern drugs no one need suffer to an intolerable level.
- Euthanasia devalues life by making it disposable.
- Euthanasia is a form of murder.
- It is "playing God" to decide that a person's life should end. Who has the right to judge when euthanasia should be carried out? We should not ask any person to carry the responsibility for deciding that someone should die.
- It's impossible to have real safeguards and voluntary euthanasia is only one step away from compulsory euthanasia.

BILL

Bill's wife, Mary, is 71 and she has developed Alzheimer's disease. Her mind is gradually going and Bill has to keep a constant eye on her. He is 74 and suffers from arthritis, which makes it painful and difficult for him to get around their house. He knows that he cannot cope with looking after Mary any more. Even with a home help coming twice a week and the meals-on-wheels service, it has become impossible. He dreads going into residential care and is terribly worried how Mary would react to that. He knows his small amount of savings will soon be gone. He doesn't wish to be a burden on anyone and so he often groans that he wishes he and Mary could escape from this life now in a painless way.

7 Discuss Bill's situation. What advice would you give him?

8 Organise a class debate. The motion could be: "This house believes that 'mercy killing' should be allowed if a terminally ill patient requests it."

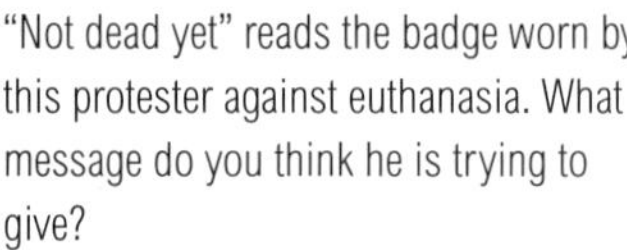

"Not dead yet" reads the badge worn by this protester against euthanasia. What message do you think he is trying to give?

Religious responses to the euthanasia debate

RELIGION FILE

BUDDHISM 

- The first of Buddhism's five moral precepts states that people should not harm any living thing (ahimsa). Part of the Eightfold Path is Right Awareness. Motives need to be taken into account in considering the issue of euthanasia. Is advocating euthanasia a way of avoiding responsibilities towards an elderly person or is it an expression of compassion towards someone who is suffering and wishes to die? Each case needs to be considered individually. The action supported should be the one that causes the least amount of pain and suffering.
- The action taken will affect karma (kamma). Involvement in euthanasia needs to be thought about carefully in terms of the spiritual harm done to oneself. Euthanasia can never be an escape from suffering, because a person's karmic forces continue into another life. Euthanasia with the wrong intention will lead to negative karma and bring about more suffering in a future life.

“We have to look at the problem from the point of view of the ill person. Is the mind still awake, alert, capable of thinking and reasoning? If yes, it is of capital importance to let that person live, even just one more day, for he or she still has the possibility of developing virtuous states of mind, such as compassion and altruism. If they have sunk into a deep coma, where the mind cannot function in any case, we must then take into consideration, among other things, the desires of the family and decide who will be responsible for euthanasia. It is a delicate problem, one that cannot be answered on the basis of general suggestions. Above all, one must consider the motivation behind the act.” [The Dalai Lama, *Beyond Dogma: the challenge of the modern world*, Souvenir Press, 1994]

1 What are the main principles that guide a Buddhist on issues such as euthanasia?

2 Why do Buddhists wish to consider each case on its merits?

3 If voluntary euthanasia were legal, how should the seriousness, stability, and informed nature of a request be judged?

RELIGION FILE

CHRISTIANITY 

- There are many references in the Bible which emphasise that life is God's gift [God created all life, Genesis 1] and therefore it is only for God to take away life. The sixth commandment is “Do not murder” [Exodus 20: 13]. God's Spirit lives in people and so ending a human life is destroying “God's temple” [I Corinthians 3: 16-17]. However, the euthanasia debate is complex and there are a variety of Christian views. Some Christians are against euthanasia in every case. Others support passive euthanasia, as in turning off the life-support system if the patient is already "brain stem dead". Some apply the commandment "Love your neighbour as you love yourself" to extreme cases of suffering and say that, in such cases, no further active treatment should be given.

- Roman Catholics say that euthanasia is "a grave violation of the law of God". "Nothing and no one can in any way permit the killing of an innocent human being . . . Furthermore, no one is permitted to ask for this act of killing, either for himself or herself or for another person entrusted to his or her care. For it is a question of the violation of the divine law, an offence against the dignity of the human person, a crime against life, and an attack on humanity." [Catholic Church Declaration on Euthanasia, Catholic Truth Society, 1980]

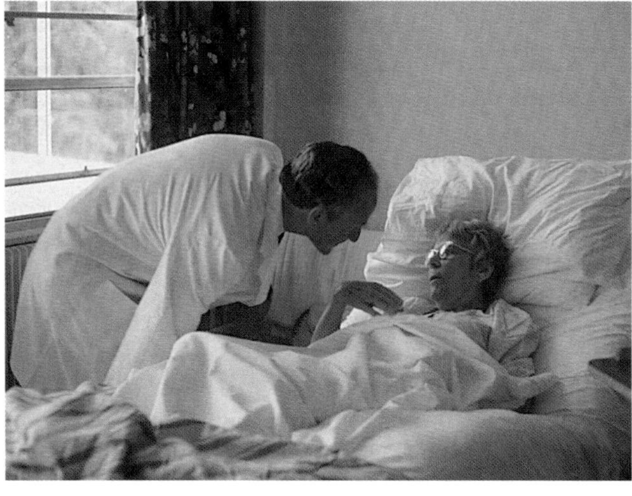

The word "hospice" refers to a resting-place for travellers. Today there are many hospices which provide a resting place for terminally ill patients who are "travelling between this world and the next". The Hospice Movement was founded by Dame Cicely Saunders, who believed that all people should be allowed to die with dignity.

- In 1992 the Church of England issued this statement: "Because human life is a gift of God to be preserved and nourished, the deliberate taking of human life is prohibited except in self-defence or the legitimate defence of others . . . The fact that it is now possible medically to keep people alive in circumstances where death might otherwise have brought relief from intolerable suffering, does not place on doctors an overriding obligation to prolong life by all available means. Crucial decisions in such circumstances should be made collaboratively and should involve more than one medically qualified person. It is a Christian imperative and a duty of the state to protect the interests of the most vulnerable, particularly those who may feel themselves to be burdensome to others or unwanted, and who thus might be under pressure to seek the hastening of their own deaths." [The Board of Social Responsibility, House of Bishops Statement, 29 October 1992]

Founder of the Hospice Movement, Dame Cicely Saunders said:

"All those who work with dying people are anxious that terminal care everywhere should become so good that no one need ever ask for voluntary euthanasia."

4 Find out and record how the Hospice Movement helps the terminally ill.

5 (a) Outline the main Christian beliefs concerning euthanasia.
(b) How do the Roman Catholic Church and the Church of England differ in their position on euthanasia?
(c) Under what circumstances might some Christians support the ending of a person's life?

6 Explain how, for some Christians, euthanasia is a matter for absolute morality and, for others, a matter for relative morality.

RELIGION FILE

HINDUISM

- Hinduism teaches that helping to take someone's life is both a crime and a sin. The terminally ill must wait until the right time (kala) comes for them to die. Respect and support should be given to the elderly, and to people who are weak and terminally ill, to enable them to perform their dharma until the right time comes for them to die naturally.
- To kill oneself or assist in someone else's death would attract bad karma and suffering in future rebirths. To avoid this, the motive for euthanasia would have to be totally selfless. "The result of a virtuous action is pure joy; actions done out of passion bring pain and suffering; ignorance arises from actions motivated by 'dark' intentions." [Bhagavad Gita 14: 16]
- Some Hindus believe that a "willed death" (that is, when an old and weak person refuses to eat and drink as he or she waits for death) may be a right action in individual cases.

7 How do most Hindus believe they should treat the elderly?

8 What effect would euthanasia have on a person's karma?

9 What is meant by "willed death"?

10 Do you think that, if euthanasia were legal, some people who consider themselves a burden, but whose lives are worth living, would feel that they ought to volunteer for it?

RELIGION FILE

ISLAM

- Islam teaches that Allah is the creator, He has created everyone for a purpose, and He should determine whether you live or die. Allah gives all life and takes it away when it is the right time [Qur'an, 40: 69-70]. "No-one dies unless Allah permits. The term of every life is fixed." [Qur'an, 3: 145]
- The Shari'ah lists conditions under which life may be taken, and they do not include or make allowance for mercy killing. The concept of a life not worth living does not exist in Islam.
- It is wrong to take one's own life. The Prophet Muhammad taught: "There was a man . . . who had an affliction that taxed his patience, so he took a

knife, cut his wrist and bled to death. Upon this God said: 'My subject hastened his end. I deny him paradise.'" [Hadith]. Another of the Hadith says that the person who kills himself with either a sword or with poison or by throwing himself off a mountain will be tormented on the Day of the Resurrection by his action.

- If a person suffers in this life, it is the will of Allah. Allah is compassionate and knows the reasons for the suffering and the tests we go through. Patience and endurance in suffering are highly regarded and rewarded in Islam [Qur'an, 39: 10].

"In his/her defence of life . . . the Doctor is well advised to realise his limit and not transgress it. If it is scientifically certain that life cannot be restored, then it is futile to diligently keep the patient in a vegetative state by heroic means or to preserve the patient by deep freezing or other artificial methods. *It is the process of life that the doctor aims to maintain and not the process of dying.* In any case, the doctor shall not take a positive measure to terminate the patient's life." [Islamic Code of Medical Ethics, 1981]

Q

11 Why do Muslims oppose voluntary euthanasia?

12 Does anyone have the right or ability to decide whether a life is worth living?

13 Is it possible for a compassionate God to allow people to suffer?

14 (a) What is meant by the words in italics in the quotation from the Code of Medical Ethics?
(b) Why might a Muslim support passive euthanasia?

RELIGION FILE

JUDAISM

- Euthanasia is not allowed in Judaism. Everything should be done to save life. In Judaism the great blessing is life. In fact, when Jewish people drink a toast, they raise their glasses and say "L'chayyim", which means "To life". Judaism teaches that life is so important that a person may break the 613 commandments given by God in all but three ways, in order to save life. (The three things still not permitted are murder, incest, and idolatry.)

- "It is forbidden to cause the dying to pass away quickly." [Shulchan Aruch, The Jewish Legal Code]. This view is supported by a number of texts in the Hebrew Bible. Life is sacred and a gift from God [Genesis 1: 27]. It is God who decides when we are to be born and when we should die [Ecclesiastes 3: 2]. Euthanasia is therefore playing God. However, Judaism teaches that it is acceptable to switch off a life-support machine when a person will not recover; keeping the person alive hinders God's will.

The character Tevye in the musical "Fiddler on the Roof" sings a song called "To Life! (L'chayyim!)": "Here's to the father I've tried to be, Here's to my bride to be, Drink L'chayyim, To Life!" Why do you think this photograph has been chosen to illustrate Jewish teaching on euthanasia?

"'Mercy killing' is totally unacceptable to Orthodox Judaism. And we should not tell an individual of his plight, in extremity, if such knowledge will unduly frighten him or weigh heavily upon him . . . We can tell him 'white lies'. Even if the doctor is asked a direct question by the patient, the doctor must judge whether the patient can withstand the hard reality of the truth. If not, and if such communication will lessen the will to survive, then the doctor should not disclose his prognosis." [Moshe Davis, *I Am A Jew*, Mowbray, 1978]

15 (a) What do Jews teach about the value of life?
(b) What do you think Jews mean when they say that euthanasia is "playing God"?

16 Is there a difference between killing someone and letting someone die?

17 Do you think people who are dying should be told the whole truth?

18 "Voluntary euthanasia could be the first step on a slippery slope." Do you agree?

RELIGION FILE

SIKHISM

- Sikhism teaches that life is a gift from God [Guru Granth Sahib 1239].
- The elderly and people who are suffering should be cared for. Some Sikhs believe that nature should be left to take its course: we should accept what God gives as an expression of the divine will [Guru Granth Sahib 1239]. Other Sikhs believe that the quality of life is of prime importance. If a person is just a living corpse, then mercy killing might be acceptable. Euthanasia might also be an option if a very weak elderly person wished to die because of the heavy burden he or she was placing upon the family. Medical and legal safeguards would need to be in place.

19 What are the main Sikh teachings about life and the elderly?
(b) What is meant by the quality of life?

20 (a) Is it ever justifiable to consider a life not worth living?
(b) Describe the circumstances where euthanasia might be acceptable to a Sikh.

"The Gurus regarded suffering as a result of man's karma. Man must have the moral courage to bear his suffering without lament. He should pray for the grace of God to enable him to put up with pain in a spirit of resignation and surrender. There is no place for mercy-killing in Sikhism. The Gurus tackled the problem of sickness and suffering by providing medical relief and alleviation of pain . . . After all, suffering is a part of the human condition and has a place in God's scheme. Suffering also prompts man to turn his thoughts to God: 'Suffering is a medicine; happiness is a disease.' . . . Even the expert physician has no right as such to end life. If he cannot cure or heal, he should not destroy life." [*Introduction to Sikhism*, Sikh-seek.com website]

Sample Examination Questions

Statement A: "People have the right to end their own lives when they wish." [from a Humanist statement on euthanasia]
Statement B: "If better methods were developed to care for the dying, euthanasia would not be needed." [from a Methodist statement on euthanasia]
(a) State and explain two religious reasons why some Christians disagree with Statement A. [4 marks]
(b) State and explain three circumstances in which euthanasia is regarded by some people as acceptable. [6 marks]
(c) Do you agree or disagree with Statement B? Give reasons for your opinion. [3 marks]
[NEAB Syllabus D Paper 2, June 1997]

CHAPTER

Is it ever right to go to war?

UNIT ONE

As you read this, more than forty wars and conflicts are taking place around the world. Some appear on television news; others go unnoticed. Sometimes people go to war to conquer land and people (the motives are aggressive). Sometimes people go to war in order to defend land and people (the motives are defensive). In this chapter you will be thinking about the morality of war and studying what the religions say about the importance of peace.

War and peace

As you read this unit, bear in mind these questions:

- Is a soldier who kills in war different from a murderer who kills in ordinary life? If so, how?
- Should all wars be regarded in the same light, or should we look differently on different types of war: nuclear, conventional, guerrilla, international, local, religious, and so on? Are some wars more justifiable than others?
- What moral questions are raised by the use of nuclear weapons, chemical and biological warfare, saturation bombing, and the use of torture?
- Is a nuclear war ever justified? If so, under what conditions? If not, why do certain countries own nuclear weapons?

On Wednesday, 16 December 1998, Britain and the USA used laser-guided bombs to attack Iraq. This was "Operation Desert Fox", a war which cost the Allies £1 billion. Tony Blair, UK Prime Minister, defended the action: "Whatever risks we face today, they are nothing compared to the risks if we do not halt [the leader of Iraq] Saddam Hussein's programme of developing chemical and biological weapons of mass destruction." One commentator described the attack as teaching "a bad world citizen" a lesson.

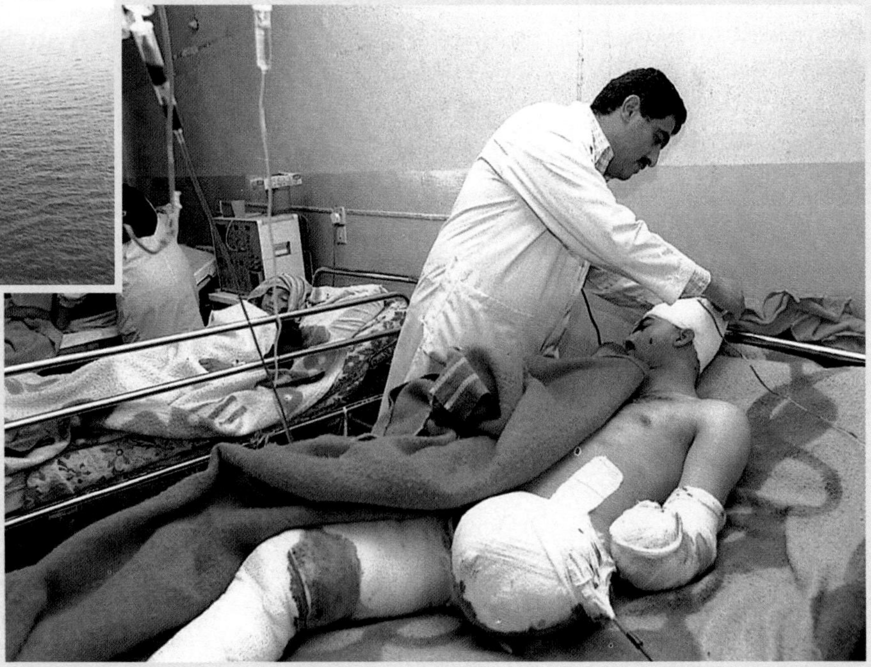

Above: This picture appeared in the press in January 1999 captioned "An RAF tornado of the type that has carried out successful bombing raids on Saddam Hussein's military machines and come back unscathed."
Right: An Iraqi victim of the Allied bombing, 18 December 1998.

1 Which of the statistics in "Did you know that . . . ?" surprises you the most? Explain why.

Did you know that . . . ?

- 60 million people were killed in wars during the 20th century.
- 332 British servicemen were executed during the First World War (1914-18) for cowardice. (Relatives have recently campaigned successfully for a pardon for these men.)
- In the Second World War (1939-45) between 30 and 55 million people died. Of these, two thirds were civilians.
- The atom bomb on Hiroshima in 1945 caused the deaths of 140,000 people.
- After the Second World War there were 30 million displaced people or refugees.
- Since 1945 over 120 wars have been fought – and there are only 165 countries in the entire world.
- In the 1990s more than 1.5 million children died in wars and 4 million were disabled.

"A single death is a tragedy: a million deaths is a statistic." [Joseph Stalin, 1879-1953, Russian Premier]

"It is striking how casually most people accept the reasons offered by governments for acts of war." [Jonathan Glover, *Causing Death and Saving Lives*, Penguin, 1990]

Attitudes to war and peace

People's reactions to killing in war are contradictory. On the one hand, a soldier who kills an enemy in war is not usually regarded with the same horror as someone who kills a fellow civilian in ordinary life. On the other hand, deaths in war may cause more horror than deaths from disease. 8,538,315 soldiers died fighting in the First World War (1914-18) – which people learn about in History and see as one of the worst wars of the 20th century. But in an influenza epidemic which broke out in 1918, between 20 and 40 million people died [statistic quoted in the *Daily Mail*, 24 December 1998] – and yet this event is given much less importance in History than the 1914-18 war. Perhaps the difference in attitude is because deaths in war are the result of deliberate killing, or because of the violence.

2 The photographs on page 132 show two sides of the same event. Do the two photographs give the complete picture of the situation? If not, what is missing?

3 How would you explain the fact that most people have heard of the First World War but not of the influenza epidemic which broke out in 1918?

4 Do you think Jonathan Glover's comment is correct? If so, why?

5 (a) Brainstorm reasons why people go to war.
(b) Is it possible that war is sometimes the lesser of two evils? Can you think of an example when this was the case?
(c) Is there a moral difference between an aggressive and a defensive war? Provide an example of each.
(d) Do you think war is a justifiable means of teaching "a bad world citizen" a lesson?

Combat as it was in "olden times": the battle of Crécy, 1346 (one of the first battles in the Hundred Years War), in a drawing from a 14th-century history of Western Europe by Jean Froissart.

MURDERERS

The Master was allergic to ideologies. "In a war of ideas", he said, "it is people who are the casualties." Later he elaborated: "People kill for money or for power. But the most ruthless murderers are those who kill for their ideas."

On another occasion the Master and his disciples attended a meeting at which people were protesting against the government's manufacture of nuclear bombs. Loud applause greeted the statement, "Bombs kill people!" The Master shook his head and muttered, "That isn't true. People kill people!" When he realised he had been overheard by the man standing next to him, he leaned over and said, "Well, I'll correct that: ideas kill people." [Anthony de Mello, *One Minute Nonsense,* 1992]

6 In "Murderers", what does the Master mean when he says people "kill for their ideas"? What sort of ideas do you think he is talking about?

"Wars arise from a failure to understand one another's humanness . . . The nature of war has changed during the last century: In olden times . . . it was a human-to-human confrontation. The victor in battle would directly see the blood and suffering of the defeated enemy. Nowadays, it is much more terrifying because a man in an office can push a button and kill millions of people and never see the human tragedy he has created. The mechanization of war, the mechanization of human conflict, poses an increasing threat to peace." [Dalai Lama, *Ocean of Wisdom: Guidelines for Living*, Clear Light Publishers]

"I have come to the conclusion that the potential destructiveness of modern weapons of war totally rules out the possibility of war ever serving again as a negative good. In a day when sputniks dash through outer space and guided ballistic missiles are carving highways of death through the stratosphere, nobody can win a war. The choice today is no longer between violence and nonviolence. It is either nonviolence or nonexistence." [Martin Luther King, in J. M. Washington, ed., *I have a Dream: Writings and speeches that changed the world*, ScottsForesman, 1992]

7 In what ways has the nature of war changed in the last hundred years?

8 (a) What do you think Martin Luther King means by war "serving . . . as a negative good"?
(b) Do you think King is right that the choice today is between violence and non-existence?

9 Complete the sentence, "For me peace is . . .".

What is peace?

Is peace just the absence of war, and war the absence of peace? Since the early 1990s, the former Yugoslavia has been torn apart by vicious civil wars. A resident of Sarajevo, the capital of Bosnia, describes peace as follows:

"When they talk about peace on the TV it's big things. It's who controls what and who governs whom. But for us peace is the little things. It's going shopping, meeting your friends for a drink, fetching a newspaper without fear of being shot at by snipers in the next street. Peace means sleeping soundly in your bed.” [quoted in *Looking Inwards, Looking Outwards*, CEM, 1997]

10 (a) What counts as a Just War?
(b) Do you think there can be such a thing as a Just War? Do you know of any war which would satisfy these conditions?
(c) Do you think a war which used nuclear weapons could ever be a Just War? Explain your answer.
(d) Do you think any other condition needs to be added today, in the light of modern technology and warfare?

11 "War can never be justified." How far do you agree with this statement? Show that you have thought about different points of view and give reasons for your answer.

A Just War?

Some people consider all wars wrong. Others believe that there are certain occasions when war is the right or just thing to do.

Over the centuries Christianity has worked out the conditions of a Just War. Different conditions have been set, to meet changing times. In the 4th century Saint Augustine set out two conditions for a Just War:

1. There must be a just cause (for example, self-defence).
2. A proper authority (e.g. a government, not private citizens) must start the war.

In the 13th century Thomas Aquinas added a third condition:

3. The war must have a good intention, and fighting must stop when that aim is achieved.

In the 16th century Francisco de Vittoria added a fourth condition:

4. The war must be waged in a just way. In other words, one can only use the correct amount of violence in order to achieve the just aims. The safety of innocent civilians must be protected.

In the 19th century other conditions were added:

5. There must be a reasonable chance of success. If you know you would lose, it would be wrong to send people in to battle.
6. War must be a last resort. Before war is waged all other forms of ending the conflict must be tried (including wide-ranging negotiations at every stage).
7. A war should only be waged if it is possible that the good achieved will outweigh the evil that is leading to the war.

Hinduism, Islam, and Sikhism also contain the concept of a Just War.

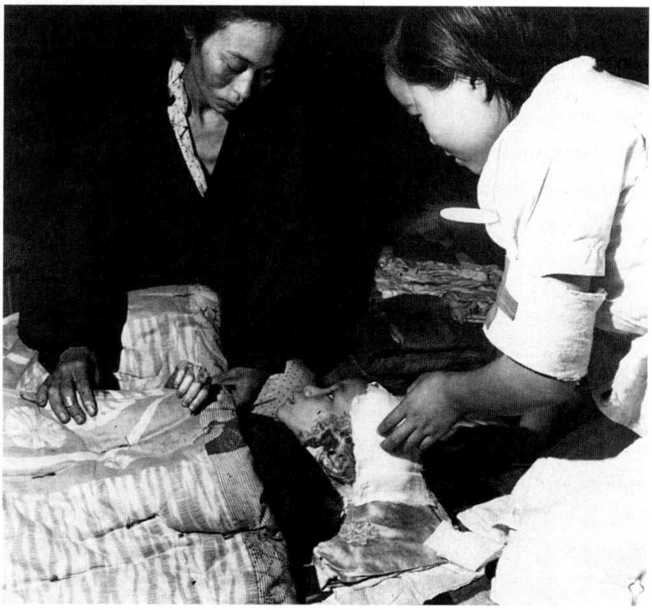

Caring for a young victim of the world's first atomic bomb, dropped on Hiroshima in August 1945. The heat and light of the explosion killed or maimed thousands of people in less than a second. Some people near the centre of the explosion were vaporised or burnt to a cinder. People further away, like this child, had their hair and skin burned off. Many of the survivors were scarred for life.

12 Do you think that there can ever be such a thing as a holy war – a war justified on grounds of religion?

Holy wars

Sometimes people fight a holy war – that is, they make war against people they see as "unbelievers", including people who follow a different religion from their own. There were holy wars in biblical times as the Israelites fought to capture the Promised Land. In the 11th and 12th centuries CE there were holy wars between Christians and Muslims. Pope Urban II urged the Christian "Crusaders" to "rescue the Holy Land from that dreadful race", by which he meant the Muslims. On 8 August 1990, Saddam Hussein, the leader of Iraq, called for a holy war against the USA.

Afghans poised for a jihad against Iran

The call to arms was made last week in Kabul at a national gathering of clerics who ordered a jihad, or holy war, to be waged in the event of an Iranian attack.

[*The Telegraph*, Sunday, 27 September 1996]

The concept of holy war raises certain issues:

- The suggestion is that a religion should not tolerate the existence of any other – but should conquer and convert people. Do you think religions have a right to do this?
- People making a holy war believe that their religion is the repository of Truth, and is therefore better than other religions. What do you think about different religions? Do you think they are all the same or does one religion contain the Truth more than others?
- All religions promote peace, so how can a holy war be justified? If people with a belief in an all-powerful God were beaten in a holy war, would their belief in God be adversely affected?

"All is fair in love and war", or is it?

The United Nations War Crimes Tribunal, based in The Hague, is one of several organisations which bring war criminals to justice. The role of the Tribunal is to put on trial people charged with violating customs of war and principles of international law.

The Nuremberg Trials were held in 1945-46 by the victors in the Second World War – Britain, the USA, and the Soviet Union. Twenty-one Nazi leaders were tried for war crimes and genocide. After this, the newly established United Nations (UN) attempted to define crimes that should be tried by the international community. These would include "war crimes" such as the massacre of unarmed civilians.

Events in the former Yugoslavia in the 1990s led the UN International War Crimes Tribunal to charge Serbian leader President Slobodan Milosevic and others with crimes against humanity. Milosevic is seen here with his wife, Mirjana Markovic, reviewing a guard of honour in Belgrade, July 1999.

13 (a) Once a war has begun, should there be any moral restrictions on the kinds of activity allowed? Is all fair in war?
(b) In groups, brainstorm behaviour which should not be allowed in times of war.
(c) Write a set of rules which you think should govern the behaviour of soldiers towards their enemies in war. Justify your list.

14 Are all war crimes wrong? Can you think of a situation where breaking the rules of war would be justified? Consider bombing a hospital where a dictator like Hitler is lying ill. Hospitals are granted immunity from attack. But would such a bombing be justified in this case?

THE TENTH CIRCLE OF HELL

Rezak Hukanovic is one of the thousands of Muslim and Croat citizens who witnessed acts of torture in the concentration camps during the conflict in Bosnia (1992-95). In his autobiographical book, *The Tenth Circle of Hell,* he describes life in the camps:

"'On all fours, I said – like dogs!' Ziga bellowed, like a dictator. He forced the three men to crawl up to a puddle . . . and then ordered them to wash in the filthy water. Their hands trembling, they washed the blood off their faces. 'The boys have been eating strawberries and got themselves a little red,' said Ziga, laughing like a madman . . . Another prisoner, Slavko Ecimovic, a Croat, and one of the first to rebel against local Serb rule, was in the same room where they had just been tortured. At least, it seemed like him. He was kneeling, all curled up, by the radiator. When he lifted his head, where his face should have been was nothing but the bloody, spongy tissue under the skin that had just been ripped off. Instead of eyes, two hollow sockets were filled with black, coagulated blood." [R. Hukanovic, *The Tenth Circle of Hell*, Abacus, 1993]

Pacifism and non-violent resistance

A pacifist is someone who is against war. In the First World War (1914-18), 16,000 men in Britain refused to fight, on grounds of conscience. They became known as conscientious objectors, or "conchies".

Two famous pacifists were Mahatma Gandhi (1869-1948) and Martin Luther King (1929-68). As leaders of protest movements, both used creative methods of non-violent resistance, including mass marches, meetings, and boycotts; sit-down protests and strikes; sit-ins; refusal to pay fines and bail for unjust arrests; and prayer pilgrimages.

15 (a) Some parents don't allow their children to play with toy guns. Why do you think this is? Did you play with toy guns, or other toys connected with war and fighting, when you were younger? What effect do you think such toys have? What message might children get from their parents' attitudes to these toys?
(b) If you were a parent, would you allow your child to play with violent computer games where the aim is to kill as many aliens and people as possible? Explain your reasons.

16 What is non-violent resistance? Why do you think it works?

How is peace created?

The purpose of the Security Council of the United Nations (UN), founded in 1948, is to maintain international peace and security. The Security Council provides peacekeeping forces, made up of soldiers from member states of the UN, to particular trouble spots. UN peacekeeping forces were awarded the Nobel Peace Prize in 1988.

Governments around the world have increasingly turned to the UN to deal with ethnic and nationalist conflicts in their countries. UN peacekeeping forces have been called upon to monitor ceasefires, demobilise former fighters, maintain buffer zones, train and monitor civilian police, and organise and observe elections. The soldiers serving these UN peacekeeping operations carry light weapons and are allowed to use minimum force in self-defence, or if armed persons try to stop them from carrying out their authorised tasks.

17 (a) Who are UN peacekeepers?
(b) What work do they do? Explain how each of their activities contributes to peace.
(c) Why do you think governments call in UN peacekeepers?
(d) What is the difference between peacekeeping and peacemaking?
(e) Find out more about the UN peacekeeping force on www.un.org.

Mostar, Bosnia, 1995: Professor Nigel Osborne and Brian Eno hold a music workshop on behalf of War Child.

An organization called War Child, founded in 1993 by two filmmakers who had been in former Yugoslavia, states that its main aim is "to advance the cause of peace through investing hope in the lives of children caught up in the horrors of war." The filmmakers had been shocked by the plight of the children caught up in the fighting in Yugoslavia. They decided to use their entertainment background to raise money to provide aid to war zones and to support children in refugee camps. Brian Eno writes: "the world of the very near future is going to be made up of these same children, and the less damaged and traumatised they are, the better it's likely to be for all of us. Remember – the future is the long now." [*War Child Bulletin* 4]. War Child now works in war zones around the world, providing medical care, food, reconstruction, and educational and social welfare programmes.

18 (a) Why was War Child founded?
(b) Why are the entertainers in War Child concentrating on helping children? How will this investment in children's lives further the cause of peace?
(c) Find out more about War Child on http://www.warchild.org.

Religious responses to war and peace

RELIGION FILE

BUDDHISM 

- At the heart of Buddhism is the principle of non-harming, ahimsa. The first of the five moral precepts, which all Buddhists keep, is "I will not harm any living thing." "Laying aside the cudgel and the sword he dwells compassionate and kind to all living creatures." [Digha Nikaya I.4]. The idea of ahimsa springs from the recognition that all beings are interconnected. For a Buddhist, to deliberately harm another would be to deny this interconnectedness.

  For this reason many Buddhists are pacifists. For example, many Tibetan Buddhists have adopted a policy of peaceful resistance to the Chinese invasion of their country in 1950. It is estimated that a million Tibetans died and 6,000 monasteries were destroyed in the aftermath of the invasion. Members of an organisation called the Buddhist Peace Fellowship are involved today in disarmament work and in non-violent campaigns for human rights in countries where Buddhists are oppressed, such as Bangladesh, Burma, Vietnam, and Tibet.

The Buddhist peace pagoda in Battersea Park, London.

- *The story of Emperor Ashoka*. Ashoka Maurya became emperor of India around 268 BCE and extended the empire greatly, through conquest. However, after a particularly bloody battle, Ashoka experienced remorse and turned to Buddhism. For the rest of his long reign he ruled by Buddhist principles of tolerance, non-violence, justice, and respect.

- Violence is not always ruled out. In the Mahayana tradition it is sometimes regarded as necessary. For example, if a gunman were about to kill many people, Mahayana Buddhists believe that, to care for fellow human beings, it would be better to kill the gunman. Yet the act of killing the gunman would still be a sin.

  Mahayana Buddhists are willing to commit sinful acts against themselves in order to save other beings. For example, during the Vietnam War, Vietnamese Buddhist monks burned themselves in the hope that their act would draw attention to the horror of the war and would help to bring an end to the fighting. There have also been examples in history of Buddhists waging war.

"We must do something to bring about an end to war and conflict, and one of the things that we have to seriously think about is the question of disarmament." [Dalai Lama, *The Power of Compassion*, HarperCollins, 1996]

1 Why are Buddhists, on the whole, pacifists?

2 (a) What is the arms trade?
(b) Is it moral to sell arms?
(c) Why do you think rich Western countries sell arms to poor countries who cannot afford to buy enough food?

3 (a) What is disarmament?
(b) Find out the difference between multilateral and unilateral disarmament.

4 Design a poster showing the Buddhist view on war and peace.

RELIGION FILE

CHRISTIANITY ✝

- Jesus was called the Prince of Peace, who called people to love each other. He preached about the Kingdom of God in which peacemakers would be "God's children" [Matthew 5: 9]. Jesus taught that you should not seek revenge [Matthew 5: 38-42] but should "love your neighbour as you love yourself" [Matthew 22: 39; see also Romans 12: 17-21] and "love your enemies and pray for those who persecute you" [Matthew 5: 43-48].
- Jesus adopted a middle ground. On the one hand, he told his disciples not to seek violence. When the soldiers came to arrest Jesus, one of his disciples drew his sword. Jesus told him to put it away [Matthew 26: 51-55]. On the other hand, Jesus accepted that violence could be necessary to defend yourself. In Luke 22: 35-38, Jesus warned his disciples that whereas, when he first sent them out to do his work, the local communities had accepted them and given them hospitality, now the situation had changed. People would not be so willing to welcome the disciples after Jesus had been crucified as a rebel. The disciples must be ready to avoid conflict and, in the last resort, to defend themselves: "whoever has no sword must sell his coat and buy one".
- Many Christians accept the concept of a Just War. However, force should be used only as a last resort and never intentionally against innocent civilians.

Archbishop Oscar Romero spoke out against the government in El Salvador, especially when dissenters were arrested and made to "disappear" (i.e. were killed). In supporting the fight for freedom, he said: "The violence we preach is ... the violence that wills to beat weapons into sickles for work." Romero was assassinated on 25 March 1980, when he was saying Mass.

- Christians are called to defend the oppressed. A way of thinking called "Liberation Theology" has grown within Christianity. The idea is that Christians are called to liberate people from their oppression and to bring about justice. For example, Oscar Romero (1917-80), a bishop in El Salvador, believed that it was right to fight for freedom in places where people have no justice and are being treated unfairly.
- Some Christians emphasise Jesus's call to be peacemakers [Matthew 5: 9] and have become pacifists. The Society of Friends (Quakers) is a pacifist Christian denomination which opposes all violence and war. Some individual Christians have also been notable for their use of non-violent forms of struggle. Two examples are Martin Luther King, in his fight for equal rights for blacks in the USA, and Bruce Kent, in his fight against nuclear war and the arms trade.

"The Christian pacifist does not necessarily condemn the use of every kind of force, but refuses to employ force unnecessarily or to destroy others, for example in either personal or state violence." [The Methodist Church, in *What the Churches Say*, CEM, 1995]

5 Why is peace an important concept in Christianity?

6 Explain why Christianity is not necessarily a pacifist religion. What reasons would a Christian give for going to war?

7 (a) What dilemmas would face a Christian considering service in the armed forces?
(b) How might these dilemmas be resolved?

The Roman Catholic pacifist priest Monsignor Bruce Kent, seen here in 1989, was general secretary of the Campaign for Nuclear Disarmament (CND).

RELIGION FILE

HINDUISM 

- The concept of ahimsa means "non-violence", avoiding harm to others, and having reverence for all life. The Indian leader Mahatma Gandhi (1869-1948) put this teaching into practice in his fight against foreign British rule. He became famous for his non-violent ways of protesting against the injustices he saw around him. Gandhi's concept of non-violent resistance is called "satyagraha". ("Satya" is truth which equals love, and "graha" is force; so satyagraha means truth-force or love-force.) One of his well-known sayings is: "An eye for an eye and we shall soon all be blind." In 1983, after interest in Gandhi had been raised by a film about him, the Gandhi Foundation was formed to show how his principles can apply to everyday life.
- Hindus believe it is important to work for and maintain a peaceful society. To this end, the warrior group in Hindu society (the Kshatriyas – meaning "who protect from harm") are expected to be noble in character [Bhagavad Gita 18: 43]. The main duty (dharma) of the Kshatriyas is to protect the innocent and especially the following five groups: women, children, the elderly, Brahmins, and cows. They should not use their weapons against innocent citizens.
- Armed conflict is allowed – it is right to fight against evil. The Laws of Manu suggest that killing is acceptable if it is to prevent something worse happening, and that killing may be necessary to fight evil, to liberate an oppressed nation, and to maintain the social order. However, conquest should not be made by fighting if there is another way.

8 What does ahimsa mean?

9 Gandhi said, "Non-violence is the way of men". Do you agree? Is it ever necessary to go to war?

10 In groups, make a list of non-violent ways in which people can protest.

11 What else does Hinduism say about the use of violence?

RELIGION FILE

ISLAM

- The word Islam comes from a root word that means "peace". Whenever Muslims meet or speak to each other on the telephone, the first thing they say is "Peace be on you". In a world which seems full of conflict and hatred, Muslims see themselves as committed to bringing about a new world order, fulfilling the command of Allah that people should live in justice, peace, and responsible brotherhood. They recognise that fighting may be necessary to bring about the new world order. This fight for justice is called "jihad" (striving).

  Muslims speak of "greater jihad", meaning the personal inner struggle that always goes on against evil (i.e. against temptations to sin); and "lesser jihad", which is a military struggle. The only time a lesser jihad is allowed is in defence of Islam [Qur'an, 22: 39-41]. Words in the Qur'an support military jihad: "strike terror into the enemy of God and your enemy ... all that you give in the cause of God shall be repaid to you. You shall not be wronged." [Qur'an, 8.61].

  There are rules for fighting a jihad: (1) It must be started and controlled by a religious leader; (2) It must have a just cause; (3) Good, not evil, must be brought about; (4) It must be a last resort; (5) It should never be fought out of aggression or to gain territory; (6) Killing must not be indiscriminate; (7) Innocent civilians should not suffer; and (8) Trees, crops, and animals should be protected. The Qur'an states that those who are killed in jihad are martyrs, and they will enter Paradise on the Day of Judgement. Fighting can never be a true jihad if it is carried out against another Muslim nation [Qur'an, 49: 9].

The Prime Minister of Israel, Ehud Barak (right), and the Palestinian leader Yasser Arafat met for the first time in July 1999. The aim was to foster trust between the two men, in preparation for difficult Israeli-Palestinian peace negotiations. Why do you think Barak presented Arafat with an olive-wood box containing a Qur'an and a Jewish Bible? What message was he giving?

- The Qur'an teaches that Muslims should seek reconciliation, and not revenge. It is for Allah to punish, not for people to return evil with evil. Forgiveness is important in Islam: "Paradise is for those who curb their anger and forgive their fellow men." [Qur'an, 3: 134]

- The Prophet Muhammad said that it was important to treat the enemy humanely. He believed that children were often the innocent victims, so the killing of children was forbidden. "Hate your enemy mildly; he may become your friend one day." [Hadith]

12 (a) What do Muslims mean by "jihad"?
(b) What is the difference between greater and lesser jihad?
(c) Give examples of greater jihad.

13 What rules govern lesser jihad? Could nuclear war be regarded as jihad?

14 What do you think it means to "treat the enemy humanely"?

RELIGION FILE

JUDAISM 

- Jews regard peace as the highest good. The word used for greeting someone is "Shalom" ("Peace be with you"). A rabbi in the Talmud says that three things keep the world safe: truth, judgement, and peace. A Midrash says: "The Torah was given to establish peace." The Jews hope for a time of peace and harmony between all people. They look forward to the Messianic Age which will be a time of peace: "Nation will not lift up sword against nation; there will be no more training for war." [Micah 4: 3-4]

  However, most Jews are not pacifists. They believe it is right to defend your own life, although war should be a last resort. Unnecessary violence is not allowed. Strict rules about going to war are spelled out in Deuteronomy 20 and amplified in the Mishnah. Jews are instructed to make an offer of peace before they attack [Deuteronomy 20: 9-12]. It is also important to cause as little damage to the environment as possible [Deuteronomy 20: 19-20].

  Judaism distinguishes three types of war: (a) obligatory wars (milchemet chovah) because of enemy aggression; (b) wars commanded by God and the Torah (milchemet mitzvah) – e.g. Joshua 8; and (c) optional wars (milchemet ha-reshut), of political significance only. Optional wars may only be undertaken for good reasons. Fighting to take revenge or to colonise is forbidden.

- The image of God in the Tenakh is sometimes of a warrior God, who fights on behalf of His people, the Israelites. For example, in Deuteronomy 25: 17-19 the Israelites are commanded to "Be sure to kill all the Amalekites, so that no one will remember them any longer."

15 (a) What is "shalom"?
(b) Why is peace important in Judaism?

16 If peace is so important, why do Jews go to war?

17 (a) Do you have a vision of an ideal world? Try to describe it.
(b) What is the Jewish vision of the Messianic Age?
(c) Do you think this vision will come about?

Many Jews believe that at times it is a religious duty to fight in a war. It is a "milchemet mitzvah". Israel's army, seen here on a training exercise in 1998, is called the Israel Defence Force (IDF). This draws attention to Judaism's emphasis on defence as a motive for war. Judaism teaches that war should be the last resort.

RELIGION FILE

SIKHISM 

- Sikhs should be ready to fight a just war, a "dharam yudh" (war in defence of righteousness), but they may only fight in defence, as a last resort. They must have no wish for revenge, and all land or property they may capture during the war must be returned. Guru Gobind Singh fought 14 battles, but he never took any land or captives, and never damaged a place of worship of any religion.

  Guru Gobind Singh wanted Sikhs to be ready to give their lives in defence of the religion. He formed the Khalsa, the Sikh community, and introduced the five Ks for Sikhs to wear. One of these five symbols is a sword (kirpan).

With India and Pakistan both carrying out nuclear tests, Sikhs from the Punjab, on the border between those two countries, were particularly concerned. They protested in New Delhi in July 1998.

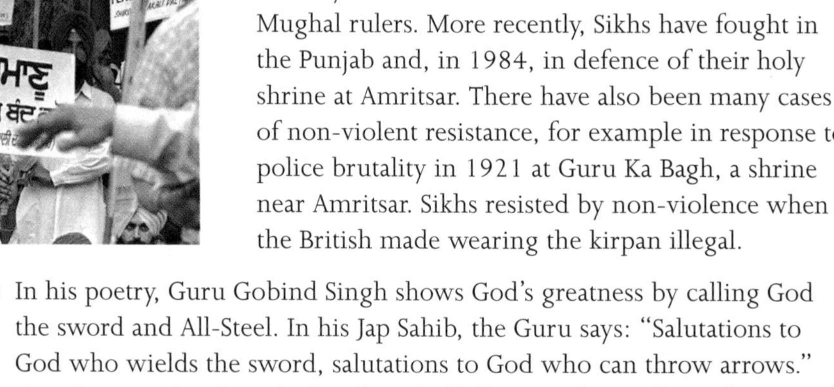

- Some Sikhs believe in ahimsa (non-violence). The first five Gurus taught non-violence. Guru Nanak was a pacifist and suggested that if somebody ill-treated you, you should bear it three times and then the fourth time God would fight for you. However, Guru Hargobind and Guru Gobind Singh became military leaders to counter the harsh rule of the Mughal rulers. More recently, Sikhs have fought in the Punjab and, in 1984, in defence of their holy shrine at Amritsar. There have also been many cases of non-violent resistance, for example in response to police brutality in 1921 at Guru Ka Bagh, a shrine near Amritsar. Sikhs resisted by non-violence when the British made wearing the kirpan illegal.

- In his poetry, Guru Gobind Singh shows God's greatness by calling God the sword and All-Steel. In his Jap Sahib, the Guru says: "Salutations to God who wields the sword, salutations to God who can throw arrows." Elsewhere God is described as "musket", "cannon", and "lance". As well as describing an aspect of God's nature, such terms also served to help Sikhs feel brave in battle.

  Other stories emphasise the need for compassion, even on the battlefield. In a battle between Sikhs and the forces of Emperor Aurangzeb, a Sikh called Bhai Kanahya gave water both to Sikh fighters and to enemy soldiers who had been wounded. Guru Gobind Singh proclaimed that Bhai Kanahya was a true and faithful Sikh, because all Sikhs must serve those in need, no matter who they are.

18 Under what conditions would a Sikh fight in a war?

19 On what grounds do you think Sikhs are protesting against nuclear testing?

20 Is it possible for a soldier to show compassion on the battlefield? Do you think there should be rules governing treatment of enemies during wartime? If so, what should they be?

Sample Examination Questions

(a) Explain why religious beliefs might lead people to campaign for peace. [7 marks]
(b) Explain how some religious people can justify going to war. [8 marks]
(c) Some people say that more wars are caused by religion than are stopped by religion. Do you think this is a fair comment? Show that you have thought about different points of view and give reasons to support your answer. [5 marks]
[SEG Summer 1997]

CHAPTER

How should we care for planet Earth?

UNIT ONE

How was the world formed? Is planet Earth the result of an accident or has it been created? In this unit we will look at both scientific and religious views.

How did the world begin?

The universe is estimated to be more than 10 billion years old. Scientists believe that the sun and its solar system, including the earth, were formed 4.6 billion years ago, that life started in the seas about 900 million years ago, and that the first mammals emerged about 250 million years ago. All this seems to contradict the religious creation stories, that the earth came about in a short space of time as the result of a supernatural power. But are the scientific and the religious accounts mutually exclusive? Or can a person believe in both?

The big bang

The most popular scientific theory of the universe is that everything started with a big bang. A gigantic explosion caused the matter of the universe, which was densely squashed together, to suddenly expand outwards.

The stars are one of the clues in the universe which point to this theory. Each star is a great ball of fire, like the sun. The stars are grouped in galaxies, and these are moving apart from each other. Scientists point out that this movement is what you would expect if all matter had started from the same place and then exploded apart. They use the present position of the galaxies and the rate at which they are moving apart to work out when the big bang occurred.

Scientists say that the long-term future depends on how much mass there is. There may be enough mass for the universe to eventually stop expanding and begin to contract because of the power of gravity. This could lead to everything being crunched up together (the big crunch) until there is another explosion; then an endless cycle of expansion and contraction could occur. On the other hand, there may be too little mass to slow down the expansion, and so the universe may go on expanding for all eternity.

Q

1 What is meant by (a) the big bang, and (b) the big crunch?

2 Does Science get rid of the need for a creator God, or do we still need God as the ultimate explanation of why the world and human life exist? What do you think?

A Hubble Space Telescope coloured image of a far-off region of galaxies, 1995. The image showed that there were many more galaxies in the universe than had previously been believed.

The theory of evolution

In the nineteenth century, Charles Darwin went on a scientific expedition on board a government vessel, HMS *Beagle*. The object was to look at the different forms of coral islands and to investigate the geographical distribution of animals and plants. During this voyage (1831-36) to many parts of the Southern Hemisphere, Darwin noted how the animals and plants had adapted to their environment. He concluded that their survival depended on their ability to adapt to their surroundings and to changing circumstances. This gave rise to the idea that, in nature, only the fittest survive, with the adapted characteristics being passed on to the next generation. So, over millions of years, as complex changes occur, life forms evolve into increasingly complicated ones. Darwin's book *The Origin of Species by Means of Natural Selection* was published in 1859. His studies led him to believe that humans had evolved from lower members of the animal kingdom.

Q

3 Does the evolutionary theory mean that humans are no more than animals? What do you think?

4 Do you think life has any purpose when seen from an evolutionary perspective? Does the universe care anything for us?

“From so simple a beginning endless forms most beautiful and most wonderful have been, and are being, evolved.” [concluding words of *The Origin of Species*]

A creative power

The belief of many religious traditions is that the universe did not happen by chance but by design; there is a power beyond the world which deliberately caused creation to take place.

The Jewish-Christian story of creation

Jews and Christians share the same story of creation. It is found at the beginning of their holy books in Genesis 1. It tells how God created the heavens and the earth out of nothing, filled the earth with living creatures, and made human beings, all in a period of "six days". On the seventh day God rested. There are various interpretations of this story.

“God created the world in six days just as it is written in the Bible.” [Aaron]

“The story of creation is not to be taken as literally true. However, that doesn't mean that there are not some important truths in this biblical story.” [Angie]

“The creation story is just a myth – a make-believe story.” [Paul]

“It's important to have in mind that ancient cultures generally passed along their wisdom in the form of stories. The stories about creation are of that sort. So they are not intended to teach scientific truths, as we would understand them today. They are actually intended to teach religious truths. For example, they teach us that the universe was created by God, that it didn't just come into existence on its own, and that the universe as a whole is good.” [Professor Nancy Murphy, quoted on *The Question Is . . . ?*, BBC Open University video]

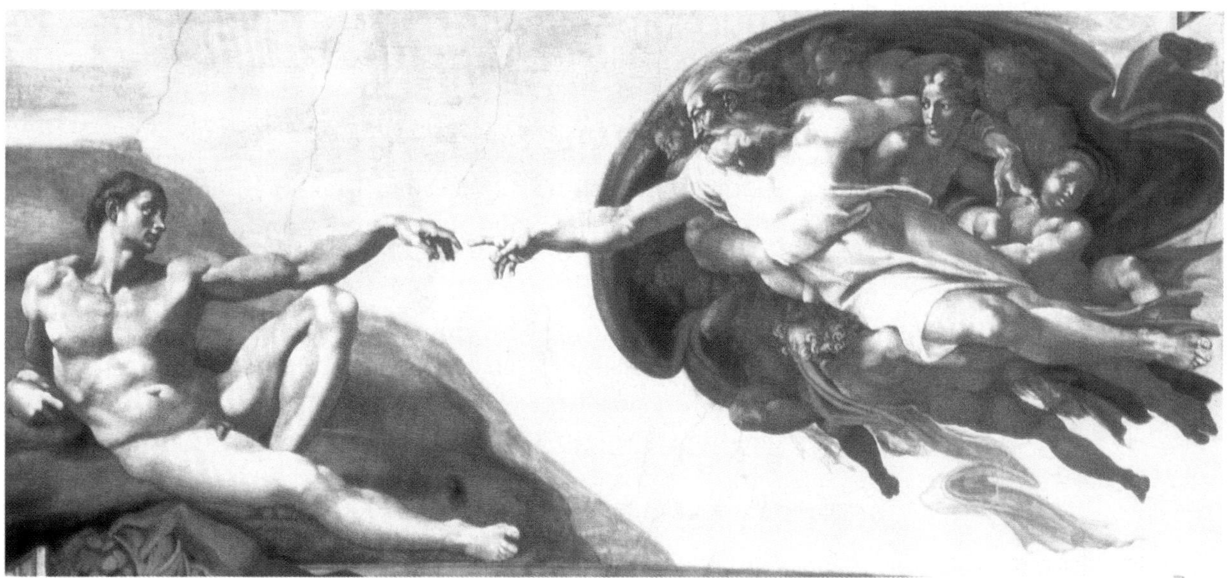

"The Creation of Adam" is one part of Michelangelo's paintings (1508-12) on the ceiling of the Sistine Chapel, in the Vatican, Rome. Eve, not yet created, is shown looking out from under God's left arm.

5 How would you reply to the following opinion? "The biblical creation story is just make-believe. Everyone knows that the earth was not made in six days!"

6 One Christian has written that "God makes the world make itself" [Austin Farrer, *The Science of God*, 1966]. What do you think he means?

Hindu creation stories

Hindus believe that many universes have, do, and will exist, and that, compared with the whole story of creation, scientific knowledge is very small. There are several Hindu stories explaining the creation of the world. They are designed to show the cycle of creation, evolution, destruction, and re-creation. Brahma (the creator), Vishnu (the Preserver), and Shiva (the Destroyer) are the main figures in the stories.

One story tells how Vishnu was asleep, resting on a great snake called Ananta as it floated on a vast ocean. From Vishnu's belly grew a lotus flower, and from the flower came Brahma. Brahma then split the lotus flower into three. He made one part into the heavens, another became the earth, and from the third came the sky. Next Brahma created the grass, flowers, trees, plants, animals, birds, and fish.

In the figure of the dancing Shiva, the fiery circle represents the cycle of destruction and re-creation.

7 How does the Hindu idea of a cycle of universes compare to the scientific theory of the big bang and what may follow?

8 Does it matter if the religious stories of creation are not all literally true?

9 (a) What questions concern the scientist?
(b) What questions are religions trying to answer?

Earth, our home

What rights and responsibilities do humans have concerning the natural world? In this unit you will learn about the use and abuse of natural resources and the need to care for the planet.

Planet Earth is our only home. Scientists know of no other planet that could provide the things humans need to breathe, drink, eat, provide clothes, and sustain life. Earth is unique, and if people destroy it, they will almost certainly destroy themselves in the process. However, today the planet is under threat.

A major problem is the massive growth in world population. In the time it takes to draw one breath, 500 babies are born. At the present rate of growth, the world's population will be 14-15 billion at the end of the 21st century, three times the present figure.

"The world's growing population and unsustainable consumption patterns are putting increasing stress on air, land, water and energy resources." [Agenda 21]

1 (a) Make a spider diagram of the major environmental problems.
(b) Why is the earth in danger? What can be done?

2 Write a poem starting with the words "If the land could speak", drawing attention to environmental dangers. What might the earth say in response to what humans are doing to it?

3 The world is very big. Does it matter if we exploit or abuse it? Is it ours to do with as we wish?

SOME THREATS TO THE ENVIRONMENT

- Pollution of rivers and seas by oil, pesticides, and nitrates kills plants and wildlife.
- Emission of gases from vehicles, power stations, and factories leads to the greenhouse effect and global warming. This causes the ice caps to melt and so sea levels rise.
- Chlorofluorocarbons (CFCs) in refrigerators, aerosols, and air-conditioning equipment have been destroying the ozone layer of the atmosphere, which naturally blocks some of the dangerous ultraviolet light getting through from the sun.
- Cutting down forests destroys natural habitat: animals and plants can become extinct. Deforestation also affects world climate, and speeds the greenhouse effect.
- Increasing amounts of waste, including non-biodegradable materials, cause problems of disposal. Toxic and nuclear waste cause particular difficulties.
- Natural resources, such as fossil fuels, are used up more quickly than they naturally replace themselves.

A recent concern

Many environmental problems can be seen as a result of technological progress, of which the downside became obvious later. Concern about the environment is relatively new. In 1972, representatives of 70 governments met at a conference in Stockholm to share concerns and, as a result, the United Nations Environment Programme (UNEP) was set up. Its aim was to push governments to take more care of the environment. In June 1992 an Earth Summit was held in Rio de Janeiro. It was the largest ever meeting of world leaders; 179 nations were represented. Together they created a document called "Agenda 21" (the agenda for the 21st century), a blueprint for saving planet Earth.

Information File: Environmental friendliness

Green: careful of the environment; acting to protect it from harm by human activity and manufactures. Many "green" products are now produced, designed to cause less damage to the environment than the products they are replacing. People are encouraged to think and act green by, for instance, **recycling** paper, glass, metals, and other products; producing or buying **organic** food (no pesticides or artificial fertilisers are used); and walking, cycling, or using public transport rather than using a car.

Ecology: scientific study of living things in relation to each other and their environment.

"The greatest challenge of both our time and the next century is to save the planet from destruction. It will require changing the very foundation of modern civilisation – the relationship of humans to nature." [Mikhail Gorbachev, quoted in *Rescue Mission Planet Earth*, Kingfisher, 1994]

Greenpeace and **Friends of the Earth** are two pressure groups which were formed in 1971, as people realised that the environment was in danger. Greenpeace aims to protect the environment through peaceful direct action. It registers its objection to activities by being present where they are happening. Greenpeace volunteers have been involved in protests against whaling, nuclear testing, air and water pollution, and the exploitation of wildlife. Friends of the Earth campaigns for more protection to be given to the environment. Part of its work is trying to educate the public about the dangers of abusing the environment. They have published books, briefings, and reports.

In 1997 the "eco-warrior" Swampy (real name Daniel Hooper) hit the headlines. He sabotaged efforts to develop a new runway at Manchester airport and set up home in trees to protest against the development of new roads. In April 1997 he declared his intention to stand for parliament, saying: "The real issues are not being addressed by the politicians' narrow agenda." He would, for instance, stop airport expansion, put national targets on traffic reduction, and stop planning permission for out-of-town shopping centres.

Humans in control

Human knowledge about how the world works has grown and grown. By the late 20th century, scientists had discovered enough about genes to be able to change or control the characteristics of living things (microbes, plants, animals, and humans). The general public became particularly aware of this in 1999, when concern suddenly erupted about genetically modified (GM) foods.

GM crops are grown from seeds which scientists have genetically engineered, to produce qualities such as resistance to disease. People are concerned about whether such crops may upset the balance of nature; and about the power that the technology gives to the seed manufacturers.

"The earth does not belong to man, man belongs to the earth. All things are connected like the blood that unites us all. Man did not weave the web of life, he is merely a strand to it. Whatever he does to the web, he does to himself." [Chief Seattle, a North American Indian, quoted by Joseph Campbell, *The Power of Myth*]

4 What does Chief Seattle mean when he says, "Whatever he does to the web, he does to himself"?

5 Find out more about the work of either Greenpeace UK, (Canonbury Villas, London N1 2PN, and www.greenpeace.org.) or Friends of the Earth (26-28 Underwood Street, London N1 7JQ).

UNIT THREE

Animal issues

What do you think about the animal world? What are animals for? To what extent are animals different from humans and what is their value compared to the value of people? What rights, if any, do humans have over animals? Do animals have rights? In this unit you will be thinking about issues involving animals.

"The greatness of a nation and its moral progress can be judged by the way its animals are treated." [Mahatma Gandhi]

ANDROCLES AND THE LION

Androcles, a Roman slave, was taken to Africa. He was so badly treated that he ran away and hid in a cave. He was petrified when a lion entered the cave, but he saw that the lion was in great pain because of a thorn in his paw. Androcles removed the thorn and the two became friends.

For three years the lion hunted and Androcles cooked the meat in the fierce midday sun. Eventually Androcles became homesick and set out to return to civilisation. On the way he was captured and taken to Rome. As a runaway slave, he was sentenced to be torn to death by lions. The crowds watched as the lion was released into the arena and Androcles waited for his end. But the lion, instead of roaring fiercely and tearing his victim limb from limb, rubbed gently around Androcles' legs. By an amazing coincidence it was the same lion that had befriended Androcles in Africa.

1 (a) The story of Androcles and the lion could have been a much shorter one. What dangers were ignored and what risks were taken?
(b) The lion and Androcles worked together as partners and equals, helping each other. List some of the ways in which animals help humans.

2 (a) What should be the relationship between humans and the animal world?
(b) Is one more important than the other?

Human rights for chimps

New Zealand could be the first country in the world to give the great apes "human" rights that could be enforced by a court. A group of 38 lawyers, scientists, and philosophers has submitted a new clause to a Bill going through Parliament which would give gorillas, chimpanzees, and orang-utans the right to life, the right not to suffer cruel or degrading treatment, and the right not to take part in all but the most benign of experiments.

[*The Times*, 11 February 1999]

The term "animal rights" was first used in a book by that title, written by Henry Salt (1851-1939). Since then many organisations have formed to protect the rights of animals. Their fundamental principle is that non-human animals deserve to live according to their own natures, free from harm, abuse, and exploitation. The organisations say that animals have the same right as humans to be free from human cruelty and exploitation. Many animal rights groups are united in their fight against factory farming, vivisection, and the use of animals for entertainment. However, there are areas of debate among animal rights supporters: for example, about whether research that harms animals is ever justifiable and about what forms of civil disobedience should be permitted in standing up for the rights of animals.

In talking about animal rights, it is justified to ask: Where do these rights come from? Have they been granted by law, or do animals have natural rights given by God?

Blood sports

In some communities, for example among the Inuit of the Arctic, hunting is done only for food. In the Arctic there is little plant life and so the Inuit hunt to survive. But in some parts of the world people hunt for sport. Fox hunting, stag hunting, hare coursing, grouse shooting, and fishing are country pastimes that have existed for centuries.

Anti-hunt campaigners distract the dogs from the scent of the fox by calling false commands, befriending them, spraying false scents, and running amongst the pack to give the fox more time to escape.

There are around 200 fox hunts in Britain, with over 12,000 hounds. The hunters enjoy the thrill of the chase and are hunting an animal which is a pest to farmers, killing lambs, poultry, and other wildlife. Approximately 300,000 foxes are killed each year, but less than 10% are killed by fox hunting. Most foxes die from road accidents, shooting, snaring, and natural causes.

Supporters of hunting for sport argue that hunting is a normal part of the cycle of life, helping to keep a balance in nature. They point out that, in a hunt, the animal has a fair chance of escaping and is therefore in a better position than animals bred and kept in a field to be slaughtered for food. However, many people disagree with hunting. The National Anti-Hunt Campaign argues that "every year in Britain tens of thousands of wild animals are chased, terrified, and brutally killed in the name of 'sport'." Anti-Hunt campaigners also say that hunting is unnecessary, since humans in most communities can gain enough food without it. They say that hunting is a mis-use of human power.

Bear-baiting, cockfighting, and badger-baiting are illegal, but bullfighting is still allowed in Spain. With its pageantry and challenge to the matadors, it entertains thousands of visitors to Spain every year.

3 (a) Could you hunt and kill animals?
(b) Is there a difference between hunting for sport and hunting for survival?
(c) Are blood sports cruel? Should they be banned?

4 (a) Are there morally any differences between bullfighting, fox hunting, shooting, and fishing?
(b) How is slaughtering animals different from hunting them? If you eat meat, isn't slaughtering just a matter of getting someone to do the hunting for you?

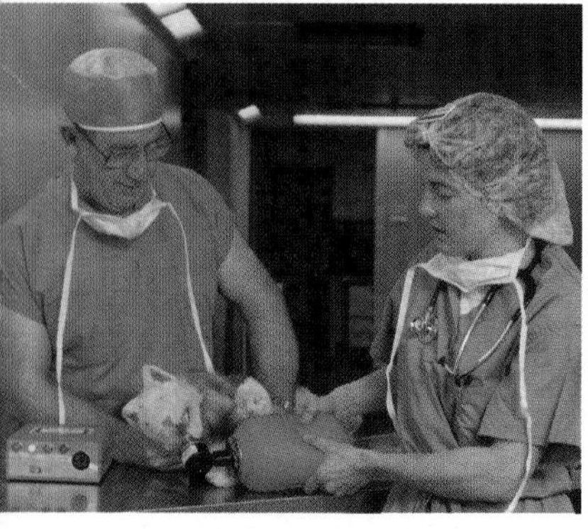

A student vet learns to resuscitate a cat, using a "resusicat". Her professor, Dr Short, invented resusicats in order to reduce the killing of real cats for veterinary education.

Animal experimentation

Many medical advances have resulted from experimentation on animals. Animal experimentation was used in the development of insulin treatment for diabetes, vaccines against whooping cough, diphtheria, rubella, and polio, and vaccines against distemper in dogs and enteritis in cats.

Vivisection literally means "the cutting up of living animals". Nowadays the term is often used to describe all the various experiments that are carried out on animals. For example, as well as in medical research, animals are used in testing for possible side-effects of cosmetics and weedkillers. Toxicity tests are carried out by injection, feeding, or putting drops in the eye. Inevitably some of these tests are painful: for instance, the Draize test where a possible irritant is dropped into a rabbit's eyes.

Animal welfare groups argue that most experiments on animals are not needed, especially those for testing cosmetic products. "The Body Shop" and "Beauty without Cruelty" are two successful businesses which do not use animal testing. The British Union for the Abolition of Vivisection (BUAV) disagrees with all forms of animal testing. It argues that tests on animals do not help, as the results are not necessarily the same on humans. It points out that there are alternatives to testing on animals: artificial cells and tissues can be used.

The number of animal experiments is being reduced both for humane reasons and because other methods give results more quickly and cheaply. Using cell culture, computers, and in-vitro research, scientists have reduced the level of animal experiments to less than 3,000,000 a year. Over 85% of these experiments are on rodents (e.g. rats and mice).

Scientists are currently investigating the use of animal organs for human transplants.

5 How has animal experimentation helped medical advances?

6 Is all animal research wrong, or does it depend on the aims and achievements? Give reasons for your opinion.

Meat or veg?

Some people choose to be vegans (to eat no animals or animal products) or vegetarians (to eat no meat). This may be for religious reasons or because they do not wish to harm animals. Some are concerned about modern farming methods, such as keeping hens in cages or rearing calves in crates. Others think that vegetables (particularly if grown organically) are safer to eat than meat and animal products, especially after the scares of salmonella in eggs and BSE. For most people, however, meat remains a major source of protein.

"Factory farming" describes a system in which animals, like these hens, are kept indoors for most of their lives, with their feeding regulated and their movement restricted. The farmer's aim is to produce enough food at affordable prices for an ever-increasing population.

7 Should animals be used for food? Are some forms of meat more acceptable than others? If so, what makes them so?

8 What is the difference between a vegan and a vegetarian? Give reasons why some people choose to avoid eating meat.

9 "For too long animals have been treated like objects, used by human beings for food, clothing, transportation, entertainment, and often cruel scientific experiments done solely for human satisfaction." Do you agree? What do you think about the rights of animals?

Religious attitudes to the environment

An event was held in Assisi, Italy, in September 1986 to celebrate the 25th anniversary of the founding of the World Wide Fund for Nature (WWF). Representatives of conservation organisations and representatives of some of the major world religions gathered for a conference, to share insights into the relationship between humans and nature. As a result, each religion published a "Declaration" setting out its stance on environmental issues.

Assisi was chosen as the place for the conference, in honour of St Francis of Assisi. In modern times this 13th-century saint has been referred to as the Green Saint, because of his teaching on conservation and the love of animals.

RELIGION FILE

BUDDHISM 

- Questions about the origin of life are left unanswered by the Buddha. He did not discuss unnecessary metaphysical questions since he considered speculation a "wilderness of opinions". Buddhists believe that worlds evolve and follow a cycle of decay, death, and rebirth. This is in keeping with modern scientific views, but Buddhists believe that there is much more to life than can be proved by scientific research.
- Buddhism is a religion of love, understanding, and compassion and Buddhists are committed to the ideal of non-violence (ahimsa). Great importance is attached to wildlife and the protection of the environment, on which every living thing in the world depends for survival.

  "All breathing, existing, living sentient creatures should not be slain or treated with violence, nor abused, nor tormented, nor driven away." [Anchoranga Sutra]. "All things should be happy and at one." [Metta Sutra]

"There is a striking similarity between exterminating the life of a wild animal for fun and terminating the life of an innocent fellow human being at the whim of a more capable and powerful person." [Buddhist Declaration, Assisi, 1986]

- There is some discussion among Buddhists about whether or not to be strict vegetarians. At the time of Buddha, eating meat was not forbidden, but members of the sangha were not allowed to kill animals for food. In some Buddhist societies, like Tibet, it was difficult to grow sufficient vegetables and so it was necessary to eat meat, even though it involved taking life. It is left to the individual's conscience to decide. Many Buddhists in Britain are vegetarians.

"According to Buddhism the life of all beings – human, animal, or otherwise – is precious, and all have the same right to happiness. For this reason I find it disgraceful that animals are used without being shown the slightest compassion, and that they are used for scientific experiments. I have also noticed that those who lack any compassion for animals and who do not hesitate to kill them are also those who, sooner or later, show a lack of compassion toward human beings." [The Dalai Lama, *Beyond Dogma: the challenge of the modern world*, Souvenir Press, 1994]

1 Is discussing questions such as "How did life begin?" or "How or why was the universe formed?" a fruitless exercise? Give reasons for your opinion.

2 What do Buddhists mean by there being more to life than can be proved by scientific research?

3 In what ways do you think the concept of non-violence affects Buddhists' treatment of the universe?

4 What teachings might influence a Buddhist in making decisions concerning animal experimentation, fur trading, and blood sports?

RELIGION FILE

CHRISTIANITY

- Among the biblical references that Christians use to formulate their ideas about the environment are the following:

  God created the universe and declared it to be good [Genesis 1: 1-4]. Christians therefore affirm the goodness of creation. Jesus himself affirmed the value of every living creature, even each individual sparrow [Luke 12: 6].

  God gave people the responsibility of looking after the world for Him, as stewards [Genesis 2: 15]. The environment should be treated with care and land should not be over-exploited [Exodus 23: 10-11]. A number of references in the Bible give guidance on what responsible stewardship means: for example, Exodus 23: 10-11; Deuteronomy 20: 19; Deuteronomy 22: 6. However, there is also a statement in the creation story that people are to bring the earth "under their control" [Genesis 1: 28]. This is seen to have led to exploitation of the earth's resources and of animals. Most Christians agree that this was not God's intention.

"Nature is the art of God." [Teilhard de Chardin, 1881-1955]

"The world was created by God and is an expression of his love. As children of God, we have a responsibility to care for it." [Major Christine Parkin, Training and Development Officer, Salvation Army]

- Pope John Paul II issued a statement in 1988 based on the following principles:

  The earth and all life are a gift from God, given to us to share and develop, not to dominate and exploit.

  Our actions have consequences for the rights of others and for the resources of the earth.

  We have the responsibility to create a balanced policy between consumption and conservation.

  ["Sollicitudo Rei Socialis", quoted in *What the Churches Say*, CEM, 1995]

"The health of the environmental system is critical to all life and immensely fragile in the face of the demands of a consumerist and technologically powerful culture." [Methodist Conference, 1991, quoted in *What the Churches Say*, CEM, 1995]

- A number of Christian aid agencies (including Christian Aid, CAFOD, and Tear Fund) draw attention to the plight of the earth. Many of their projects are concerned with the environment.

  The Reverend Arthur Broome and other Christians started the RSPCA in 1824, in response to cruelty against animals. It was the first animal welfare organisation in the world.

- Some Christians believe that animals are different from humans, since people are created in the image of God [Genesis 1: 26]. Essential animal experiments to aid medical advances are tolerated by most Christians, provided the animals are treated as humanely as possible. Testing cosmetics on animals is not so acceptable. Other Christians apply Jesus's teaching "Do as you would be done by" to animals as well as humans.

Q

5 If creation was perfect, why do we have so many environmental problems?

6 (a) What does it mean to be a steward?
(b) In your opinion, how well have most humans carried out their role? Did God make a mistake in giving humans the responsibility of looking after the world?

7 A minority view expressed in Christianity is that we can do what we want to the world. Which biblical teaching might be used to support the exploitation of the environment?

8 In what ways are animals exploited? Is there a difference between using animals for the benefit of humans and exploiting them?

9 "In the end, lack of respect for the life and wellbeing of an animal must bring with it a lowering of man's own self-respect. 'In as much as you do it to these, the least of my little ones, you do it unto me.'" [former Archbishop Robert Runcie]. Discuss.

Here's an example of the difficulty of maintaining a balance between "consumption and conservation". This boy in Madagascar is standing in front of a forest which has been burnt in order to grow food. People need to use land to grow food. What would you say is the difference between using it and "over-exploiting" it?

RELIGION FILE

HINDUISM ॐ

- Everything in the universe comes from God and is therefore part of Him – see the story about salt on page 44. Therefore reverence for the whole of creation is essential. Some Hindus believe that the world is the work of God's creativity. It is therefore sacred and precious, and must be cared for.

  In the Bhagavad Gita, Lord Krishna says: "Everything rests on me as pearls are strung on a thread. I am the original fragrance of the earth. I am the taste in water. I am the heat in fire and the sound in space. I am the light of the sun and moon and the life of all that lives." [7.7-9].

- Hinduism teaches that all living things are bound up with samsara (the cycle of birth, death, and rebirth) as the Atman (soul) assumes different forms. Therefore all living things should be treated with the same respect. It is part of a Hindu's dharma (duty) to protect and not exploit other living things.

- Ahimsa, which means avoiding harming others, is a very important value in Hinduism. No harm should be done to any living thing [Laws of Manu 5: 51]. Ahimsa expresses the sanctity of all forms of life – insects, fish, birds, animals, and human beings.

  Stories about Krishna's life as a cowherd show him to be closely in touch with and caring of the environment: he is pictured playing the flute, surrounded by cattle for which he is responsible. Krishna sets an example for the Hindu community: "Elsewhere Krishna cleaned the river. He defeated the serpent Kaliya and purified the Yamuna River. He swallowed the forest fire to protect the forest. He looked after the cows. He spoke to the birds in their own language. Krishna was always protecting nature." [R. Prime, *Hinduism and Ecology: Seeds of Truth*, WWF/Cassell, 1992]

Cows are especially sacred in Hinduism and should not be mistreated or killed. The Bhagavad Gita advises Hindus to protect the cow. Cows are therefore allowed to roam free in India.

- Hindu gods and goddesses have particular animals as their vehicles (vahana). For instance, a bull called Nandi is usually linked with Shiva. Vishnu took the form of various animals, including a fish and a tortoise, to save the world from particular dangers. Some Hindu deities appear as an animal, for example Ganesh as an elephant. The association of animals with the gods and goddesses gives animals a special place in Hinduism.

“No person should kill animals helpful to all. Rather by serving them, one should attain happiness.” [Yagur Veda 13: 47]

10 Do you think it is possible to avoid harming all living things? Give reasons for your opinion.

11 (a) Explain how ahimsa affects Hindu attitudes to animal life.
(b) Most Hindus are vegetarians. Explain why this is.
(c) Why might Hindus oppose animal experimentation?

12 To Hindus, what is the value of animals compared to humans?

RELIGION FILE

Smog covered Borneo, Malaysia, and Indonesia in 1997, causing breathing problems for millions of people. Combined causes of the smog were a drought in the area and the burning of forests to clear land. What do you think would be the Muslim attitude to these events?

ISLAM

- Islam teaches that the universe was created by and belongs to Allah [Qur'an, 2: 29; 2: 117; 3: 190; 45: 11-12]. “All Creation is like a family of God; and He loves the most those who are the most beneficent to His family.” [Hadith]

  The Qur'an [21: 31] may support the big bang theory: “Are the disbelievers aware that the heavens and the earth were but one solid mass which We tore asunder?”

- Islam teaches that humans have been given the role of khalifa (vice-regent or trustee). “The Earth is green and beautiful, and Allah has appointed you His stewards over it.” [Qur'an, 6: 165]. Abusing the authority that Allah has given is a form of blasphemy against Him. On the Day of Judgement everyone will have to answer to Allah about the way they have carried out their khalifa-ship – what they have done and what they have failed to do.

  The Islamic Declaration made at the Religion and Nature Interfaith Meeting in Assisi in 1986 acknowledged that “often while working as scientists or technologists, economists or politicians, we act contrary to the environmental dictates of Islam” and that there needed to be a return to “unity, trusteeship, and accountability, the three central concepts of Islam”.

“The central concept of Islam is tawhid or the Unity of God. Allah is unity; and His Unity is also reflected in the unity of mankind and the unity of man and nature. His trustees are responsible for maintaining the unity of His creation, the integrity of the Earth, its flora and fauna, its wildlife and natural environment.” [Islamic Declaration, Assisi, 1986]

- An important concept in Islamic law (the Shari'ah) is that of hima. Hima is an area of undeveloped land left for pasture. A hima can be set aside by the government on public land, or by an individual on private land. Muslim law-makers have used the same concept (of protected areas) in formulating laws to conserve forests and water resources, for example, and even to limit the growth of cities.

- Muslims believe that God loves and cares for all creatures and so cruelty to animals is forbidden. "There is not a creature on the earth but God provides its sustenance." [Qur'an, 11: 6]. "A good deed done to a beast is as good as doing good to a human being; while an act of cruelty to a beast is as bad as an act of cruelty to a human being." [Hadith]

  Hunting is allowed only for food, not for pleasure. "If someone kills a sparrow for sport, the sparrow will cry out on the Day of Judgement, 'O Lord! That person killed me for nothing! He did not kill me for any useful purpose!'" [Hadith]

  Animal experimentation is allowed if it helps humans to make medical advances. Needless suffering should be avoided. Experimenting on animals for cosmetics or luxury goods is forbidden.

  While in a state of ihram, for example when on Hajj, Muslims must harm no living creature [Qur'an, 5: 97-98] because they should be in a state of peace and purity with all.

- There are a number of rules governing food in Islam. Certain animals, including the pig, may not be used for food; all other animals must be slaughtered in the most painless manner, and the slaughterer must say "In the name of Allah, Allah is most Great". (This is Halal slaughter.) "He has forbidden you … any flesh that is consecrated other than in the name of God." [Qur'an, 2: 173 and 16: 115].

  Muslims may choose to be vegetarian, but eating meat is part of their religion – for example, at the feast of Eid-ul-Adha animals are slaughtered and the meat distributed to the community.

13 What does it mean to be given the role of khalifa?

14 (a) Why do Muslims believe that they must take great care how they treat the environment?
(b) Brainstorm ways in which people can show care in their treatment of the environment.

15 Explain Muslim attitudes towards eating meat.

16 (a) Why is cruelty to animals strictly forbidden in Islam?
(b) How might this affect a Muslim's choice of luxury items (e.g. clothes, cosmetics)?
(c) What would be the Muslim attitude towards (i) factory farming? (ii) zoos?

RELIGION FILE

JUDAISM

- Among the biblical references used by Jews to formulate their ideas about the environment are the following:

  God created the universe and declared it to be good [Genesis 1: 1-4]. Jews therefore affirm the goodness of creation [Psalm 24: 1]. Genesis 1 shows that the web of life encompasses all.

  God gave people the responsibility of looking after the world for Him. Adam is placed in the garden of Eden to till it and look after it [Genesis 2: 15], and he names the species [Genesis 2: 19]. The environment should be treated with care and land should not be over-exploited [Exodus 23: 10-11]. Other Bible passages giving guidance on what responsible stewardship means include Deuteronomy 20: 19 and Deuteronomy 22: 6. People should share the land [Numbers 35: 2].

In March 1958, David Ben-Gurion, Prime Minister of Israel, planted the first of a million trees in a plan to create "the Jerusalem Forest". The importance of planting trees goes back to the early days of Judaism. When the Jewish tribes originally approached the land of Israel they were told: "When you shall come to the Land, you shall plant all types of trees." [Leviticus 19: 2-3]. In 1949, as Prime Minister of the new state of Israel, Ben-Gurion said: "I do not know if there is a more fruitful enterprise, whose results are so useful, as the planting of trees, which adds beauty to the scenery of our country, improves its climate and adds health to its inhabitants."

THE ROWING BOAT

A first-century rabbi told the story of two men who went out together in a rowing boat. After a while one of the men suddenly started sawing a hole in the boat underneath his feet. The other man was alarmed and asked him to stop immediately. "Why should I?" was the reply. "I have the right to do whatever I like as this spot belongs to me!" "If you continue to make a hole you will sink both of us because we are in this boat together," answered his companion.

17 "We are in this boat together." What message do you think the rabbi was trying to convey?

- In the creation account, God gives human beings "dominion" over all living creatures [Genesis 1: 26]. Animal life does not have the same value as human life. However, humans have responsibility for the animal kingdom, and should not abuse it. After the flood, God gave Noah seven commandments (the Noahide Code) including "Man must not be cruel to animals."

  Abraham Isaac Kook (1865-1935), the first Ashkenazi Chief Rabbi of Palestine, wrote "The Prophecy of Vegetarianism and Peace", in which he says that dominion over the animals is not "the domination of a tyrant tormenting his people and his slaves only to satisfy his personal needs and desires. God forbid that such an ugly law of slavery should be sealed eternally in the word of God who is good to all, and whose tender mercies are over all his works." [quoted in A. Rose, ed., *Judaism and Ecology*, WWF/Cassell]

  Judaism teaches that animals should be treated with kindness and consideration [Deuteronomy 25: 4; Proverbs 12: 10]. Animals were created to be of use to humankind. This does not justify cruelty, but does make legitimate the use of animals in medical research, and for organ transplants, for example.

18 Judaism says that we have a religious obligation to protect the environment so that all may enjoy it. Which teachings support this idea? What does having a "religious obligation" mean?

19 (a) How does Judaism understand the relationship between humans and animal life?
(b) When were humans given permission to eat meat? What rules apply?

20 What might Jews think about
(a) zoos,
(b) keeping pets,
(c) using animals for cosmetic experiments?

"Teachers must see that children respect the smallest and largest animals, which, like people, have feelings. The child who gets enjoyment from the convulsions of an injured beetle will grow up to be insensitive to human suffering." [Rabbi S. R. Hirsch]

- In Judaism, humans are given permission to eat meat. At first, God provided "all kinds of grain and all kinds of fruit for you [humans] to eat" [Genesis 1: 29]. After the flood, God promises never again to send a flood to destroy all living creatures and Noah is told that animals may also be his food. [Genesis 9: 2-3]

  Laws were given about which animals may be eaten [Leviticus 11]. Animals and birds may only be eaten if they have been killed by shechitah. This involves killing the animal instantaneously by a short, quick slit in the carotid artery.

  Some Jews still choose to be vegetarian, following the example of the prophet Daniel [Daniel 1: 12-16].

"Now, when the whole world is in peril, when the environment is in danger of being poisoned and various species, both plant and animal, are becoming extinct, it is our Jewish responsibility to put the defence of the whole of nature at the very centre of our concern . . . Judaism has maintained . . . that this world is the arena that God created for man, half beast and half angel, to prove that he could behave as a moral being . . .

We have responsibility to life, to defend it everywhere, not only against our own sins but also against those of others." [Jewish Declaration, Assisi, 1986]

RELIGION FILE

SIKHISM 

"You, Lord, are the river wherein all things dwell; apart from you nothing can be. All that has life owes that life to your purpose ... Wondrous Creator, the Maker of all things, apart from you nothing can be." [Evening Prayer]

- Sikhs do not try to explain how the universe came to exist but believe it "comes into being by God's will" [Guru Granth Sahib 1]. They believe that God created everything, and that when everything else disappears, only God will remain. God created many universes and creation evolved slowly [Japji 33, 34]. Evidence of God is seen in the whole of creation. "I see the creator pervading everywhere." [Guru Granth Sahib 21]

  No one can learn the full truth about creation. Guru Nanak answered "Only the Creator knows" to the question of when the universe was created. Human knowledge is limited and cannot be compared to the knowledge of God. Science cannot, therefore, provide all the answers to the origins and development of the world.

Sunflowers grown in the Punjab for the production of sunflower oil.

- The belief that God dwells in all things influences Sikh attitudes to nature and wildlife. Sikhism teaches that humans are custodians of the earth. Human superiority is not an excuse to mistreat animals.

Many Sikhs are vegetarians but diet is a matter for individual choice. "All food is pure, for God has provided it for our sustenance." [Guru Granth Sahib 472]. The Namdhari Sikhs, in east central Punjab, set a particular example: they are strict vegetarians who also wear homespun cloth and emphasise the simple life. The Rahit Maryada forbids the eating of halal meat (animals killed in the Muslim way), and some Sikhs regard this as meaning a total ban on meat; others think that animals killed by other methods may be eaten. The food of the langar is always vegetarian, so that everyone who comes to the gurdwara can join in.

Sikhs oppose cruelty to animals but the decision whether to support or oppose hunting, vegetarianism, or animal experimentation is largely a matter of individual conscience. Some of the Gurus hunted. Guru Har Gobind and Guru Gobind Singh are often pictured carrying a bow and arrow and hunting with falcons.

“I care for the animals I use and have respect for them. I don't eat meat because that is inflicting pointless suffering; experiments are not pointless. What I do benefits mankind; so I do what I do with a heavy heart, but I trust God – he knows that my intentions are pure. My work makes life better for many at the expense of a few. Sikhs believe that suffering for the greater good will be looked upon favourably by God.**”** [Ranjit Singh, research scientist, quoted in Joe Walker, *Their World: Religion and Animal Issues*, Hodder & Stoughton, 1999]

21 What attitude do Sikhs have towards scientific explanations of the origins of the universe?

22 To what extent do you agree that "Only the Creator knows" how and when the universe was created?

23 If God created the world and everything in it, what responsibilities do humans have towards the earth?

24 Explain the different Sikh attitudes towards using animals for food.

25 What is the Sikh attitude towards hunting and animal experimentation?

Sample Examination Questions

(a) Explain the work of ONE religious organisation OR person helping to conserve the planet and its resources. [2 marks]

(b) "Religious people should spend less time praying for the environment and do more to save it." Do you agree? Give reasons for your answer, showing that you have considered another point of view. [8 marks]

[London Examinations GCSE (Short Course) Syllabus A Paper 1, June 1997]

PART C: ACTING

Your perspective on the world affects the way you act within it. In this third part of the book, we will look at how people's actions are influenced and inspired by their religious beliefs and values and by the guidance their religion gives on how to behave.

Louder than words

Many religious believers are passionate about their world view. We say that they are committed to it. Some have even been willing to die for what they believe. A person's actions may teach us more about his or her beliefs than if the person tried to tell us in words about them. Actions speak louder than words.

"You catch religion much as you catch measles, from people – as much from what they are as from what they say."

1 (a) What does it mean to say that religion is "catching"? Do you agree?

2 Is it always possible for religious believers to live up to the teachings of their religion? What happens if they don't?

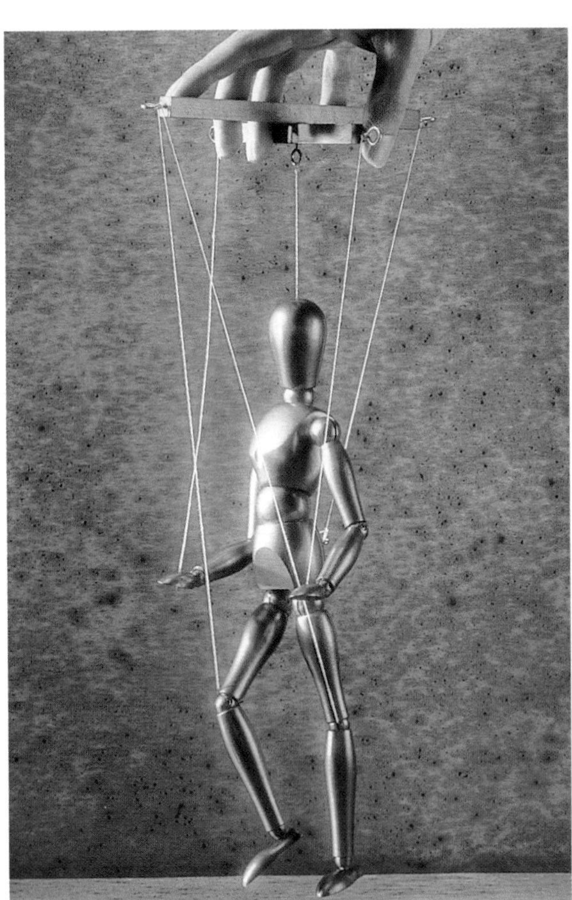

A puppet's actions depend on its strings and who is working them. People are not puppets, but you could perhaps say that their actions depend on the beliefs and motives which support them and pull them in certain directions.

Two perspectives

The religions of the world all stress that people should aim to be morally good. They say that this is more important than striving after power, wealth, beauty, or knowledge. But the religions have different reasons for stressing the importance of goodness.

Followers of Judaism, Christianity, and Islam emphasise that God is a moral God who has revealed how people should behave and has given laws by which they should live. They believe there will be a Judgement Day at the end of time and they see their actions in this world from the perspective of what will happen to them on and beyond that Judgement Day.

On the other hand, followers of Hinduism, Buddhism, and Sikhism employ the concept of the natural law of karma when stressing the importance of being good. Karma literally means "action" but also includes the sense of motives for the action. The law of karma states that each action has a cause and a consequence. People are rewarded and punished as a natural consequence of their actions. The process guarantees morality since, given time, justice will win – people will get what they deserve.

3 (a) What makes an action good or bad?
(b) Is lying always wrong? What makes it right or wrong?
(c) Is stealing always wrong? What makes it right or wrong?
(d) Is it always good to be selfless in one's dealings with others?

Cultivating a good heart

Religions teach that it is not just what you do, but why you do it, that matters. They stress the importance of intention and motive. They speak of the importance of "cultivating a good heart". For example:

"If a man speaks or acts with a pure mind, joy follows him as his own shadow." [Buddhism: Dhammapada 2]

Buddhists say that actions motivated by greed, hatred, and delusion are bad (akusala). Actions motivated by non-attachment, benevolence, and understanding are good (kusala).

In the Sermon on the Mount, Jesus teaches: "You have heard that people were told in the past, Do not commit murder; anyone who does will be brought to trial. But now I tell you: whoever is angry with his brother will be brought to trial." [Christianity: Matthew 5: 21-22]

"Samsara, the transmigration of life, takes place in one's mind. Let one therefore keep the mind pure, for what one thinks, that he becomes: this is the mystery of Eternity." [Hinduism: Maitri Upanishad]

"God does not look at your forms and your possessions, but He looks at your hearts and your deeds." [Islam: Hadith]

"Every human being has been given free-will. If he wishes to incline himself toward the good way and to be righteous, he is free to do so; and if he wishes to incline himself toward the evil way and to be wicked he is free to do that . . . Every individual is capable of being righteous like Moses or wicked like Jeroboam, wise or foolish, merciful or cruel, mean or generous." [Judaism: Mishneh Torah 5: 1-3]

"Truth is higher than everything; but higher still is living the truth." [Sikhism: Guru Granth Sahib 62: 11]

In Christianity, Jesus likened good actions to good fruit on a tree: "There is no such thing as a good tree producing bad fruit," he said, "nor yet a bad tree producing good fruit ... you do not gather figs from brambles or pick grapes from thistles. Good people produce good from the store of good within themselves; and evil people produce evil from the evil within them." [Luke 6: 43-45]

CHAPTER

Relationships

UNIT ONE

In this unit you will learn about the purpose of marriage. You will consider whether the institution of marriage is out of date, and how people choose their life partners.

Marriage

KEY ISSUES IN THIS CHAPTER

- the reasons some people get married
- the differences between getting married and living together
- how people choose a marriage partner
- the reasons why some people get divorced
- whether it matters if a person has sex before or outside marriage
- the debate on homosexuality

1 (a) Can you see yourself getting married?
(b) What do you think is the purpose of marriage? Why do people decide to take marriage vows instead of just living together?

“The concept of marriage is extraordinary: to promise to spend the rest of your life with one person.”

Fifty or so years ago, most people in Britain got married. But today a growing number of people are deciding against marriage. Of the people who do get married, up to a third later get divorced. Are the facts telling us that marriage is becoming out of date, or are there still good reasons for people to get married?

“Married people will soon be outnumbered by those who are unmarried for the first time since central marital records began in 1801. The decrease reflects not so much an increase in the divorce rate, as a sharp rise in the number of people choosing never to marry at all.” [*The Times*, 9 January 1999]

THE PURPOSE OF MARRIAGE

The religions of the world share many ideas about the purpose of marriage.

Procreation. Men and women were created to have children. Marriage establishes a secure setting in which to raise children and bring them up in a religious tradition.

Mutual support. Men and women were created to support each other, to give each other comfort and companionship, and to form a unity.

Sex. Marriage is the correct context in which to enjoy sexual intimacy, as an expression of love.

The religions also stress that marriage is a **committed** relationship. It is life-long.

Total number of marriages in England and Wales

1985
1995

Total number of births in England and Wales

1997

Total number of births outside marriage in England and Wales

1985
1996

In August 1996, Dave Lawrence and his bride, Jane Harland, had their marriage blessed on the wings of two 50-year-old biplanes, in a ceremony 1,500 feet above ground level. The Rev. Anthony Kelton, who performed the ceremony, was strapped to the wings of a third plane.

“I want to get married in my early twenties and have three children. I come from a large family. For me, families are very important. Getting married is a commitment for life. This provides the best environment for raising a family.” [Rebecca, 17]

“I don’t see the point of getting married. These days it’s acceptable to live together. My parents lived together for years. They married when I was born.” [Jeremy, 16]

“If you live together and it doesn’t work out, then you are free to split up and start again. Marriage ties you down too much.” [Mike, 18]

“These days, people live much longer. It’s becoming more unrealistic to think that you will marry someone for the rest of your life.” [Sue, 17]

Living together

In very recent times, living together (“cohabitation”) has become an alternative to getting married, especially in the West. There are several reasons for this trend. Although many people practise religion, society in the West is less religious than in the past. Since the 1960s, society has become morally more liberal. It has become more accepted to have a sexual relationship outside marriage. In the past, sexual activity was closely tied to having children. Today, because of the availability of contraception, having sex does not have this tie. Couples may feel that, if they are not going to have children, they do not need the security of the marriage bond.

Often couples decide to live together before they marry. It is like a trial period to see whether their relationship is going to work. In England and Wales, people who cohabit have fewer legal ties to each other than a married couple do. For example, if one person dies and there is no will, the partner does not have automatic inheritance rights. Governments set tax laws which give advantages to married couples, because they want to encourage the family as the basic social unit.

Most cultures recognise that children born within marriage are “legitimate”, whilst those born outside marriage are “illegitimate” (bastards). This is an important point when property is passed on from parents to children.

2 (a) What do the figures (left) tell you about (i) the trend in people getting married; (ii) the trend in people having children outside marriage?
(b) What reasons can you suggest for the increase in people who never marry?

3 Write a newspaper headline and the first paragraph of a journalistic article based on the figures in the table. The theme should be “The State of Marriage in the Nation”.

Information File: Partners and Families

Marriage: the relationship between husband and wife.
Monogamy: the state or custom of having a sexual relationship with only one partner. The word is also used for the state of marriage to one partner.
Serial monogamy: the state or custom of having a series of long-term sexual partners, one at a time, or of being married several times in your life – usually as a result of divorce.
Polygamy: the custom in some societies of being legally married to more than one person at the same time. Polygyny is where a man has more than one wife.
Adultery: having sexual intercourse with someone other than your marriage partner.
Nuclear family: father, mother, and children.
Extended family: parents, children, and the wider family – grandparents, nephews, etc.

4 *Options* magazine asked seven leading advertising agencies in London to design a poster which would persuade people to get married. We have published two of the results. What reasons for getting married is each poster presenting? Do you think they are good reasons?

"Marriage is the ultimate proof of commitment" was the message this advert was designed to convey.

JUST COHABITING

E298 KYM

NOT QUITE THE SAME IS IT?

NOBODY HAS TO GET MARRIED. THAT'S WHAT MAKES IT SO MEANINGFUL.

MARRIAGE.

KIDS can be BASTARDS

EVEN IN THESE enlightened days, prejudice survives. In school playgrounds everywhere. Get married for your child's sake. Because kids can be bastards. Especially when they find a real one.

MARRIAGE

A BETTER START FOR THE FAMILY

The creators of this advert thought that the most persuasive argument for marriage was "very old fashioned – that marriage is the basis for a family". In Britain today, 40 per cent of children are born out of wedlock.

What does getting married mean?

Although marriage ceremonies differ across continents and religions, many include a number of the same ingredients. In Christianity, Hinduism, and Sikhism, marriage is considered a sacrament, a divinely blessed union which people should not break. It is a lifelong union given by God. The marriage rituals create a bond between the man and woman. Sikhs talk about the fusing of two souls in marriage, so that they become spiritually inseparable. Christians speak of the couple becoming "one flesh".

A religious marriage carries with it some important expectations. In Christianity and Hinduism, these are made explicit in religious vows (promises) which the couple make publicly to each other. The different religious ceremonies contain a variety of vows; commonly found are vows of faithfulness and mutual support, that the marriage will last until death, and that children will be born.

Christianity requires that there should be a formal legal registration of the marriage, whilst Islam regards its marriage ceremony as a legal, binding contract between the man and woman. In contrast, Hinduism insists that a marriage is brought about only by the religious ritual. However, people may be living in a country where it is desirable for all marriages to be recognised legally. For example, Sikhs living in the West mostly have a civil marriage in the Registry Office near the time of their engagement, but do not live together until after their religious marriage ceremony. The legal registering of a marriage gives the couple legal rights, according to the laws of the country in which they live.

Today, many marriages in the West take place in a registry office. These are called civil ceremonies. In the UK, whether the marriage takes place in a place of worship or in a registry office, the law requires that two statements be repeated by both the bride and groom, in the presence of witnesses:

"I do solemnly declare that I know not of any lawful impediment why I [full names must be said] may not be joined in matrimony to [full names]."

"I call upon these persons here present to witness that I [full names] do take thee [full names] to be my lawful wedded wife/husband."

The marriage ceremony is a public affair, which draws attention to the belief that marriage brings together not just two individuals but two families. Marriage ceremonies therefore can include hundreds of people, sometimes the whole community (in Judaism, Hinduism, and Sikhism). Hindus, Muslims, and Sikhs stress the concept of marriage as a social contract. In Islam the public declaration of a marriage is essential; secret marriages are not allowed. Furthermore, to avoid friction in the future, these religions often emphasise the need for people to marry people of the same religion and to have similar backgrounds, for example in levels of education and income. However, these are not religious requirements. Judaism lays importance on marrying within the faith not only because the religion is centred on the home but also because no non-Jewish partner can help a Jewish child fulfil the essential role of keeping alive the Jewish heritage.

Who chooses? How do you decide whom to marry?

In some parts of the world people choose their own marriage partner. The romantic picture is of searching for the one person who can make you happy, falling in love, and getting hitched for life. However, the divorce statistics tell us that this might be an unreliable way of choosing a partner. Are young people prepared enough to make such a big choice?

In Hinduism, Islam, and Sikhism the emphasis is less on love than on a shared set of values. This does not mean that love is not considered important, but it is something that can develop after marriage, not necessarily before. Each of these religions has marriages which are arranged by the parents.

5 (a) If you had the freedom to choose your own marriage partner, which qualities would you look for in him or her? Look through the list of qualities you make: are they the kind that would secure a life-long relationship?
(b) How might the qualities you list differ from your parents' view?

6 How important is it to marry someone with a similar background and similar interests to you? Does it matter if they are, for example, a different colour, a different race, and a different religion?

7 Dating agencies are very popular these days. How do you explain their popularity? In what sense are they providing arranged marriages?

“Marriage is pot luck. Until you're actually married to somebody you don't know exactly what they're like. I think there's a lot to be said for arranged marriages. It's far harder for girls now. Men get everything they want from girls before they marry them and perhaps women want husbands more than men want wives.”

“Fairy tales end with the first kiss. In real life, that's when the relationship, and the work of love, begins.”

8 In the extract from the poem, what advice "On Marriage" is given in each of the lines in italics? Do you think this is good advice for a marriage?

9 "The most important thing in marriage is friendship." Discuss.

10 Design your own poster advertising marriage. What message are you trying to get across?

ON MARRIAGE

The following is an extract from a poem by Khalil Gibran (1883-1931), in which a Prophet of God gives advice on marriage.

Love one another, but make not a bond of love:
Let it rather be a moving sea between the shores of your souls.
Fill each other's cup but drink not from one cup.
Give one another of your bread but eat not from the same loaf.
Sing and dance together and be joyous, but let each one of you be alone
Even as the strings of a lute are alone though they quiver with the same music.

Give your hearts, but not into each other's keeping.
For only the hand of life can contain your hearts.
And stand together yet not too near together:
For the pillars of the temple stand apart, and the oak trees and the cypress
Grow not in each other's shadow.
[Khahil Gibran, *The Prophet*, Heinemann]

UNIT TWO

Divorce

When a couple get divorced, this means that their marriage is officially declared by the courts to be at an end. Sometimes a couple undergo a period of separation before they get divorced. In this unit you will consider and evaluate the reasons why people get divorced.

Changing attitudes and the law

The rise in divorce during the last twenty years – about a third of marriages end in divorce – is a sad fact, and a personal tragedy for the people concerned. One factor explaining the rise is that divorce, which used to be seen as a matter of shame, has become accepted in society. This change in attitudes is reflected in the law. Between 1857 and 1936, in the UK, the only ground for divorce was adultery (known then as "marital crime"). In 1937, desertion and insanity became grounds for divorce. With the start of the women's liberation movement in the 1970s, a divorce reform movement began. The 1971 Divorce Reform Act granted divorce on grounds of agreement by both partners, after a separation of two years. If only one partner wanted a divorce, the separation had to be five years.

The 1984 Matrimonial and Family Proceedings Act allowed divorce after one year of marriage. In 1995, a White Paper set out the government's proposal that divorce should be allowed without the need to prove "fault" in the marriage; the couple must, however, spend a year working in mediation. The Family Law Act 1996 allows divorce on the basis of failure of marriage alone, after a period of "reflection and consideration".

In the UK, when a couple divorce, the custody of any children from the marriage may be awarded to either partner, with fair regulations being made about visiting rights and support of the children. Today more divorcing couples are working out joint-custody arrangements rather than taking this matter to court.

1 (a) It is no longer necessary to show that one partner is at fault, in order to get a legal divorce in England. Do you think that "fault" is a useful term when talking about divorce? Why do you think the law was changed?
(b) Why do you think the law now requires a couple who want a divorce to undergo a period of reflection and consideration?

The main reasons for divorces and the rise in divorce

Too high expectations.
Romantic ideals.
"Young people get married with more hope than planning."

Children (or lack of them).
Children cause tension in marriage.
NB This is not saying that children cause divorces.

Lack of commitment.
People unwilling to work through difficulties.
Too willing to jump boat at the first signs of trouble.

Money problems – expense of running a home, in materialistic society. Concerns about money lead to tensions and fights – a reason for divorce.

Divorce is easier to obtain.
No social stigma.

Societal pressures.
TV shows extra-marital sex as acceptable.
More wives go out to work – more opportunity for men and women to have extra-marital relationships.

2 When people seek a divorce they give many reasons. Some of them are:
"We aren't really suited to each other."
"There's no spark left, we don't get excited by being together."
"She's had an affair with her boss."
"We've fallen out of love."
"We're unable to have children together."
"He hits me."
"She's unreasonable."
(a) Do you think all these reasons are valid?
(b) What do you think "unreasonable behaviour" is?
(c) What do you think the law would count as unreasonable behaviour?

QUICKCOURT: ELECTRONIC DIVORCE

In the state of Arizona in the USA, husbands and wives can now divorce each other without telling their partner, courtesy of the QuickCourt. A person walks up to one of the computer terminals – they look like cash-dispensing machines – where an on-screen counsellor asks, "Are you sure you want to get divorced?" The machine takes names and addresses and details about property and any children the married couple have. After digesting the information, QuickCourt prints out a form which the person takes to a clerk in the court building. When the person leaves, his or her marriage is no more. The whole process takes only 20 minutes! QuickCourt makes divorcing easier than getting a driving licence.

One abused wife explained how QuickCourt helped her: "I don't know that I would have had the courage to divorce him if I'd had to use a lawyer." Another said: "When I pressed the yes button, I felt so good. It was like I was erasing all the pain, like one of those video games when you blast aliens off the screen."

QuickCourt machines have processed more than 10,000 divorces since they were introduced in 1994. The average age of partners was 28.

The religions' response

In the context of the changing attitudes, religions have had to do a lot of thinking. They place high value on the marriage vows. So what should their attitude be to divorce? Should they allow people who have been divorced to remarry, making the vows again? Some religions have accepted some compromise. They recognise that, sadly, marriages do break down and divorces happen. Some religions (e.g. Judaism, Islam, Buddhism, Sikhism) allow people to remarry. Other religions affirm the life-long nature of marriage and will not allow the marriage ritual to be performed for people who have been divorced.

3 (a) What do you think of the QuickCourt? Is it something you would like to see in Britain? What are the disadvantages and advantages?
(b) Do you think it makes divorce too easy?

4 Which members of a family – husband, wife, or children – suffer most in the case of divorce? Give reasons for your answer.

“Marriage, like any relationship, will break down when people stop listening to each other. All relationships need working at, with each person taking responsibility for his or her own actions. However, we live in a 'blame culture', where people are all too willing to blame others when things go wrong.” [Don]

Affairs

One of the big news stories of 1998 was the revelation that the US President, Bill Clinton, an apparently happily married family man, had had a sexual affair with 25-year-old White House employee, Monica Lewinsky. Why do people have affairs? Dr Shirley Glass, who carried out research on affairs, points out that an affair is not just about sex:

“There can be an affair without any kind of touching at all ... Three elements determine whether a relationship is an affair: (1) secrecy; (2) emotional intimacy; (3) sexual chemistry.” [*Psychology Today*, July/August 1998]

A common myth is that people have affairs because they are unhappy in their marriages. Dr Glass found that 56% of men interviewed who had affairs said their marriages were happy. The figure for women was 34%.

“My research shows that there are many men who do love their partners, who enjoy good sex at home, who nevertheless never turn down an opportunity for extramarital sex.” [*Psychology Today*, July/August 1998]

The Clinton family was “on show” in the summer of 1998, as people imagined how the president's wife Hillary and daughter Chelsea were reacting to the news of his affair.

Sometimes affairs are less a reflection on the marriage than a result of pressure from a society that accepts affairs as normal. Surveys show that women often enter affairs in search of love and emotional intimacy, and that men enter them often for sex. Statistics tell us that only 10% of people who leave their permanent relationship for an affair end up living permanently with the affair partner.

When a person discovers that a marriage partner has been unfaithful, his or her world falls apart:

“Affairs aren't really about sex; they're about betrayal. The infidelity is that you took something that was supposed to be mine, which is sexual or emotional intimacy, and you gave it to somebody else. I thought we had a special relationship, and now you have contaminated it; it doesn't feel special any more, because you shared something very precious to us with someone else.” [Dr Shirley Glass, *Psychology Today*, July/August 1998]

Marriages can survive affairs if the couple are willing to build up their trust in each other again. Despite the hurt and anger, love can still survive.

5 What is an affair? Why do people have affairs? Is one partner's having an affair a strong enough reason for a married couple to get divorced? Can marriages survive an affair?

Sexuality

We are all sexual beings, but what difference does that make? Is it important how we express our sexuality? In this unit you will be considering different expressions of human sexuality.

The change in attitudes

In the past, in the West, it was less accepted than it is today for people to have sexual intercourse outside marriage. In certain Middle Eastern and Asian cultures today, a young woman may be cast out of her family home for disgracing her family in this way. Reasons for the change in attitude in the West include:

- Religious moral codes play less of a role than before in modern society.
- Secular culture, as portrayed in the media, encourages permissiveness.
- Widely available contraception reduces the risk of pregnancy.
- Modern society has a greater number of single parents, and so less stigma is attached to unmarried mothers than used to be the case.

What do you think should be the content of sex education classes at school?

A dark side to the increased tolerance of sex before marriage has been an increase in the incidence of sexually transmitted diseases. In 1983 the virus HIV was identified. It has been estimated that by the year 2000 between 30 and 40 million people will have been infected with HIV.

1 Choose a magazine aimed at teenagers. How much of it is concerned with boy/girl relationships? What kind of issues are dealt with? Do you think the magazine encourages these relationships? Does the magazine give a balanced message on the subject?

2 Many television programmes today show people entering into sexual relationships before marriage. What moral message do you think such programmes are presenting?

Information File: Sexual experience

Celibacy: the state of not having sexual intercourse with anyone for some time or for a particular period of life. It also refers to the state of being unmarried.

Chastity: the state of being sexually pure. This can apply to (a) a person who does not have sex with anyone or (b) a person who has sex only with his or her marriage partner. It can also refer to not having forms of sex condemned by moral guidelines or religion.

Virginity: the state of never having had sexual intercourse.

Promiscuous: having sex with many different people.

Heterosexual: sexually attracted to people of the opposite sex.

Homosexual: sexually attracted to people of the same sex.

Rape: the crime of forcing someone to have sexual intercourse, usually by violence or threats of violence.

Recreational sex: sex treated as a leisure-time activity, not necessarily involving commitment or relationship.

Age of consent: the age at which a person can legally agree to having a sexual relationship.

Why have sex?

"Prove you're a man – do IT!"

"Everybody's doing it."

"So what's wrong with me? Don't you find me attractive?"

Have you ever heard any of these reasons? Have you used them yourself? Sometimes it seem that every time you turn on the TV someone is having sex – at least, after nine o'clock at night! But why do people have sex? What are the good reasons for having sex?

Sex before marriage

The main world religions teach the importance of saving sex until you are in a permanent married relationship. Some religions say that sex is a gift from God, a way of expressing love, and not to be abused.

How far do you think the couple in the photograph should go in physically expressing their love? What would you want to know about these people, in order to give your opinion? What factors might affect the advice you would give?

"Losing your virginity is a very big thing in a teenager's life. If you are not committed to a person you can get very seriously hurt." [Van Vyke, 17]

"Recreational sex leads nowhere. It is very rare for both partners to be able to treat it equally casually." [Libby Purves, in *The Times*, 26 September 1998]

One response to modern sexual attitudes has been the "True Love Waits" campaign. It started in Baptist churches in the USA but has spread to England and Europe. The campaign teaches the importance of chastity (abstaining from sexual intercourse) before marriage. People who join the campaign make this pledge:

> *"Believing that true love waits, I make a commitment to God, myself, and my family, those I date, my future mate, and my future children, to be sexually pure until the day I enter a covenant marriage relationship."*

Not all people who make the pledge are virgins:

"I wanted to start again. I was 20 years old and had slept with people I didn't even know the names of – one-night stands at parties, that sort of thing. I didn't feel good about myself. At times I felt used by men. Inside I was losing my own self-respect, whilst at the same time not getting the love I really craved. By making this promise I was pledging myself not to have sex until I married a person whom I really loved. True love waits." [Sue, 21]

3 Why did Sue take the "True Love Waits" pledge? Why do you think people feel it is important to make this promise in public? How do you think they would feel if they broke the promise?

4 What attitudes do the media show towards homosexuality? Which television programmes show homosexual relationships? How are they presented?

Homosexuality: the "love that dares not speak its name"

A shift of attitudes towards homosexuality took place from the mid-1990s. Television soaps started to include people in homosexual relationships. Members of Parliament "came out", declaring their homosexual orientation. However, not all reporting was positive. For example, *The Sun* newspaper in November 1998 demanded of the Prime Minister: "Tell us the truth Tony. Are we being run by a gay mafia? . . . The public has the right to know how many homosexuals occupy positions of high power."

A question of equality

The law in Britain treats heterosexuals and homosexuals (gays) differently. Gay men and women are not allowed to be married (or enter into "domestic partnerships"). Section 28 of the 1988 Local Government Act banned councils from intentionally promoting a positive view of homosexuality, for example, in schools. The homosexual community has been campaigning for equal rights.

"We have had a Race Relations Act since 1965, a Sex Discrimination Act since 1975, and a Disabilities Act since 1995, but discrimination on the grounds of sexuality is still not barred by statute." [Martin Bowley, *The Guardian*, 15 April 1997]

5 The gay community has campaigned for the legal age of consent to be made the same (16) for homosexuals as it is for heterosexuals. In groups, consider the arguments that can be raised on both sides of the debate.

6 Should gay couples be allowed to get married? If the law prevents gay marriages, is it practising a form of discrimination?

"The outing campaign is cruel, wicked, and evil." [Edwina Currie]

Outing

"Outing" is a term used for forcing someone to "come out" and declare their homosexual orientation. Peter Tatchell, a member of the gay direct-action group Outrage, campaigns for people in prominent positions in society, such as MPs and priests, to "be honest about their homosexuality".

Tatchell believes his campaign is a moral duty. However, not all of the gay community agree with his outing tactics. In a poll conducted in *Capital Gay*, a London gay newspaper, 46% of respondents said they believe outing does more harm than good.

7 (a) Should all people have the right to keep their sexual orientation private?
(b) Why do you think Peter Tatchell wants people to be honest about their homosexuality?
(c) Why do you think some homosexuals keep their sexual orientation private?
(d) Do you think the outing campaign has a moral purpose or is it "cruel, wicked, and evil"? Give reasons to support your opinion.

Gay pair insist on right to "family child"

Two gay men are seeking a surrogate mother for a "family child". The couple who say they have "a God-given right to be parents", are looking for a mother or a lesbian couple who would have a child by artificial insemination. "We are deeply committed to one another. We love each other very much. We feel that the love and respect that a child brings would complete our lives. We all have a right to have children. It doesn't matter who or what we are. I just want to be able to hear someone call me 'Dad'." The proposal was strongly criticised by Nicholas Winterton MP, who said the needs of the child were being overlooked: "it wouldn't be beneficial for the child to be brought up in such a strange situation".

[*The Guardian*, 28 May 1997]

8 (a) What issues are involved in the news story about the "family child"?
(b) Should gay people be parents? Do you agree that all people have a right to have children? Give reasons for your answer.
(c) What reasons does the man in the news report give for wanting a child? Do you think these are good reasons?
(d) Do you think that a gay couple is able to meet the needs of a child? Explain your answer.

The press took a great deal of interest in some discussions at the Lambeth Conference of Anglican bishops in 1998. Nigerian bishop Emmanuel Chukwuma tried to cast out what he called "the demon of homosexuality" from a gay priest. Here he is in an argument with Richard Kirker, the general secretary of the Lesbian and Gay Christian Movement. Why do you think lesbian and gay people have formed this movement?

Celibacy

Some people choose to remain unmarried and not to have sexual relationships. This is called celibacy. In some religions, some people are required to be celibate – for example, Roman Catholic priests and Buddhist monks and nuns. Their commitment to celibacy is a commitment to remain sexually pure, and to channel all of their energies into religious work; it is a commitment to their religion:

“As long as I remain a monk in the Theravadan tradition I have vowed to be celibate, to concentrate on my own enlightenment and to be of help to other people seeking the dharma.”

“There's a lovely phrase that I picked up from a man in South America, a Brazilian. He said to me, 'Are you a priest?' I said, 'Yes'. 'No, you're not; you're a man becoming a priest.' And that really struck hard. It's a very simple statement, and I think it's true to say that people are not married, they are becoming married; I am not celibate, I am becoming celibate. I'm talking about celibacy as a way of life ... it's about making an act of love which says I am prepared to explore the value and meaning and worth of this person and that person.” [A Roman Catholic priest]

In Susan Howatch's novel *A Question of Integrity*, one of the characters, a priest called Father Lewis, describes celibacy: “The successful celibate life isn't about repression but about sublimation, which is a different kettle of fish altogether. Repression means refusing to think of sex, locking up one's sex-drive and always feeling exhausted – not to mention neurotic – because it takes an enormous amount of mental energy to convince yourself nobody has any genitals. Sublimation means facing up to sex, standing eyeball to eyeball with one's sex-drive and, by the grace of God, figuring out how to expend all that energy creatively and productively in some way outside the bedroom.” [Warner Books, 1998]

11 What is celibacy? For what reasons (religious and non-religious) might people choose celibacy? Do you think it is a positive or negative choice?

Most Buddhist monks and nuns shave their heads, to renounce vanity, wear simple robes, and keep only the possessions that are really necessary.

Religious teachings on marriage, divorce, and sexuality

RELIGION FILE

BUDDHISM 

Marriage

- At the heart of Buddhism is the quest for enlightenment. In Theravada Buddhism the celibate life of the monk or nun is seen as the best suited for this quest. Mahayana Buddhism is more optimistic about the possibility of married people – householders – reaching Nirvana.

  There is no specific religious ceremony for marriage in Buddhism. It is thought of as a family ritual at which members of the sangha are asked to chant special texts of blessing. Buddhists live according to the marriage laws in the country in which they live. Therefore, polygamy has sometimes been practised by Buddhists.

  Vows made by the bride and bridegroom show the importance of marriage. One set of vows that is used comes from the Sigalovada Sutta, the Buddha's teaching about the responsibilities of family members. The bridegroom says: "I undertake to love and respect her, be kind and considerate, be faithful, delegate domestic management, provide gifts to please her." The bride says: "I undertake to perform household duties efficiently, be hospitable to my in-laws and friends of my husband, be faithful, protect and invest our earnings, discharge my responsibilities lovingly and conscientiously."

  Marriage, like all aspects of life, must be lived according to the five precepts (page 37). For example, looking at the first precept: are the partners draining each other of life or helping one another fully? The third precept: is the relationship based on sexual exploitation? The third precept rules out adultery. The fourth precept: are the couple honest and open with each other? Buddhists practise loyalty, honesty, and faithfulness, which help to destroy selfishness.

1 (a) What can you tell about roles within marriage from the vows quoted from the Sigalovada Sutta?
(b) Do you think husbands and wives have different roles within marriage?
(c) The Sigalovada Sutta contains the Buddha's advice to his lay followers 2,500 years ago. Do you think the vows are applicable today? How would you rewrite them?

2 In what ways is marriage based upon the five moral precepts?

3 Why does Buddhism allow divorce?

Divorce

- Because making vows is very important, marriage is for life and Buddhists are encouraged to be faithful. However, Buddhists are realistic and recognise that people and circumstances are constantly changing. Relationships can change, so divorce is allowed when it is seen to be the best course of action. What is important is the intention or motive for such a request. Selfishness is always discouraged, and loving-kindness always encouraged.

Sexuality

- The Buddhist spiritual path is a Middle Way between indulgence and deprivation. Sexual drive needs to be controlled in order to avoid causing suffering for others. Buddhists believe that sexual permissiveness usually brings suffering (dukkha). "There is a Middle Way wherein sexuality is fully acknowledged and regarded compassionately without the need to indulge in actions which lead to suffering." [Daishin Morgan, Zen monk quoted in O. Cole, ed., *Moral Issues in Six Religions*, Heinemann, 1991]

Buddhist attitudes towards sexuality are shaped by the five precepts and by the concept of right intention with regard to other people. For example, in sexual relations, we should not cause harm towards other people (first and third precepts) – this rules out rape and abuse and also less obvious things, like faithlessness and persuasion. The second precept is "I will not take what is not given", so a Buddhist should not press a person for a sexual relationship against his or her will. This would also rule out rape. Right intention would rule out lying to get your own way, or telling someone you love them when it isn't true.

Traditionally, Buddhism identified two types of sexuality: that of celibate monks and nuns, and that of married householders engaged in heterosexual family life. However, Buddhism recognises that, on the issue of homosexuality, opinions might change. Buddhists stress that people should live according to "right action". There are no absolutes with regard to heterosexuality or homosexuality. What matters is the intention of those involved.

4 (a) What do you think about the Buddhist teaching on sexuality?
(b) Do you agree that sexual permissiveness usually results in suffering?

RELIGION FILE

CHRISTIANITY

Marriage

- Christians believe that marriage is part of God's plan for humanity. God created woman from one of the man's ribs and the man said: "'At last, here is one of my kind – bone taken from my bone, and flesh from my flesh' . . . This is why a man leaves his father and mother and is united with his wife, and they become one." [Genesis 2: 23, 24]

Because marriage is created by God and is part of God's plan it is protected: "You shall not commit adultery." [Exodus 20: 14]

Some Christians say that God is the third partner in a Christian marriage. The unconditional love the two people promise, their openness and vulnerability to each other, and their willingness to show each other mercy, show what Christ's sacrificial love is like.

The Christian New Testament teaches that Christians should marry other Christians [2 Corinthians 6: 14].

Because marriage is for life, some churches prepare a couple carefully before they enter into it. The purpose of the preparation is to enable people to feel secure in their love.

The marriage ritual is a sacrament. (A sacrament is a symbol that conveys real value and meaning. Christians believe that, through the sacraments, God gives people the power of his Holy Spirit to guide, comfort, and strengthen them.) It is also a public announcement of the vows that the couple make to each other. The vows bind them in front of witnesses and in front of God. The vows made by people marrying in the Anglican Church are: "I, [full name], take you, [full name], to be my [husband/wife], to have and to hold from this day forward; for better, for worse, for richer, for poorer, in sickness and in health, to love and to cherish, till death us do part, according to God's holy law; and this is my solemn vow."

Wedding rings are a symbol of the vows a couple make to each other. They are also a symbol of the marriage, like a ring, having no end.

5 (a) What is the purpose of Christian marriage?
(b) How does Christian marriage reflect the nature of God?
(c) What do Christians mean when they speak of marriage as a sacrament?

6 (a) What are the vows which the bride and bridegroom make to each other in a Christian marriage? Give an example of what these might mean in their life together.
(b) What do you think about these vows? Would you add any others?
(c) What is the meaning of the giving of rings?

7 In some marriage services the bride promises to "obey" her husband. What do you think this means? Read Ephesians 5: 21-33: how is the relationship between husband and wife described? How do you understand the term "submit" in verse 33? Do you think the concept of obedience is relevant in today's society? Is it against the spirit of equal opportunities?

8 (a) Why do you think Christianity is generally opposed to divorce?
(b) Should divorced people be allowed to marry in church? Which part of Christian teaching would support this?

Divorce

- Christianity teaches that "Man must not separate what God has joined together." [Matthew 19: 6; see also Mark 10: 2-12]. However, many Christians recognise that sometimes a marriage breaks down past repair. Support is given to people who are going through separation and divorce. In some Christian traditions, clergy have not usually been prepared to allow divorced people to marry in church. People have a civil ceremony instead. However, Jesus also taught people not to judge others who fail to live up to the ideal – people should be forgiven if they are truly sorry for what they have done.

  The Roman Catholic Church does not accept divorce; however, if there is a just reason (e.g. impotence), a marriage can be dissolved – it is recognised as having ended. In certain situations (for example, if someone was forced into marriage; or if there is an inability to carry out marriage duties, due to mental illness), the Roman Catholic Church allows annulment – the new marriage is considered never to have existed.

Sexuality

- Christians believe that God created people as sexual beings, and that our bodies must be used responsibly in accordance with God's wishes. The Song of Solomon, in the Old Testament, celebrates God's gift of love and sexuality within the framework of marriage. However, Jesus spoke out against lust [Matthew 5: 27-30].

  Marriage is the correct context for sex. Sexual love between husband and wife is important [1 Corinthians 7: 3-4]. In sex two people become one in a very real way – yes, physically, but also emotionally and spiritually; they become completely open with each other and share their greatest intimacy. They become "one flesh" [Mark 10: 6-8].

  Some Christians point to biblical passages which say that people should not practise homosexual acts [Leviticus 18: 22, Romans 1: 26-27, Corinthians 6: 9-10; and the story of Sodom in Genesis 18-19]. In 1991, the Bishops of the Church of England declared that gay men could be priests only if they abstained from sex. Other Christians point out how society has changed since biblical times. For example, in his letters to the Romans and Corinthians, Paul accepted slavery without question. In the same way as the Christian churches have altered their thinking about slavery and the position of women, so they need to update their stance towards homosexuality. The Lesbian and Gay Christian Movement states its conviction that it is "entirely compatible with the Christian faith not only to love another person of the same sex but also to express that love fully in a personal sexual relationship".

RELIGION FILE

HINDUISM 

Marriage

- Traditionally, a Hindu's life is divided into four stages (student, householder, retirement, renunciation). Marriage, which marks a person's

At this Hindu wedding, the symbols are clearly of "tying" the two people to each other.

entrance into the householder stage, is regarded as a religious duty. A marriage is blessed by God and should be permanent. Manusmriti 3: 78 says that the householder stage is the most excellent one, because it supports people in the other stages of life.

Marriage is regarded as important for the good of society. It marks the coming together of two families. For this reason, many Hindu marriages are arranged. Great effort is put into finding suitable partners. Caste, social background, and interests are taken into account. Often horoscopes are consulted, to check that the two people are compatible and the time for the ceremony is auspicious.

Hindu marriage rituals establish an unbreakable bond between the man and woman. The bride stands on a stone, a symbol of the stability of marriage. The end of her sari is tied to the bridegroom's shawl, symbolising the gentle tying together of the couple. They then take seven steps around the sacred fire. In this ritual of saptapadi, the couple pledge total support for each other. The seven steps are (1) for the sake of food; (2) for strength; (3) for wealth; (4) for happiness; (5) for children; (6) for sustenance; and (7) for unity.

Divorce

- Divorce and remarriage are allowed but are rare in Hinduism. The evidence is that arranged marriages are less likely to break down than "love marriages". Today the main reasons for divorce for Hindus are cruelty or not having children after fifteen years. At present there is much discussion in India about whether the irretrievable breakdown of a marriage should be allowed as a reason for divorce, as it is in Britain. Many Hindus feel that allowing this reason for divorce would have bad consequences for Hindu society. However, divorce is occurring more – especially among Hindus in Britain, as women have become more aware of their rights and are less willing to live with the adultery or cruelty of their husbands.

On World AIDS Day in November 1998, Hindus in New Delhi joined in a candelight vigil to spread awareness of HIV and AIDS.

Sexuality

- Hindus should maintain a balance between the four aims in life [Manusmriti 2: 224], one of which is kama (see pages 48-49). Kama means sensual pleasure, including sexual pleasure within marriage. There are many religious stories about sexual activity. For example, the god Shiva is often represented by the lingam (an erect penis). The Kama Sutra is a religious book encouraging the enjoyment of sexual pleasure in a way which can make sex a religious experience.

  Sex outside marriage is wrong. The major concern is to protect female chastity. However, among many young Hindus today there is a growing feeling that pre-marital sex is acceptable for a couple who are to marry.

Hindu religious texts say little about homosexuality. However, unless a Hindu becomes a celibate monk or nun, it is his or her duty to marry and have children. In reaction to the growing threat of AIDS, more and more people in India are saying that the only way to avoid disease is to prohibit any form of sex outside marriage.

The first, third, and fourth stages (student, retirement, and renunciation) of a Hindu's life are celibate.

9 Hindus believe that marriage is important for society and is not just the concern of the two individuals involved. (a) Why do you think this is so? (b) What do you think?

10 Do you think that Hindus have a positive attitude towards sex? Explain your answer.

RELIGION FILE

ISLAM 

Marriage

- For Muslims marriage is a legally binding social contract. There must be two witnesses and the groom gives a gift (dowry) of money to his wife. The two families could simply meet together to sign the agreement. However, the imam (leader of the mosque) is often present and will recite relevant verses from the Qur'an. The marriage contract mentions mutual respect. The couple make vows of mercy, love, peace, faithfulness, and co-operation. Rings are exchanged.

Because of the importance of modesty and chastity before marriage, traditionally marriages have been arranged by the parents. However, it is important that the partners consent to being married to each other.

Marriage is such an important relationship that it cannot be based only on personal attraction. Most Muslims marry other Muslims (Muslim women must only marry Muslim men). "You shall not wed pagan women . . . nor shall you wed idolators." [Qur'an, 2: 220].

Monogamy is the norm, but polygyny (having more than one wife) is allowed [Qur'an, 4: 3]. Because marriage is a social contract, people retain their personal rights: the wife does not become merely an addition to her husband. Husband and wife should understand each other, and show each other kindness, love, and companionship. "They [wives] are your garments and you [husbands] are their garments." [Qur'an, 2: 187]. Each has the responsibility of fulfilling the other's sexual needs. Marriage is a partnership of two equal people. Allah is the only master.

Divorce

- Marital breakdown is recognised as a sad fact. "Divorce is the most detestable in the sight of God of all permitted things." [Hadith]. Divorce should be the very last resort. A process of "waiting periods" (iddah) is followed: in the periods between three announcements of intended divorce, efforts are made to reconcile the couple.

11 (a) In what sense is marriage in Islam a social contract?
(b) Why is the wife given a dowry?

12 (a) Discuss what equality in marriage means.
(b) Do you think it is possible for a husband who has more than one wife to treat each equally?

13 (a) What rules govern divorce in Islam? Do you think these are helpful? Write your own rules to govern divorce.
(b) Discuss reasons why Muslims might be against lifelong settlements for divorced wives.

Settlement must be fair and equal rights are stressed. The husband cannot take back from the wife anything he has given her [Qur'an, 2: 230; 4: 19-20], nor should he fight with the wife – he should let her go with kindness [Qur'an, 2: 232]. Both parties must act towards the other with kindness and charity, as if the marriage bond were still intact. It is interesting to note that there are more grounds on which a wife can seek divorce than a husband [Qur'an, 4: 128]: for example, long absence without knowing where her husband is. Both parties are allowed to remarry.

It is not usual for Muslim men to pay maintenance for long periods after divorce. The divorced woman is supported by her family or by Islamic government.

Sexuality

- Sexual intercourse is considered a gift from Allah, through which people's emotional needs are met. Through sex Muslims contribute to God's act of creation. It is therefore a noble and holy act. To maintain the importance and value of sexual intercourse, Islam prohibits sex outside marriage. To assist people in being faithful, the Qur'an states that Muslims must help other people not to be tempted by them. For this reason both men and women dress, and behave, modestly [Qur'an, 24: 30-31]. Any form of privacy between unmarried couples is forbidden. Adultery is regarded as a form of theft [Qur'an, 17:32].

Modest dress for Muslim women, as shown in Ankara, Turkey, means keeping their bodies covered, except for their hands, feet, and faces.

Sex is compared to a pilgrimage. By going on pilgrimage a Muslim achieves union with Allah. A sexual relationship enables Muslims to achieve a physical union where love and commitment can be shown.

Homosexuality is forbidden because it is unnatural and a deviation from the norm. "What! Of all creatures, do you approach males and leave the spouses whom your Lord has created for you? Indeed, you are people transgressing [all limits]" [Qur'an, 26: 165-166]. Homosexuality is regarded as a depraved practice. [Qur'an, 4: 16-18].

14 (a) Explain the importance of sex in Islam.
(b) Why do you think it is important for Muslims to protect young people's chastity before marriage?
(c) How does the Muslim view of sex differ from that of Western society, as portrayed on television?

RELIGION FILE

JUDAISM

Marriage

- "A man without a wife lives without joy, without blessing and without good." [Talmud]. Judaism stresses the importance of marriage. The marriage ceremony is called kidushin, which means "sanctification".

Marriage in Judaism is a contract. At the ceremony, the husband gives his wife a written contract (the ketubah). The rabbi supervises rather than performs the ceremony.

Judaism is a religion centred on the home, and marriage is about creating a home, and having children. Jewish couples get married under a canopy, the chuppah, which is a symbol of an open home. A marriage brings together not just two individuals, but two families, and this is shown at many weddings by the presence of the large extended families.

In Judaism it is important to marry someone of the same religion. The Jewish tradition is against Jews marrying non-Jews, since one reason for marriage is to propagate the Jewish people, and to keep the Jewish heritage alive. In Orthodox Judaism only the child of a Jewish mother is recognised as Jewish. In other more liberal branches of Judaism it is possible for someone to convert to Judaism. There is lively debate in Jewish society today about "who is a Jew?"

15 In Judaism the marriage promises are written down in a contract called a ketubah.
(a) Do you think this makes them more permanent than just saying the words?
(b) Read the qualities of a wife in Proverbs 31: 10-31. Do you think these qualities are applicable today?

16 (a) Summarise the Jewish attitude towards divorce.
(b) Why might one partner refuse to agree to a divorce?
(c) How do you think this would affect the couple themselves, and any children they have?

Divorce

- Although marriage should be for life, Judaism accepts that marriages can break down, and a compassionate view is shown. Divorce is permitted and can be easy to obtain. However, if there is a chance that the marriage can be saved, all efforts must be made at reconciliation. The couple are counselled, usually by the rabbi.

Divorce proceedings are carried out very quickly so that both people can start to rebuild their lives. All that is necessary is the mutual agreement of the two partners and the giving of a divorce document (the get) by the husband to the wife. Without the get, a woman cannot remarry. It is done this way because, at the marriage, it was the husband who entered into the contract, giving his wife the ketubah. The promises were made by him to her; therefore, if there is to be a divorce, only he can break the contract by giving the get. It is easy to see how this has led to problems, especially when the wife wants a divorce and the husband does not agree. This issue of divorce is one of the most vexing concerns within the Jewish community today.

The Talmud suggests that God is against divorce: "Tears fall on God's altar for whoever divorces his first wife." [Gittin 90a]. Remarriage is allowed but not to a previous husband [Deuteronomy 24: 1-4].

Sexuality

- Judaism speaks frankly about sexual matters. Sex is one of the great things that God has created for human pleasure. "Know that sexual intercourse is holy and pure when carried on properly in the proper time and with the proper intention." [Nachmanides, a Jewish leader, 1194-1270]. Within marriage, sex is not just for procreation; it is considered an important way of expressing love.

Technically, sex is one of the three stages of marriage (i.e. by having sex you are embarking on the marriage process) and so, technically, it is impossible to have sex before marriage. Obviously, in reality, it is possible to have sex before marriage. Doing so is thought to cheapen sex and lower

17 Describe the variety of responses to homosexuality found in Judaism today. Which response do you (i) most and (ii) least agree with?

18 Judaism has a positive attitude towards sex. How do you think this should affect its views on (a) homosexuality, (b) prostitution, (c) using sexual imagery in advertisements?

self-respect. However, a child who is born before marriage is not considered illegitimate. Only a child who is born as the result of adultery is considered illegitimate.

Sexual activity outside marriage is wrong: "Do not commit adultery." [Exodus 20: 14]. The law in Deuteronomy 22: 13-21 gives stoning as the punishment for sexual promiscuity. However, there has been no recorded case of this punishment being carried out in the last 2,000 years. The Jewish courts have made the evidence required almost impossible to obtain. Judaism also speaks out against incest (sex with a family member) [Leviticus 18: 6-23].

Judaism has traditionally opposed homosexuality [Leviticus 18: 22], the punishment for which is death [Leviticus 20: 13]. But there is no record in Jewish history of such a punishment. With the emergence of Gay Liberation, the issue of homosexuality has been hotly debated. Modern Orthodox attitudes have ranged from outright condemnation (sometimes linked with discussing AIDS as a divine punishment) to a pragmatic recognition that Jews sin all the time but this does not stop them from attending the synagogue, so why is being gay any different from not observing the Shabbat, etc? Others see homosexuality as a kind of sickness, of physical or psychological origin, which should be treated or suffered in silence, the best advice being to lead a life of celibacy. Former Chief Rabbi of Britain, Lord Jakobovits, among others, recommended gene therapy in order to heal homosexuals. The response of Reform Jews has been different. For example, in the USA, Reform Jews have created Gay Temples ("temple" is the American Reform term for synagogue). Known homosexual and lesbian rabbis have been employed by congregations in the USA and the UK.

This gay couple in New York were married in traditional Jewish style, under a wedding canopy (the chuppah) – a symbol of the openness of the home.

RELIGION FILE

SIKHISM 

Marriage

- Sikhs place a high value on getting married. The ideal of marriage is to bring together two souls so that they may become spiritually inseparable. Marriage is therefore not merely a social contract or a union of two bodies. God sees the marriage and blesses it. It is a spiritual union. "They are not husband and wife who only dwell together. Only they who have one spirit in two bodies can be called husband and wife." [Guru Granth Sahib 788; see also 58]. Marriage is the way God intended people to live. The marriage ceremony – the Lavan – draws attention not only to the joining of two people but also to the soul's gradual progression towards union with God.

  Monogamy has always been the Sikh norm. Sikhs normally marry other Sikhs, although inter-marriage with Hindus has occurred. Marriage is regarded as a union of two families. In the majority of marriages the couple's families play a large role in selecting the partners, although there is no tradition of arranged marriages in Sikhism today.

In the wedding ceremony the couple are reminded of their duties of love, loyalty, and the sharing of joys and sorrows in a life-long relationship.

Divorce

- Divorce is allowed, but discouraged. Divorce is on the increase, especially for Sikhs living in Western countries. There is no religious objection to remarriage. Parents often arrange a remarriage for their son or daughter after a divorce. A divorcee can be remarried in the gurdwara.

Sexuality

- Sikhism teaches that the only correct place for sex is marriage. The religion started in northern India, in a culture where marriage was regarded as the bringing together of two extended families and marriages were arranged at an early age. Therefore sex before marriage was unheard of. The izzat (honour) of a Sikh family is very important. Every family member must behave well. Girls especially have to show sharam (decent modesty). Traditionally, girls are not allowed to mix with boys without a chaperone. Living together and sex before marriage are considered wrong. Virginity before marriage is important.

  Lust is one of five evil passions. "Do not cast your eyes on the beauty of another's wife." [Guru Granth Sahib 274]. The Sikh underwear, the kachh – one of the Five Ks – worn by both sexes, is a reminder of the need for chastity and faithfulness in marriage.

  The Guru Granth Sahib does not mention homosexuality. However, there is an expectation that men and women should marry and have children.

19 (a) What do Sikhs mean by saying that marriage is a spiritual union?
(b) How do they show this in their marriage ceremony?
(c) Why do you think Sikh parents are often involved in choosing marriage partners for their children?

20 What attitude towards divorce do Sikhs have?

21 Sikhs live in extended families.
(a) What is an extended family?
(b) What do you think are the advantages of extended families?

Sample Examination Questions

(a) What is a nuclear family? [2 marks]
(b) State the teaching of ONE religion about the importance of family life. [6 marks]
(c) Explain why Christians have different views about divorce. [8 marks]
(d) "Living together is better than getting married." Do you agree? Give reasons for your answer, showing that you have considered another point of view. [4 marks]
[London Examinations GCSE (Short Course) Syllabus A Paper 2, June 1997]

CHAPTER

Wealth and poverty

UNIT ONE

Money is a powerful and attractive thing to many people. In this unit you will consider the value of money and how it can be used both for good and for bad.

The power of money

KEY ISSUES IN THIS CHAPTER

- the inequality between the rich and the poor
- attitudes to wealth and poverty
- religious teachings about the use of wealth

Picking over rubbish in Bangladesh, for the means to survive.

An unfair world

Wealth is unequally distributed around the world. Some people have far more than they need, whilst others are dying of poverty. Imagine that there are thirty people in your class at the moment and the classroom represents the world. Here's what your scaled-down world would be like:

- Only two of you would live to the age of 74.
- Two of you would be so underfed that you would not grow properly.
- Seventeen of you would make less than £300 a year.
- Only fifteen of you would be able to get clean drinking water.
- One of you would control 80% of the farmland.
- Only six of you would live in safe homes.

THE STATE OF THE WORLD

Achieved since 1975

- ▲ Enough food for all the world's population
- ▲ 80% of all the world's children vaccinated against major diseases
- ▲ 100 million more children attend school than in 1975
- ▲ 1.6 billion more people have safe water

But still . . .

- ▼ One fifth of the world goes hungry
- ▼ 2.5 million unvaccinated children die each year from measles, tetanus, and whooping cough
- ▼ 100 million children (mostly girls) do not attend school
- ▼ More than 2 million people die each year from effects of polluted water

[Source: Christian Aid pamphlet, "Why Christian Aid?"]

Q

1 Write a paragraph about "The State of the World", using the information here together with material you find in recent newspapers. Draw attention to the difference between your standard of living and that of other people in the world.

"Is it only thieves who steal? No, everyone who keeps back what could be of use to many."

"*Fortune* magazine annually lists the 500 richest people; no one knows the names of the 500 poorest!"

2 Why do you think there is a magazine dedicated to describing the lives of the rich? Why isn't there a similar magazine about poor people?

What reasons can you suggest for the differences between the situations shown in this photograph and the one on page 186? Are car-boot sales a sign of consumerism?

Jubilee 2000

On 16 May 1998, the international Jubilee 2000 campaign was launched. In one event, 70,000 people made a human chain around the city of Birmingham in a show of support for poor countries. Their message to the leaders of the world was: "Cancel the debts of the world's poorest countries and give a billion people a new start." These countries had been loaned money by the West. The only way for them to pay back their debts is through export earnings, and yet the amount that many of them earn through exports is much lower than the debt they owe. The interest that some countries are having to pay is three times the amount of the original loan. As a direct result, spending on health and education in these countries has fallen.

What can be done? The rich countries are very unlikely to see their money returned. The logical thing to do would be to cancel the debts and be more cautious about lending money in the future. In the past, much of the money lent to poor countries was misused by corrupt political regimes and went to line the pockets of dictators.

The aim of the Jubilee 2000 campaign is to bombard world leaders every 100 days with reminders of the needs of the poor. Many people are wearing debt lapel chains, the international symbol of the campaign.

These girls were part of the human chain made around Birmingham to launch the Jubilee 2000 campaign.

3 What do you think of the Jubilee 2000 campaign? How do you think cancelling the poor countries' debts will "give a billion people a new start"? Do rich countries have a responsibility to help poor countries?

4 (a) What evidence can you find (i) in your own town/country, and (ii) in the world at large, to support the claim that we live in an unfair world?
(b) Whose responsibility are the homeless in our society?

What thoughts might be going through these Lottery players' minds? Would you like to win the jackpot? What would you do with the money? Would you spend it all on yourself, or give some away? Would winning change your life?

A materialistic, consumerist world

Western countries, including Britain, are often described as materialistic societies, in which wealth and possessions are valued more highly than qualities such as justice and compassion for people in need.

Britain's National Lottery has become a symbol of the country's materialism. Since it was introduced in 1994, two-thirds of the adult population have become regular players, taking part at least once a week. A proportion of the money taken by the Lottery is shared between good causes, including charities, the arts, and sport, but new problems of "lottery addiction" have arisen for some of the people who play.

Lottery Addicts Swamp Gamblers Anonymous

Gamblers Anonymous have reported an influx of callers requesting help and guidance to overcome their lottery addiction. Last week the lottery claimed its first death. Timothy O'Brien shot himself after failing to buy a ticket when all six of his syndicate's numbers were chosen.

[*Sunday Times*, 16 April 1995]

Sometimes you will hear society described as consumerist. Consumerism is a preoccupation with acquiring consumer goods (goods in a finished state, ready for the buyer to use). Every day people are bombarded with adverts encouraging them to buy more and more. As people are caught up in this consumerist spirit, it is easy for them to become blind to the needs of the poor.

5 Do you think it is correct to describe Britain as (a) a materialistic society? (b) a consumerist society? Give your reasons.

"After a visit to the beach, it's hard to believe that we live in a materialistic world."

A matter of attitude

Money and possessions are not bad things in themselves. It all depends on the attitude you have towards them. Money makes a good servant but a bad master. Compare Etin's story below with Andrew Carnegie's (page 189). Carnegie's possessions had come to possess him.

ETIN

A friend who was working in the Dominican Republic met a small boy named Etin. He noticed that when Etin wore a shirt it was always the same dirty, tattered one. A box of used clothes had been left at the camp, and my friend found two shirts in it that were in reasonably good shape and about Etin's size, so he gave them to the grateful boy. A few days later he saw another boy wearing one of the shirts. When he next met up with Etin he explained that the shirts had been meant for him. Etin looked at him and said, "But you gave me two!"

6 What is Etin's attitude to wealth? How might this differ from your own?

“Money is like fertiliser: you have to spread it around everywhere, if not it stinks.” [John Paul Getty, multi-millionaire]

I COULDN'T STOP

American industrialist Andrew Carnegie (1835-1919) controlled about a quarter of American iron and steel production and became one of the richest men in the world. He was once asked: “You could have stopped any time, couldn't you, because you always had much more than you needed?” He replied: “Yes, that's right. But I could not stop. I had forgotten how to.”

7 “Money causes more problems than it solves." How far do you agree with this statement? Show that you have thought about different points of view and give reasons to support your answer.

“It's fine to make money. It isn't fine to make money your god.” [Sinead O'Connor, musician]

8 (a) In what ways can money be a good servant but a bad master?
(b) Write your own “wisdom story” about attitudes to wealth and possessions.

A RICH INDUSTRIALIST AND A FISHER

Narrator: A rich industrialist was shocked to find a fisher lying lazily beside his boat, smoking a pipe.
Industrialist: Why aren't you out fishing?
Fisher: Because I have caught enough fish for the day.
Industrialist: Why don't you catch more than you need?
Fisher: What would I do with it?
Industrialist: You could earn more money. You could use it to have a motor fixed to your boat. Then you could go into deeper water, gain more fish, and sell them for a higher profit. Then you could buy two boats and be rich like me.
Fisher: What would I do then?
Industrialist: Then you could sit down and enjoy life.
Fisher: What do you think I'm doing right now?

In December 1997 Prince Charles visited the offices of the “Big Issue” (a self-help organisation for people who are homeless). It turned out that Clive Harold, the homeless man who greeted the prince, had been in the same class as him at school. How do you think each of the two men felt when they met again on this occasion? Why do you think two people who started off in the same school came to live in such different ways?

Religious responses to wealth and poverty

All religions think it is important to have the right attitude towards wealth and possessions. A wrong attitude can lead people away from what is really important in life – the search for spiritual truth and inner happiness. Religions teach that true happiness is not found solely in material riches.

"During one of my trips to the United States a very wealthy family invited me to lunch. I observed the opulence and comfort that prevailed in their home and I thought that these people must be completely content. At the end of the meal I went to freshen up in the bathroom. I peeked discreetly into a half-open medicine cabinet: it was full of sleeping tablets and tranquillizers. I concluded that they must not be as happy as they seemed." [The Dalai Lama, *Beyond Dogma: the challenge of the modern world*, Souvenir Press, 1994]

On the other hand, people have the ability to use money for good, so much so that money has been described as "God in circulation".

RELIGION FILE

BUDDHISM

- The story of the founder of Buddhism, Siddhattha Gotama, is that of a prince who left his wealth behind in order to seek the answer to why there is suffering. It was as a poor wandering holy man that he found the answer to his question and achieved inner peace and happiness. Siddhattha even called his son Rahula, which means chains, because he felt caught in the chains of wealth.
- Buddhism is sometimes called a "Middle Way" between the extremes of having everything and having nothing. Everyone needs the basic necessities to live without anxiety – food, clothing, and shelter; but if people have too much wealth they can be so concerned about protecting it that they become attached to it. The right attitude to all material things is: "Look upon the world as a bubble, look upon it as a mirage . . . for the wise there is no attachment at all." [Dhammapada 170-1]
- To gain wealth is a proper goal for ordinary Buddhist householders. It is important that it is honestly earned by right livelihood (see the Eightfold Path, page 37) and that it is properly used. It is not right to hoard money. The proper use of wealth is in looking after family and friends. Also, lay Buddhists are called to help the poor and to provide the material necessities for monks and nuns. This generosity to the monks and nuns is called "dana". In return, the monks and nuns provide the teaching, the Dhamma. Generosity is one of the most important lay Buddhist virtues. Being able to give shows that a person is not attached to his or her wealth. "Whoever in your kingdom is poor, to him let some help be given." [Cakkavatti Sihananda Sutta].

Novice monks on the alms round in Thailand receive food from a lay Buddhist.

1 (a) Why is Buddhism sometimes called the Middle Way?
(b) What difficulties might a Buddhist face living in the West as s/he tries to live a life without greed and desire?

2 Choose THREE jobs that would not count as right livelihood. Explain your choices.

3 Describe TWO ways in which a Buddhist could demonstrate dana.

RELIGION FILE

CHRISTIANITY

- The Bible teaches that all created things are from God. "The world and all that is in it [including money and possessions] belong to the Lord." [Psalm 50: 12]. It also teaches that people should be good stewards of their money. There are a number of passages in the Bible which point to the importance of using money wisely, to help others [Matthew 25: 35-40; Acts 2: 45; James 2: 15-17].

In giving to the Church and to charity, many Christians bear in mind the idea of tithing – giving one tenth of their possessions [Genesis 28: 20-22; Leviticus 27: 30-33]. This giving is in recognition of the fact that all things come from and belong to God.

Notre Dame Cathedral in Montreal, Canada, looks rich. Why do you think the wealth of churches is a concern for some Christians? South African Archbishop Desmond Tutu said: "The church that is in solidarity with the poor can never be a wealthy church."

"Rich nations have a grave moral responsibility towards those which are unable to ensure the means of their development by themselves." [Pope John Paul II, December 1994]

"The Church should concern itself first, and indeed second, with the poor and needy, whether in spirit or in body." [Church of England, *Faith in the City*, 1985]

- Jesus warned his followers about the dangers of money, the fact that possessions can possess a person: "No one can be a slave of two masters; he will hate the one and love the other . . . You cannot serve both God and money." [Matthew 6: 24; also Luke 12: 15]. St Paul wrote to Timothy: "The love of money causes all kinds of evil." [1 Timothy 6: 10]

Christians believe that they have a responsibility to help the poor. They also recognise that having a lot of money can blind you to the needs of others. Jesus told a story about a man who was so rich that he was blind to the needs of a poor man named Lazarus. [Luke 16: 19-21]. In another story, about the end of the world, Jesus made it clear that people would be judged according to how they have treated their fellow humans – whether they have cared for the poor and needy, the hungry and thirsty [Matthew 25: 31-46].

Q

4 Why are some Christians against the National Lottery?

5 What do you think Jesus meant when he said: "It is much harder for a rich person to enter the Kingdom of God than for a camel to go through the eye of a needle." [Mark 10: 25]?

6 Why do Christians believe that they should share what they have with those who are in need?

Mary (Jesus's mother) sings a song of praise to God in which she says: "He [God] has filled the hungry with good things, and sent the rich away with empty hands." [Luke 1: 53]

- Cafod, Christian Aid, and Tear Fund are three examples of Christian organisations that give relief to the poor, whatever their race, religion, or colour. Their aims are (a) to help the poor to help themselves (long-term aid); (b) to provide emergency relief when there is sudden disaster (short-term aid); (c) to educate people in the Western world about the causes of poverty and injustice.

“In the Bible it is written that what God gave us is for us all. I often think how beautiful it would be if everyone understood this.” [Prayer from Honduras]

- Many Christians are against gambling because it encourages a love of money for its own sake [see 1 Timothy 6: 9-10]. Some feel that the National Lottery is a form of national gambling that encourages greed. "It can totally destroy lives and bring misery. It also encourages people to gamble beyond their means." [Bishop of Wakefield, *The Times*, 1 January 1996]. Others are concerned that only a small amount of the money taken (some estimate as low as 5.6%) goes to charities.

RELIGION FILE

Hindu businessmen pray to Lakshmi, goddess of wealth, during the festival of Diwali. This market stall holder in Nepal has some posters of Lakshmi hanging behind him.

HINDUISM ॐ

- Hinduism teaches that the comforts of wealth and riches may well be the result of good karma, good deeds in previous lives; so such comforts are considered earned. Wealth is not good or bad in itself. It all depends on how it is used.

  One of the four aims in life for Hindus is "artha" – to make wealth in order to support others and contribute to the economic development of the community. This aim is particularly important in the "householder" stage of life. However wealth must not be acquired by any means. A book written by Kautilya in about 300 BCE, the Artha-shastra, explains how to gain and use wealth and power in a moral way. It includes teachings about accounts, trade and commerce, weights and measures, taxation, and economic development.

“He who seeks happiness must strive for contentment and self-control; happiness arises from contentment, uncontrolled pursuit of wealth will result in unhappiness.” [Manu 4:12]

- If Hindus have more wealth than they need for survival they should consider how to use the extra wealth for the good of others. The act of giving away money, especially to religious causes, is thought to give a person merit. This is why many saintly people can be seen begging in India and also why hospitality is considered very important. Many Hindus in Britain are involved in projects that send money for education and food etc to India. Many Hindu temples in Britain collect charity gifts to help the poor.

7 (a) What is the correct Hindu attitude towards wealth and possessions?
(b) What does it mean to gain and use wealth in a moral way?
(c) List three ways in which a Hindu in Britain could use his or her extra wealth to help others.

8 "Charity begins at home". Do you agree? Do you think that people have a responsibility to help others whom they do not know?

RELIGION FILE

ISLAM

- All wealth is a gift from Allah. If a Muslim is wealthy it is because Allah has made him so; therefore Allah has the right to demand how the wealth is used. Money is of value only for what it can do, not for itself. Hoarding wealth will be punished on the Day of Judgement: "And let the hoarders not think that what Allah has bestowed upon them from His bounty is better for them ... That which they hoard will be a burden for them on the Day of Judgement" [Qur'an, 3:180; also 9: 34].
  A Muslim must not make wealth a more important thing than Allah [Qur'an, 3: 14]. Muslims should not charge interest (practise usury) on anything borrowed or lent because this exploits those in need [Qur'an, 2: 276, 278-279].

"Richness does not lie in abundance of worldly goods, but true richness is the richness of the soul." [Hadith]

- Each year, every Muslim is required to pay 2.5% of his or her cash wealth as zakah (see page 60). The money collected is used to support the poor among the Islamic community, to promote Islam through educational programmes, and to help pilgrims stranded on Hajj.
  Some Muslims also make other, voluntary, gifts to charity. This is known as sadaqah. It is said that sadaqah must be given in such a way that even the right hand of the giver does not know what the left hand is doing. Red Crescent and Islamic Relief are two Islamic organisations which use money collected by sadaqah to provide aid, for example, in international disasters.
  Through its teachings on zakah and sadaqah, Islam encourages generosity and compassion towards people in need.

"Every human being has a right that his or her basic needs should be fulfilled. The Islamic concept of property is very different from the Western concept of property because in the Islamic framework we believe that Allah is the owner, and that you have been given the possession of it so that you can use it for rightful purposes, not for exploitation of others." [S. Mohammed Reza Hejazi, in *Muslim Educational Quarterly*, Vol. 11 No. 2, 1994, The Islamic Academy, Cambridge]

9 (a) What are zakah and sadaqah?
(b) What is the difference between them?
(c) Why do you think Muslims are not allowed to lend money at interest (i.e. practise usury)?

10 What would the Muslim reaction be to the National Lottery? Explain your answer.

RELIGION FILE

JUDAISM

- In Judaism, the way a person uses his or her wealth is important. Wealthy people are allowed to own luxuries but should also put their wealth at the service of the community. Judaism warns against materialism [Proverbs 23: 4; Ecclesiastes 5: 10-12], since it can lead a person to sin [Deuteronomy 8: 11-14].

11 (a) What kind of happiness can material things give you?
(b) Do you agree with Maimonides that "the objects we physically need rate inversely to their price"?

"'Who is rich? He who is satisfied with what he has.' [Ethics of the Fathers]. There is the secret ... Maimonides observed that the objects we physically need rate inversely to their price. The primary requirement of our body is air; we can exist only a few minutes without it; and it is absolutely free! Next, we need water, and that is fairly cheap. At the other end of the scale lie gold and diamonds; they are tremendously expensive. But a man can live the whole of his life without need of them." [Moshe Davis, *I Am A Jew*, Mowbray, 1978]

THE GREEDY FOX

To spend one's existence in toiling for material possessions is likened to a fox which found a vineyard fenced around on all sides. There was just one hole. He wished to enter through it but was unable to do so. What did he do? He fasted for three days until he became very thin, and then went through the aperture. He feasted there and, of course, grew fat again. When he wanted to go out he was unable to pass through the hole. So he fasted another three days until he had grown thin and then went out. When he was outside he turned back and gazing upon it he cried, "O vineyard! What use have you been to me and what use are your fruits? All that is inside is beautiful and praiseworthy, but what benefit has one from you? As one enters so he comes out." [From A. Cohn, *Everyman's Talmud*, Dent & Sons, 1971]

- To provide for the poor is one of the most important commands of the Torah [Deuteronomy 15: 11]. The Hebrew word for charity is tzedakah, which is also the word for justice; charity is seen not so much as being generous as being just. It is fair and just that people who have should give to people who have not. Not giving tzedakah is, in effect, robbing the poor. Referring to the Torah [Genesis 28: 20-22; Leviticus 27: 30-33], many Jews try to give a tithe (tenth) of their wealth to the poor. However, some rabbis have interpreted the Torah as meaning that "A tenth of his wealth is the average amount [to give] and one who gives less than this is ungenerous." [Yoreh De'ah 249: 1]. Other rabbis have suggested that if you are rich you should give more than a tenth, but if you are poor, you should give a tenth of your disposable income.

  Many Jewish homes keep collection boxes (pushkes) for loose change, which is then given to charity. Children are taught to put some of their pocket money in the pushke.

  In 1990 some young Jews formed a charity called Tzedakah. They wanted people to become more concerned about global issues. Tzedekah

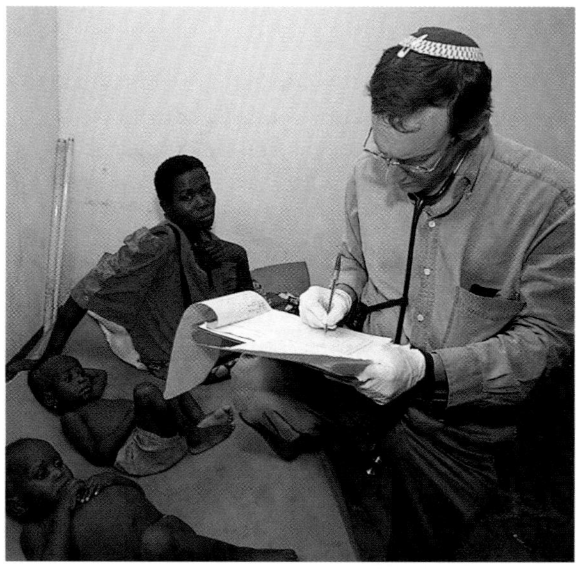

A Jewish doctor in a refugee camp in Tanzania.

offers help to anyone in need, regardless of race or religion. It runs educational programmes to inform people about issues such as trade and debt and the plight of refugees. It works alongside established agencies abroad to provide relief from suffering. Tzedakah wants people to do more than just give money. It wants them to become personally involved in trying to put right something that is wrong in society.

- Maimonides was a great rabbi who lived in Spain in the twelfth century. He described a "ladder of charity" with eight rungs. The lowest rung on the ladder is when someone gives grudgingly. The highest is when the giver gives so that the receiver becomes independent and never has to rely on charity again.

12 (a) What is tzedakah?
(b) In what way is charity associated with the idea of justice in Judaism?
(c) Why do you think that putting money in the pushke is part of Jewish family education? Do you think it is a good thing to teach children?

13 "The more easily you get your wealth, the sooner you will lose it. The harder it is to earn it, the more you will have." [Proverbs 13: 11]. Do you agree?

RELIGION FILE

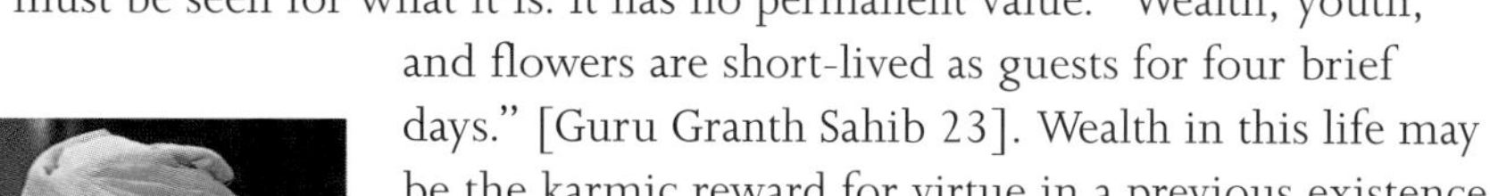

SIKHISM

- Wealth should not distract Sikhs from life's spiritual goals. Instead, wealth must be seen for what it is. It has no permanent value. "Wealth, youth, and flowers are short-lived as guests for four brief days." [Guru Granth Sahib 23]. Wealth in this life may be the karmic reward for virtue in a previous existence.

Sikhs must earn their wealth honestly and share generously. They should give at least a tenth (dasvandh) of their earnings to the needy or to the gurdwara. Often Sikhs give "in kind" – for example, food for the langar or building materials for a gurdwara, rather than cash.

Money should not be spent on things such as gambling or drinking [Guru Granth Sahib 914].

❝Be grateful to God whose bounties you enjoy. Be compassionate to the needy and the people you employ.❞ [Guru Nanak]

Sikh men prepare food for the langar. Guru Amar Das described the idea of the meal: "Each gives as much as he can spare and takes as much as he needs. Here there is no difference between kings and beggars."

GURU NANAK AND TWO PIECES OF BREAD

A wealthy man called Malak Bhago made a fortune, but showed his poor workers no mercy and paid them miserable wages. The fame of Guru Nanak reached him and he sent an invitation to the Guru to come to his house to eat supper. Guru Nanak chose instead to accept the hospitality of Lalo, a poor carpenter.

Malak Bhago wanted to know why the famous Guru had preferred the poor man's bread to his fine meal. Guru Nanak put out his hand and asked Malak Bhago for a piece of the bread from his table. In his other hand he held a piece of bread from the table of Lalo. He then squeezed the two pieces of bread. From Malak Bhago's bread came drops of blood and from the poor man's bread came sweet wholesome milk. Guru Nanak said that he preferred bread that was earned by honest means and hard work to the bread that was earned at the expense of the blood and suffering of others.

- Sewa (service, caring for those in need) is an important concept in Sikhism. God commands it: "A place in God's court can only be attained if we do service to others in this world." [Guru Granth Sahib 26] "Those who love God love everybody." [Guru Granth Sahib 557]

Gurdip Gujral fulfilled his ambition to build his own business and became a millionaire. He says: "My property comes not only from hard work but my faith in almighty God which helped me achieve my success. Everyday in my room upstairs I worship God. Hard work does pay, but according to Sikh belief worship of God is very important." [BBC *Taking Issue* Programme 3]

14 What is the langar? What happens there? How does the langar encourage sewa?

15 What does it mean to say that wealth may be the karmic reward for virtue in a previous existence?

16 Does the story about two pieces of bread condemn wealth? What attitude does it recommend?

Sample Examination Questions

(a) Explain the teaching of Christianity and of ONE other religion on wealth and poverty. [12 marks]
(b) "Only religious organisations can solve the problems of world poverty." Do you agree? Give reasons for your answer, showing that you have considered another point of view. [8 marks]
[London Examinations GCSE (Short Course) Syllabus A Paper 1, June 1997]

CHAPTER

Prejudice

UNIT ONE

Prejudice and discrimination

In this unit you will learn about the meaning of prejudice and discrimination.

KEY ISSUES IN THIS CHAPTER

- types of prejudice and discrimination
- reasons for prejudice and discrimination
- religious teachings on prejudice and discrimination

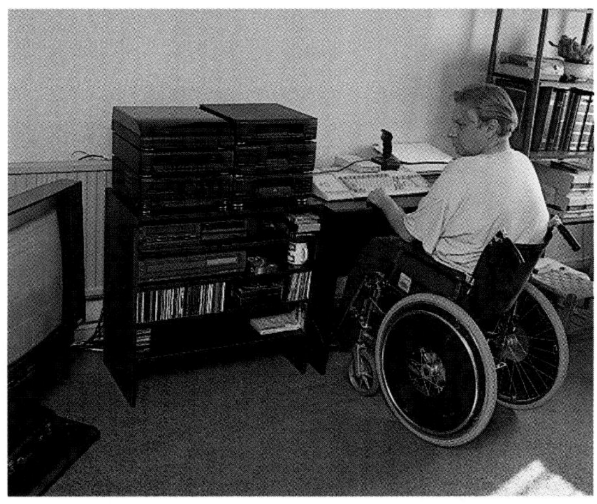

What might be this person's experience of prejudice and discrimination? Discuss the problems he could face when (a) going shopping, and (b) going for a job interview.

Prejudice and discrimination are shown towards people because of their age, their race, the colour of their skin, their gender, their sexual orientation, their religious beliefs, their abilities or disabilities, and their social class. The effects can be very destructive. People are made to feel they are vulnerable victims, rejected and hated for who they are. In the UK there are laws against discrimination, to ensure, for instance, that people all have equal rights at work or when buying goods in shops, but there are no laws against prejudice – it is very difficult to make laws about how people feel. Prejudice has to be fought by providing proper education. Schools and the media have a big role to play in this.

Information File: Prejudice and discrimination

Prejudice is pre-judging, making up one's mind before a proper examination of the facts. It is based upon feelings, attitudes, or ideas that people have about something.

Stereotyping is building an image of something or of people, based on our prejudices. Stereotypes are fixed, over-simplified mental pictures. For example, a person who has had a bad experience of violent teenagers may stereotype all teenagers as violent. Stereotypes are broken down when people are seen as individuals with their own strengths and weaknesses.

Discrimination is action taken against different groups because of prejudice. It could be described as "prejudice in action". Discrimination can be both negative and positive. We discriminate against people when we don't give them a fair chance at getting a job. On the other hand, we can discriminate positively to ensure fair treatment for groups who might otherwise lose out.

Xenophobia is a fear or hatred of foreigners.

1 (a) What is the difference between prejudice and discrimination?
(b) Provide your own examples of prejudice and discrimination in society today.

2 (a) Make a list of all the groups in society you can think of which suffer prejudice.
(b) Choose two of the groups on your list and explain how people in them can be discriminated against.

THE CIVIL RIGHTS MOVEMENT

Racial discrimination was one of the greatest problems facing America in the 1950s and 1960s. The problem had a long history. In 1619, black Africans started to be shipped in masses to America, to be employed as servants. However by 1661 their status had become that of slaves. From the beginning, slavery and second-class treatment of blacks raised moral questions that white America found difficult to answer. How could a free society deny equal rights to some of its members? Attempts were made to give equal rights to all Americans, but in the southern states of America the whites formed a common front against blacks.

At the start of the 20th century a number of black intellectuals began to argue for equal rights. The man who was to change the status quo was born in Atlanta, Georgia, on 15 January 1929. His name was Martin Luther King. He taught that the only way to achieve equality was through non-violent protest.

In the south, in Alabama, state law said that black people had to sit at the back of public buses, and had to give up their seats for white people if necessary. Martin Luther King organised a bus boycott, which went on for over a year, causing the bus company to lose income. Finally, Alabama's laws about segregation on buses were declared to be against the American Constitution. This was the start of the Civil Rights movement.

As leader of the Civil Rights movement, Martin Luther King worked continually to bring an end to all forms of black segregation. The Civil Rights Act of 1964 guaranteed all Americans equal use of public accommodations and the right to compete for employment on the sole basis of individual merit. The Voting Rights Act of 1965 made it clear that all people, including blacks, should be allowed to vote. But more importantly than individual Acts of Parliament, the mood of American people had changed. People had begun to treat each other as equals.

In 1968 a white gunman assassinated Martin Luther King. Today America pays tribute to his work by celebrating an annual Martin Luther King Day.

25 March 1965: Martin Luther King and his wife head a Civil Rights march of about 10,000 people in Alabama, USA. King was a Baptist pastor and often made references to parts of the Bible in his speeches. In particular he likened his followers in the Civil Rights movement to the Israelites in the story of the Exodus, who were led out of slavery in Egypt to freedom in the Promised Land.

REASONS FOR PREJUDICE AND DISCRIMINATION

Ignorance: people often reject and characterise people they do not know and understand.

Going with the crowd: people seek security in their own group. Other people become outsiders and enemies.

Using people as scapegoats: people often pick on other people to blame when something goes wrong.

Selfishness and greed: sometimes a nation persecutes a group of people for its own ends – for example, the treatment of black slaves in America.

Fear: people feel threatened by something strange and new.

Racial prejudice

Racism is the belief that people of some races are inferior to others. The story of Martin Luther King (page 198) is a famous example of success in combating racism. But many current news reports are evidence that racism still exists.

In the 1990s, news reports from Eastern Europe told of growing support for extreme right-wing parties. An example in Russia was the racist and anti-Semitic National Patriotic Front "Pamyat". It takes the last Tsar, Nicholas II, and Jesus as its heroes, and claims to be guided by Christian teachings. Can you explain why the rise of groups like Pamyat is a major concern for people who aim for understanding between religions?

3 (a) Why are people prejudiced?
(b) What can people do, practically, to fight prejudice in society today?

4 "Laws are no good. To stop prejudice you have first to change people's minds." How far do you agree with this statement? Show that you have thought about different points of view and give reasons for your answer.

5 What is the main message of Martin Luther King's "I have a dream" speech? How did his religious faith influence his ideas?

MARTIN LUTHER KING'S DREAM

"I have a dream that one day this nation will rise up and live out the true meaning of its creed: 'We hold these truths to be self-evident; that all men were created equal.' I have a dream that one day on the red hills of Georgia the sons of former slaves and the sons of former slave owners will be able to sit down together at the table of brotherhood . . . I have a dream that my four little children will one day live in a nation where they will not be judged according to the colour of their skin but by the content of their character . . . I have a dream today."

Religious responses to prejudice

"I think God is silly because he should have painted everybody the same colour and then they wouldn't fight." [Ricardo, 7]

RELIGION FILE

BUDDHISM

- The Buddha lived in India and was brought up within the caste system – the division of people into groups or classes. However, he rejected the caste system, teaching that all people are equal and have within them the Buddha-nature, the nature of enlightenment [Dhammapada 393-4].

"Buddhism is not the possession of any race or nation but aspires to the unity of the human race on earth. Nationalism and racism are seen as forms of greed, hatred and delusion." [World Fellowship of Buddhists in Colombo, 1984, quoted in *Ethical Issues in Six Religious Traditions*, Edinburgh University Press, 1996]

- The things which divide and separate people – race, religion, gender, social position, intelligence, etc – are all illusory. The more enlightened people are, the more they will treat people equally. However, "Many do not know that we are here to live in harmony." [Dhammapada 6]
- Friendliness and Metta (loving-kindness) towards all beings are stressed in Buddhism. Buddhism stresses Right Action and Right Speech – elements of the Eightfold Path (see pages 36-37). Right Action opposes discrimination – it includes treating all people equally; Right Speech includes a rejection of prejudiced talk.

"Tolerance is a principal virtue in Buddhism and it is a virtue that is called for when one meets different beliefs and values. People may hold very different beliefs to you or even express very strong objections to your beliefs, but tolerance, for a Buddhist, means showing love to the fellow human being holding those different beliefs to you." [Adiccabanhu, *Clear Vision*]

1 On what grounds do Buddhists oppose prejudice and discrimination?

2 Explain why loving-kindness and tolerance are important concepts in Buddhism.

RELIGION FILE

CHRISTIANITY

- Christians believe in one God who is the Creator and Father of all people. All people are made in the image of God and are therefore of equal value.
  In his life and teaching Jesus showed the belief that all people are equal. When asked "Who is my neighbour?", Jesus replied by telling the story of the Good Samaritan [Luke 10: 25-36, see page 25]. In this story he made a Samaritan, the enemy of the Jews, the hero. His message was that all

Archbishop Desmond Tutu, 1994. One reason why Tutu first became a priest was to fight the injustice of South Africa's apartheid system. He said: "To speak of God, you must speak of your neighbour ... He does not tolerate a relationship with himself that excludes your neighbour."

people are your neighbours, all people are to be loved and respected. People from different races and backgrounds should learn to love each other and live in harmony. Jesus opposed all forms of discrimination. For example, he healed the servant of a Roman centurion, even though the Romans were a foreign army occupying his country [Luke 7: 1-10]. He befriended Zacchaeus, a tax collector, though tax collectors were shunned by the Jews [Luke 19: 1-10].

Saint Paul expressed the Christian attitude when he wrote, "There is no such thing as Jew and Greek, slave and freeman, male and female; for you are all one person in Christ Jesus." [Galatians 3: 28]

- The Bible makes it clear that strangers must be accepted [Leviticus 19: 33-34] and that being prejudiced is sinning [James 2: 8-9].
- Christian churches respond in a number of ways in their fight against prejudice and discrimination. The Church of England has a Race and Community Relations Committee which addresses issues such as the operation of nationality and immigration laws, the position of black people in the prison system, and unemployment among black people. The Catholic Association for Racial Justice campaigns against racism.
- The Christian churches are sometimes accused of discriminating against women because of the different roles women have traditionally been given in the church.

3 Make a list of Christian teachings that speak against prejudice and discrimination.

4 (a) According to Christianity who is your neighbour? How should you treat your neighbour?
(b) How has the Church responded to prejudice and discrimination?

5 Jesus came from the Middle East. However, in Western art he has nearly always been painted as a white man. What effect do you think this has had in history?

6 Desmond Tutu once said: "Thank God I am black. White people will have a lot to answer for at the Last Judgement." What do you think he meant?

RELIGION FILE

HINDUISM ॐ

- Hinduism teaches that all people are equal in the spiritual realm. The Bhagavad Gita indicates that the divine is non-partial: "I look upon all creatures equally." [Bhagavad Gita 9.29]. However, there are material differences in society which help society to work. One creation story is called Purusha-sukta. It describes how Brahma made humanity in four groups from his own body. Each group was equally important but had a different role to play. In Hindu society these four groups are called varnas. They are the Brahmins (priests and teachers), the Kshatriyas (soldiers and rulers), the Vaishyas (merchants and farmers), and the Shudras (labourers and craftsmen). This system shows that each person is dependent on others.

Mahatma Gandhi (1869-1948) was a famous political and religious leader. He spoke out against the abuse of the Untouchables, whom he called "Harijans", meaning "children of God". He also took action: he led Untouchables by the hand into the temples from which they had been excluded. It was partly due to Gandhi that Untouchability was made illegal in India in 1949.

Unfortunately, this system became open to abuse and the varnas became hereditary groupings called castes. Marrying a member of a different caste became impossible. And, in addition to the four groups, a fifth grouping called the "Untouchables" was developed. Untouchables were considered unclean; they were separated from society and were not allowed to worship in temples. The use of the term "Untouchable" and society's discrimination against these people were made illegal in the Indian and Pakistan constitutions in 1949 and 1953, but the law was difficult to enforce. Today the Untouchables call themselves "dalits" (the oppressed). They have voting rights and have formed a political party.

The caste system still operates in many villages in India, but in recent years the system has started to break down in the big cities, and people mix socially much more.

7 (a) On what grounds does Hinduism teach equality?
(b) Is equality practised in Hinduism? Explain the role of the caste system.

8 (a) What is the caste system? Who are the Untouchables?
(b) Why did Gandhi oppose the caste system?

RELIGION FILE

ISLAM 

- Muslims believe that all people are equally God's creation [Qur'an, 49:13]. "All God's creatures are His family." [Hadith]. The great variety of colours, races, and languages of human beings is evidence of God's wonderful creativity. "And among His signs is the creation of the heaven and the earth and the variation in your languages and colours." [Qur'an, 30:22].

- The Ummah, the worldwide community of Muslims, is multi-racial, multi-cultural, and multi-lingual. Muslims from very different backgrounds are united in the Ummah by the five pillars of Islam.

  When Muslims go on pilgrimage (the Hajj) to Makkah, they all wear simple white garments, showing their equality before God. These simple garments are also used on the bodies of the dead before they are buried, for the same reason.

- Men and women have equal religious, ethical, and civil rights: "Whether male or female, whoever in faith does a good work for the sake of God will be granted a good life and rewarded with greater reward." [Qur'an, 16: 97]. But men and women have different roles within the Ummah. This is not to deny the fact that in some states women are not given their full rights under Islamic Law.

9 Explain why Muslims think prejudice is wrong.

10 (a) What is the Ummah?
(b) How is equality within the Ummah shown?
(c) How is the importance of equality shown on the Hajj?

RELIGION FILE

JUDAISM

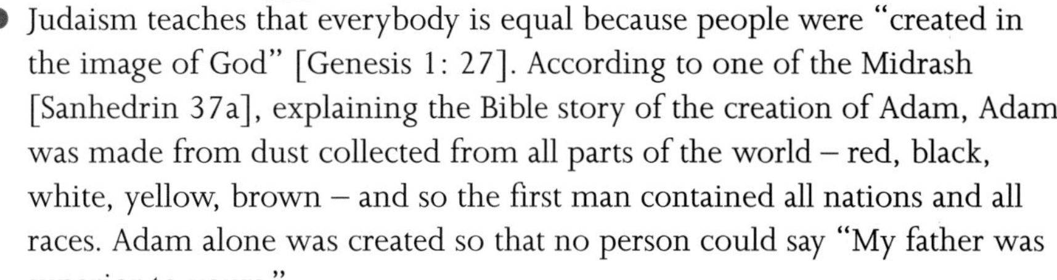

- Judaism teaches that everybody is equal because people were "created in the image of God" [Genesis 1: 27]. According to one of the Midrash [Sanhedrin 37a], explaining the Bible story of the creation of Adam, Adam was made from dust collected from all parts of the world – red, black, white, yellow, brown – and so the first man contained all nations and all races. Adam alone was created so that no person could say "My father was superior to yours."
- The Law that Moses received from God made it clear that people should live in harmony and create a just society. It commands love of strangers: "God loves the stranger by feeding him. Love the stranger because you were strangers in Egypt." [Deuteronomy 10: 18-19; Leviticus 19: 33-34]
- In both Orthodox and Progressive Judaism women and men have equal status. Progressive Judaism says that men and women can have the same roles – for example, men and women can both be rabbis. Orthodox Judaism gives men and women distinct roles. Women are given supremacy in the home. Men are given supremacy in public life, in the synagogues, and in courts. This does not mean that today Jewish women cannot pursue careers. Many Jewish men also make a large contribution to the home.

THE VISITOR

One midnight when Rabbi Moshe Keib was absorbed in mystic teachings, he heard a knock at his window. A drunken peasant stood outside and asked to be let in and given a bed for the night. For a moment the rabbi's heart was full of anger and he said to himself: "How can a drunk have the insolence to ask to be let in, and what business has he in this house!" But then he said silently in his heart: "And what business has he in God's world? But if God gets along with him, can I reject him?" He opened the door at once and prepared a bed.

11 If men and women are equal, should they be allowed to do the same things? What would (a) an Orthodox Jew and (b) a Progressive Jew say?

12 What is the message of the Visitor story?

13 What is anti-Semitism? How has it shown itself in this century?

14 The Jewish world makes a distinction between Jews and non-Jews.
(a) Why do they do this?
(b) Is this a form of prejudice?

Anti-Semitism, a particular example of prejudice

According to the Hebrew Bible, the Jews are God's chosen people: "You shall be for me a kingdom of priests and a holy nation." [Exodus 19: 6]. This sets them apart from all other people in the world.

The Jewish people's separateness has made them subject to prejudice and discrimination. Anti-Semitism (hatred of Jews) has a very long history. Christians in the Middle Ages blamed Jews for the crucifixion of Jesus. In the 20th century anti-Semitism led to the extermination of over 6 million Jews in the Second World War, mainly in concentration camps. Persecution of Jews has not ended today: newspapers still report acts of anti-Semitism.

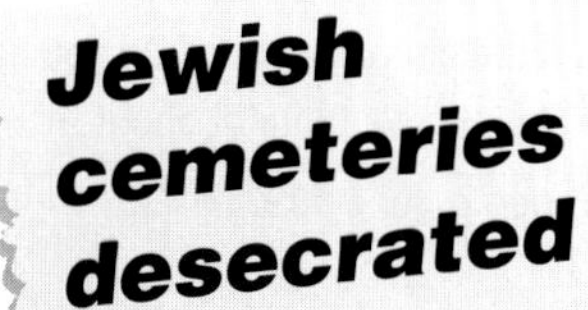

Historian denies holocaust ever happened

RELIGION FILE

SIKHISM 

Young women provide the music for a Sikh festival, at which five men (in the background) represent the "Panj Piarey" (the Five Beloved Ones), the very first members of the Sikh Khalsa.

15 (a) Why do Sikhs think equality is important?
(b) How do Sikhs demonstrate equality between people in the gurdwara?

16 (a) Is there equality in our society today? Are there people who are not treated as equal?
(b) Why do you think this is the case?

- The Sikh Gurus stressed that God is the source of all life, and that all people are equal. The Guru Granth Sahib stresses "All men and women are equal" and "All are children of God." Sikhs therefore condemn all forms of prejudice and discrimination. A practical expression of the belief that all people are equal is the langar – the meal shared after a service in the gurdwara. Everyone is welcome to the langar, including people of other faiths.

  "We need to recognise the oneness of all humanity . . . Though they use different dresses according to the influence of regional customs, All men have the same eyes, ears, body and figure, Made out of the compounds of earth, air, fire and water." [Guru Gobind Singh]

- Sikhs teach that men and women need each other. They are equal in status. According to Guru Nanak: "It is through women . . . that we are conceived and from her that we are born. It is to women that we get engaged and then married. She is our lifelong friend and the survival of our race depends on her ... Through women we establish our social ties. Why denounce her, the one from whom even kings are born?" [Guru Granth Sahib 473]

"In stressing the equality of all human beings, men and women, their emphasis on social and religious tolerance and their brave and forthright attack on all notions of caste, class or racial superiority [the Gurus] gave us, in a sense, the forerunner of the United Nations ideal. Different cultures, different ways of life, are not barriers between people, but gateways to a fuller understanding and enrichment of life itself." [Indarjit Singh, "Thought for the Day", BBC, 23 October 1985]

"Sikhs have never managed to shake off the caste system entirely, especially in the case of marriage . . . In one town there may be a Bhatra Sangat Gurdwara, Ramgarhia Sikh Gurdwara and Singh Sabha Gurdwara, each attended by a different section of the community. Prejudices are sometimes encouraged to preserve separation." [Piara Singh Sambhi, in O. Cole, ed., *Moral Issues in Six Religions*, Heinemann, 1991]

Sample Examination Questions

(a) Explain, using examples, the difference between prejudice and discrimination. [4 marks]

(b) What teaching is given about prejudice and discrimination in the sacred texts of ONE religious tradition?

(c) Describe how the teachings you have outlined in part (b) are put into practice in this tradition with regard to (i) people of different races and (ii) women. [6 marks]

(d) An Anglican bishop has argued that it is not always wrong to discriminate against other people; it depends on the circumstances. Do you agree with his view? Give reasons for your opinion, showing that you have thought about more than one point of view. [5 marks]

[NEAB Syllabus D Paper 2, June 1997]

CHAPTER

Work and leisure

UNIT ONE

One of the biggest choices people make in their lives is the kind of work they want to do. People spend up to 60% of their life at work. It is important that the work people do is connected with what they believe is important in life.

Why work?

KEY ISSUES IN THIS CHAPTER

- reasons why people value work and leisure
- values promoted in the work place
- the spiritual quality of work and leisure
- whether some jobs are forbidden by religious believers

1 (a) Do you know what career you would like? What attracts you to it?
(b) What factors will influence you in choosing a job?

2 In groups, brainstorm reasons why work is a good thing. What purposes does work fulfil?

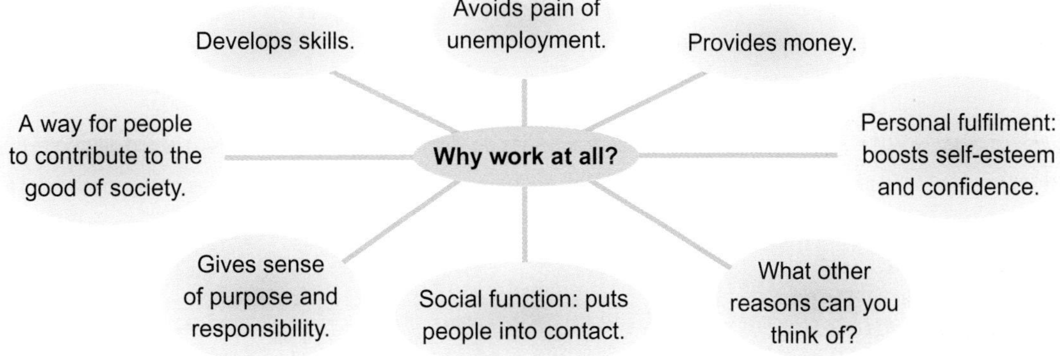

What makes a happy work place?

In a survey, supervisors and employees were given a list of ten things to rank in order of importance. Here's how the employees listed what they wanted most, and how the supervisors listed what they thought would most motivate the employees.

Employees want	Supervisors think employees want
Appreciation	Good wages
Feeling "in" on things	Job security
Understanding attitude	Promotion opportunities
Job security	Good working conditions
Good wages	Interesting work
Interesting work	Loyalty from management
Promotion opportunities	Tactful discipline
Loyalty from management	Appreciation
Good working conditions	Understanding attitude
Tactful discipline	Feeling "in" on things

3 What conclusions can you reach from the survey of employees and supervisors?

4 (a) Why is work important in a person's life?
(b) Do all people have a right to work?

5 Describe THREE main problems which unemployment may cause.

"For me, the work place is much less a factory for the production of goods and much more an incubator for the human spirit. It is where a continuous sense of spiritual education can take place, and where self-esteem gives us the ability to express ourselves and to contribute selflessly to a greater good." [Anita Roddick, founder of The Body Shop, quoted in J. Canfield and J. Miller, *Heart at Work*, McGraw-Hill, 1996]

6 (a) What does Anita Roddick mean when she says that the work place is "an incubator for the human spirit"?
(b) Why do you think it is important for an employer to value his or her workers? How can an employer do this?

The value of leisure

People have more leisure time these days than in the past, and leisure time is more likely to increase in the future.

7 Why do you think people have more leisure time today than in the past?

8 (a) Do you think people have a right to engage in any leisure activity they wish? Are there some they should be protected against?
(b) Write a label for each of these four photographs showing leisure activities. Give your view on each.
(c) Which leisure activities do you think religious believers (i) would advocate, (ii) would forbid? Explain your answer.

Religious teachings on work and leisure

All religions encourage a right attitude to work. They speak out against the dangers of unemployment, both for the individual and for society, and offer support to the unemployed. Some jobs and some types of leisure may be ruled out if they involve activities that are against religious beliefs. Work and leisure, like all areas of life, have a spiritual dimension.

RELIGION FILE

BUDDHISM 

Nuns at a Tibetan Buddhist Centre in South London work at wrapping prayer wheels.

- The fifth stage of the Eightfold Path is Right Livelihood (or work). The way a person earns his or her living is important in Buddhism. Work which would involve a person in going against one of the precepts (e.g. not harming a living thing, not lying) is not allowed. Some jobs that have traditionally been forbidden for Buddhists are: dealing in arms, buying and selling meat, and any work that involves alcoholic drinks or drugs.
- Buddhists must show right effort in their work: "he who does not get up when it is time to get up, who, though young and strong, is full of sloth, who is weak in resolution and thought, that lazy and idle man will not find the way of wisdom." [Dhammapada 280]
- One modern British Buddhist group, the Friends of the Western Buddhist Order, organise "Right Livelihood Co-operatives" which seek to put into practice Buddhist ideals with regard to work. They say that "work should never become so dominant in a person's life or be so boring and unpleasant that it can only be done for the sake of rewards." [D. Subhuti, *Buddhism for Today*, Element, 1983]. Buddhists emphasise that any work situation can be used to practise mindfulness.
- Leisure is important for a balanced life. Buddhists keep the precepts in mind in choosing their leisure activities. Many lay Buddhists spend leisure time at dharma centres, meeting Buddhist friends, and getting teaching from the monks.

1 Name THREE jobs forbidden to Buddhists. Explain why they are forbidden.

2 (a) What does it mean for a Buddhist to show right effort in his or her work?
(b) If you were a Buddhist employer, how would you create a positive work environment?

RELIGION FILE

CHRISTIANITY 

- Christians believe that all of life, including work, should be lived according to God's will. Work is not just a way of earning money to stay alive; it can also be good in itself. "Through work humankind not only transforms nature, adapting it to its needs, but it also achieves fulfilment." [Pope John Paul II]

- Christians believe that God has a purpose for each individual life and that God wants each person to use his or her talents. Work should be done to the glory of God. Christians believe that work is sharing with God in being creative and active in the world. Some Christians support the view known as the "Protestant Work Ethic": that work is a duty to God and hard work is a virtue. The harder you work the more pleasing this is to God. [Colossians 3: 23; Ephesians 6: 7]

  Christians sometimes refer to a particular kind of work as a vocation. This comes from the Latin "vocare" (to call). A person feels called by God to do a particular job. Some Christians believe that we all have a vocation from God.

- Christians consider that some work is opposed to their beliefs: for example, many Christians will not work in betting shops or in hospital wards where women are enabled to have abortions.

- Christianity teaches that all people are of value in God's eyes. The Church recognises that unemployment can make people feel not valued by the world. Ways in which Christians might therefore try to help include giving financial support; offering counselling; engaging people in worthwhile tasks in the community.

- Christians believe that God commands them (in the Ten Commandments) to keep one day of the week holy (separate). This is why many Christians are against Sunday trading.

3 Try to summarise Christian attitudes to work.

4 (a) How would you describe the difference between a job and a vocation? Give TWO important differences.
(b) Give THREE examples of jobs that Christians might feel are vocations. Explain your answer.
(c) Are there some jobs that Christians would choose not to do? Give reasons.

5 (a) "Unemployment has the power to corrupt the soul of any man or woman." [Archbishop William Temple]. Discuss.
(b) How might the Church help the unemployed?

6 "Leisure is good if used for the glory of God." [Methodist Conference, 1974]. Which leisure activities (a) would glorify God, (b) would not glorify God?

7 In 1994 the law was changed to allow shops in Britain to open on Sundays.
(a) Do you shop on Sundays? Why do you think many people like shopping on Sundays?
(b) Why are many Christians against Sunday trading?

RELIGION FILE

HINDUISM ॐ

- In the traditional Hindu caste system different jobs were assigned to each caste. For example, the Vaishyas were mainly agriculturalists and traders whereas the Kshatriyas were the rulers, leaders, and soldiers. The idea was that the groups were interdependent, each making a valuable contribution to the good of society as a whole. Unfortunately, the system was abused (see pages 201-202). However, it did ensure that the poor were fed and provided for, since each person had his or her role.

- All work is considered good if it is what a person's dharma demands. "Do the work allocated to you according to your dharma, for work is better than idleness." [Bhagavad Gita 3:8]. Hindus are encouraged to work for the good of others and to care for others.

- Leisure and pleasure (kama) are one of the four main aims of Hindu life. It is important to keep a balance between work and enjoyment.

8 The Hindu caste system accords different jobs to different groups of people in society. Do you think this is a sensible way of dividing roles, or do you think that people should be able to choose to cross over caste lines?

9 (a) Should people be paid different salaries for different jobs?
(b) What would be the advantages and disadvantages of paying all people the same wage, irrespective of which job they do?

RELIGION FILE

ISLAM

Relaxing on the river at Stratford-upon-Avon

- Muslims value work as a way of serving God. No honest job is considered degrading. What matters is the dignity and attitude with which the work is done. "God loves that when any of you does anything, he should do it in the best way." [Hadith]. However, jobs which harm others are forbidden: i.e. work involving dishonesty, exploitation, gambling, cheating, etc.
  Muslims should not become so involved with work that they forget Allah. It is for this reason that Muslims are called to prayer five times a day. At these times a Muslim must stop what he or she is doing to perform salah (prayer).

- Every Muslim should contribute to the good of the Muslim community. Islam discourages idleness. Whilst prayer is an important element in Islam it is not a full-time activity in itself. The Prophet Muhammad was told about a man who spent all his time in prayer. He asked, "Then who feeds him?" "His brother," was the reply. "Then his brother is better than he," said the Prophet.

- Women are allowed to earn money outside the home, so long as this is not at the expense of their role in the home. The money women earn is their own.

- Time and life are gifts from God. Time should be used wisely. Apart from working and serving humanity, Muslims are encouraged to spend some time on their own or with close friends and family, enjoying activities of personal interest. It is important to live a balanced life, because this contributes to the balanced nature of the Ummah. The Prophet Muhammad took care to preserve his physical energy: he liked to swim, shoot arrows, and ride horses. Gambling, drugs, and alcohol are not leisure activities in Islam.

10 What is the Muslim attitude to work?

11 Name THREE jobs that would be forbidden to Muslims. Explain why they would be forbidden.

12 Do you think a wife and mother should work outside the home? What is the Muslim attitude to wives working?

RELIGION FILE

JUDAISM

Visiting family on Shabbat in Jerusalem. The whole city comes to a standstill on Shabbat. This day of complete rest from the bustle of the week is a time for people to refresh themselves.

- Work has a high value. "No labour, however humble, is dishonouring." [Talmud]. The Talmud commands: "Teach your son a trade or you teach him to become a robber." Judaism does not contain a monastic order – people who withdraw from the world to devote themselves to spirituality. It teaches that people serve God by bringing His will to every part of life. In the Mishnah the image of work is used to talk about the relationship between God and humanity. Rabbi Eliazar says: "Know before whom you are toiling and who your employer is who will pay you the reward of your labour." [Pirkei Avot 2: 19-21]

- The Ten Commandments state that people should work for six days and rest on the seventh [Exodus 20: 9-10]. The Mishnah and the Talmud describe 39 types of work forbidden on the Sabbath. These 39 actions fall into five groups: (1) producing food, (2) making cloth, (3) writing, (4) building, (5) carrying something from private property to public property or in public property.

- Jews believe that they are always answerable to God for everything that they do. It is important that they act justly in their businesses (e.g. not charging too high a price, using honest advertising, fulfilling their contracts as employees as well as employers). The rabbis have taught that the first question Jews will be asked on Judgement Day is whether they have acted justly in their work.

13 (a) Which of the following actions would not be allowed on the Shabbat? Explain why. (1) making a cake, (2) moving a chair to your neighbour's house, (3) writing a letter to a friend, (4) eating cake, (5) reading a letter.
(b) Explain why Shabbat is a special day for Jews.
(c) Do you think that it is good to have one day a week free from all work? What are the advantages of this day?

14 Describe TWO business practices that a Jew would consider dishonest and unjust.

15 How do you think Judaism would regard trade unions?

RELIGION FILE

SIKHISM

- Sikhs have a reputation for hard work and taking the initiative. The Gurus taught that work is a way of serving God. Sikhs are expected to work hard and to keep their families. "He alone has found the right way who eats what he earns through toil and shares his earnings with the needy." [Guru Granth Sahib 1245]

  "Every work is noble if performed in the right way." [Guru Granth Sahib 568]. The only unacceptable jobs are those which contradict Sikh beliefs: for example, selling alcohol and, in particular, selling cigarettes and tobacco.

16 Give two reasons why Sikhs think hard work is good.

17 Explain why certain jobs are forbidden to Sikhs.

CHAPTER

Religion and Science

UNIT ONE

For the last thousand years or so Science and Religion have been like brothers and sisters – sometimes fighting with each other, at other times on common ground. In this chapter you will trace the Religion and Science debate, and consider the questions which Science has raised for religious people.

1 Study the Time Line, which starts below and runs through this chapter. What are the main issues over which Science and Religion parted company? Choose one of the issues and explain why it was important.

2 Read the text on pages 211-12, under the heading "Science and the Creation". Write a paragraph summarising the opinions given. Provide your own evaluation.

KEY ISSUES IN THIS CHAPTER

- the historical debate between Science and Religion
- explanations of the origins of life
- Science and Religion, in conflict or two sides of the same coin?

The Science and Religion debate

It has been said that Religion is the "Queen of the Sciences". It is certainly true that Religion has played a large part in the development of Science and that many scientists have at the same time been religious people. So why has conflict arisen in the relationship between Science and Religion? The Time Line below (pages 211–215) shows some of the main issues at stake.

Science and the Creation

The discussion between Religion and Science has not always led to disagreements. Many thinkers have concluded that scientific findings inform us about the way God created the universe and works within it.

- Physicist Mehdi Golshani of Sharif University in Tehran, drawing on the Qu'ran, believes that natural phenomena are "God's signs in the universe" and that studying them is almost a religious obligation. The Qur'an asks humans to "travel in the earth, then see how He initiated the creation". Research "is a worship act, in that it reveals more of the wonders of God's creation." [*Newsweek* , 27 July 1998]
- "Science is thinking God's thought after Him just as truly as when we read the scripture." [Charles Garman, *Letters, Lectures, Addresses*, 1909]

800-1000

The sciences of astronomy and mathematics develop in the Islamic Empire. They are considered to provide glimpses of the work of God.

1268-1273

Thomas Aquinas shows how the rational ideas of the ancient Greek philosopher Aristotle (above left) can be brought together with Christian thought. Medieval scientists consider their role as uncovering the divine plan.

1543

Copernicus publishes "De Revolutionibus" ("On the Revolutions of the Celestial Spheres"), concluding that the earth moves around the sun. Previously it has been taught that the earth – and therefore humans – were at the centre of God's universe.

- "How could science be an enemy of religion when God commanded man to be a scientist the day He told him to rule the earth and subject it?" [American prelate (bishop), Fulton J. Sheen, *The Life of All Living*, 1929]
- Allan Sandage has pioneered the science of astronomy in the 20th century. His findings showed how fast the universe is exploding and how old it is: "It was my science that drove me to the conclusion that the world is much more complicated than can be explained by science. It is only through the supernatural that I can understand the mystery of existence." [*Newsweek*, 27 July 1998]
- Scientists have not been able to prove the existence of God – it is not their job. However, they may be able to give clues as to what God is like. "Science may not serve as an eye-witness of God the creator, but it can serve as a character witness." [W. Mark Richardson quoted in *Newsweek*, 27 July 1998]

"Evolution is a marvellous expression of how God is working in the world." [Rev. Dr Arthur Peacocke]

- Arthur Peacocke is a biochemist. He became a priest in 1971. He accepts the scientific theory of evolution and goes further. He believes that evolutionary theory can teach us something about the nature of God. He thinks that God has chosen to limit His omnipotence and omniscience. The process of evolution suggests a divine humility. Much as a loving parent lets a child be and become, freely and without interference, so God lets creation make itself.

3 "Science is helping us understand the mind of God." Do you agree?

What type of knowledge?

One way of explaining the apparent conflict between Science and Religion is that they are two different standpoints from which to view and explain the same thing. In many areas, looking at something from different standpoints leads to different explanations. To take an example from literature,

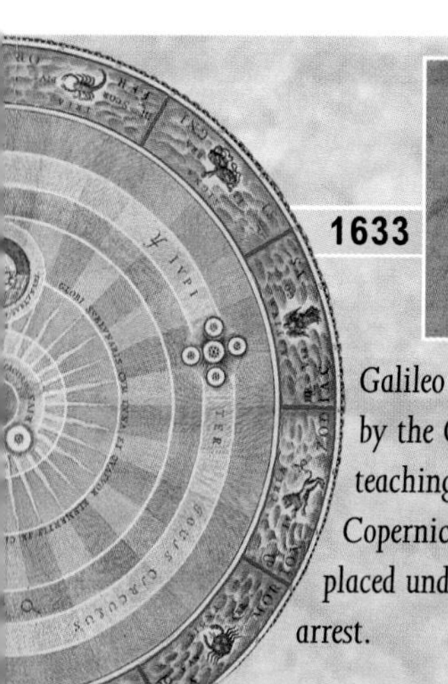

1633

Galileo is disciplined by the Church for teaching the ideas of Copernicus. He is placed under house arrest.

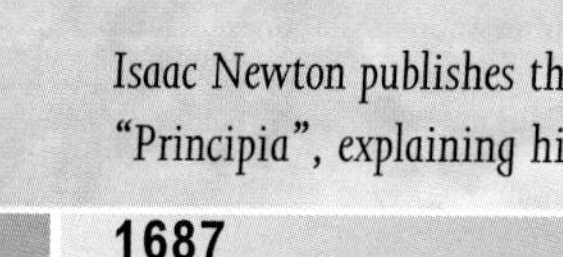

1687

Isaac Newton publishes the "Principia", explaining his theory of gravitation. The workings of the world are described in mechanistic ways.

However, Newton leaves room for God in this world view by suggesting that God was the first cause of the universe.

1802

Lamarck publishes "Research on the Organisation of Living Bodies", suggesting that animals evolve – a contradiction of the idea that God created all creatures exactly as they are.

Shakespeare's *The Winter's Tale* sets part of its action on the sea coast of Bohemia. Geographers will tell you that Bohemia has no sea coast. This does not make Shakespeare's story any less true. He was using language in a different way, to show a different kind of truth. Science and Religion offer different explanations of how life began on earth, because they are two world views trying to show different kinds of truth.

4 Try explaining things from different standpoints. For instance, how would a scientist explain what is happening when two people kiss? How would the lovers explain what is happening? How do the descriptions differ? Is one description more true than the other or are both true?

- "Science and religion seek to answer different questions. Science asks how things happen, religion asks why. Genesis is not there to give us strict, technical answers about how the universe began. It gives us the big answer that things exist because of God's will. One can perfectly well believe in the Big Bang but [also] believe in it as the will of the Creator." [John Polkinghorne, physicist and Anglican priest, quoted in *Newsweek*, 27 July 1998]
- "Human science is but the backward undoing of the tapestry web of God's science." [George MacDonald, novelist and poet, 1887]
- "The Bible teaches us how to go to heaven, not how the heavens go." [Galileo]
- "Our science tells us how to do an infinitely greater number of things, it picks apart the cog-wheels of nature; but it is not wise, it does not discriminate what is worth doing, and before the greatest problem of all, what meaning can man give to his life in this vast world, it gives a despairing 'Nescio', if not an 'I don't care'." [J. H. Randall, *The Making of the Modern Mind*, Columbia University Press, 1977]

5 Read the opinions quoted on this page and then write a paragraph explaining how religion and science may go hand in hand.

1859

Charles Darwin publishes "The Origin of Species by Means of Natural Selection", concluding that species evolve on the basis of natural selection – the fittest (best adapted) survive and reproduce. Wilberforce, Bishop of Oxford, declares in 1860 that if Darwin's theory is true, then Genesis was a lie and God was dethroned. If humans have evolved on the basis of the survival of the fittest this means that humans do not have free will. Evolution does not provide a moral guide.

1871

Darwin publishes "The Descent of Man", arguing that humankind developed from apes. This undermines the biblical doctrine that humans were created by God.

6 Bertrand Russell said: "Whatever knowledge is attainable must be attainable by scientific methods; and what science cannot discover, mankind cannot know." [Bertrand Russell, *Religion and Science*, 1935].
(a) Do you agree?
(b) Can science be sure of its findings?

Are there limits to scientific knowledge? Three professors gave their views:

Professor Daniel Dennett: "Absolute certainty is never achievable, but practical certainty is certainly possible. Scientific reasoning is our best route to practical certainty."

Professor Owen Gingerich: "As a historian of science I find that the historical record is rather different. It suggests that scientific data is ambiguous when you are at the cutting edge of science. You don't always know which facts are the good ones and which should be ignored."

Professor Bob Herrmann: "Science has changed drastically in the last few decades. We now know how tremendous the limitations are. We understand that as we delve into the recesses of matter and energy, there are limitations that are far beyond our ability to appreciate and understand. We realise that the universe is more like a cosmic onion with layer after layer. To say that science is rock solid, and that every fact is sure and secure, is to be totally arrogant."
[quoted in *The Question Is . . .*, BBC OU video]

Lessons to learn

Technology has made tremendous advances. Science can tell us how to heal; it can also tell us how to destroy. What it doesn't do is tell us which of the two to do.

When Science is seen to cause great destruction (think of the atom bomb and the gas chambers as 20th-century examples), some people question the worth of making scientific progress.

"If science produces no better fruits than tyranny, murder, rapine and destitution of national morality, I would rather wish our country to be ignorant, honest and estimable, as our neighboring savages are." [Thomas Jefferson, President of the USA 1801-9, Letter to John Adams, 1812]

1905

John William Strutt determines the age of rock to be 2 billion years. This goes against James Ussher's 1650 theory that according to Genesis the universe was created on 22 October 4004 BCE.

1916

Albert Einstein discovers the laws of general and specific relativity. He says that, looking at the great design within the universe, he became convinced that all of it could have come about by chance. In his opinion "God doesn't play dice."

1925

John Scopes, a high school teacher in Tennessee, is put on trial for teaching the theory of evolution (forbidden by law in Tennessee until 1967, because it contradicted the Bible account of creation).

It could be argued that Science helps to inform us about God, and that Science also needs the help of Religion.

“Science needs religion, to prevent it from becoming a curse to mankind instead of a blessing.” [Edgar J. Goodspeed, *Four Pillars of Democracy*, 1940]

“Science without religion is lame, religion without science is blind.” [Albert Einstein, *Out of My Later Years*, 1950]

WHAT DOES IT MEAN TO BE HUMAN?

On the first day of term, the Principal of an American High School sent his teachers a copy of this letter, which was written by a survivor from a Jewish concentration camp.

Dear Teacher,
I am a survivor of a concentration camp.
My eyes saw what no man should witness:
Gas chambers built by learned engineers,
Children poisoned by educated physicians,
Infants killed by trained nurses,
Women and babies shot and burned by high school and college graduates.

So I am suspicious of education.
My request is – help your students become human.
Your efforts must never produce learned monsters,
skilled psychopaths, educated Eichmans.
Reading, writing, arithmetic are important only if they serve to make our children more human.

7 Why do you think the Principal sent the concentration camp survivor's letter to his teaching staff? What is the main point of the letter? What comment does it make on the limitations of Science? What is it saying about the relationship between Religion and Science?

1948 George Gamow uses the term “big bang” to describe the theory that the universe began in a primeval explosion. This scientific theory clashes with the religious account of the creation.

1965 Arno Penzias and Robert Wilson find that space is filled with background radiation. This discovery supports the big bang model. In 1989 a satellite makes an image of this radiation.

1992 Pope John Paul II apologises for the Roman Catholic Church's condemnation of Galileo.

1996 The Pope says that evolution was part of God's master plan.

CHAPTER

Religion, the arts, and the media

UNIT ONE

Travelling around the world, it is hard to ignore the influence which religion has had on art, architecture, and sculpture. Religious art has fulfilled many functions: glorifying God and teaching and inspiring people. This chapter looks at the communication of religious ideas through the arts and the media.

KEY ISSUES IN THIS CHAPTER

- the ability of the arts to express religious ideas and beliefs
- the values and beliefs expressed through the media, especially the television and the Internet
- the potential dangers of the media

Information File: Arts and media

Arts: activities including art, sculpture, music, drama, dance, literature, and cinema, in which people can take part for enjoyment or to create works that express serious meanings or ideas.
Media: a term used to describe different forms of communication including newspapers and magazines, books, television, radio, and the Internet.

1 In groups, explore how music can be used to create atmosphere. For example, how is music used differently in a romantic film and a horror film? In what ways does music express emotions better than words?

2 A few years ago Gregorian Chant became very popular. It is a form of religious music used in monasteries. Listen to a piece. What does it make you feel? In what sense do you think it is religious? In what sense do you think such music communicates to people in deeper ways than either a piece of writing or a speech?

3 Many artists and composers say that they feel inspired in their work – many mean "inspired by God". Works of art and music also inspire the people who look at or listen to them. Can you name a piece of art or music that has inspired you? Why did it inspire you? What did it make you feel?

For Buddhists the lotus flower is a symbol of enlightenment. The roots of the lotus grow in muddy water (representing the anger, ignorance, and greed which darken people's minds). The flower rises above the water and gradually opens its petals as it faces the sun. So also the mind can become enlightened.

Religious expression in the arts

Words can be limiting when you want to express abstract thoughts and deep feelings. Religious traditions use art, music, and dance to help express ideas and beliefs.

In their art, religions use symbols to represent ideas that cannot easily be put into words. Religious symbols represent important ideas and make invisible things visible. A symbol can be an object, a gesture, or a sign. Symbols speak to people at a deep level.

Jewish artists have created ritual objects for use in religious celebrations both in the home and in the synagogue. These objects are part of "Judaica", things that express Jewish culture. By linking Jewish people with their spiritual tradition, Judaica has helped build a Jewish identity in the many countries in which Jews have lived throughout the centuries. Judaica uses Jewish and biblical symbols such as the menorah (the seven-branched candlestick), the star of David, the Lion (of Judah), the olive branch (of peace), and the crown (for kingship).

Traditionally, Jewish art did not contain representations of human figures, since there was a fear that people would be tempted to make these into idols. However, as Jews moved West, they sometimes took on the artistic styles of the European countries in which they lived, and did decorate synagogues and religious books with figurative paintings.

An example of Judaica: a candlestick for the Jewish festival of Hanukah. Differently from a menorah, it has eight branches.

"In my house I have a pair of silver candlesticks, a silver kiddush cup, a menorah and a havdalah set. Each of these objects fulfils a function within our religion. They are also decorative. You go into a Jewish house and you know you are in a Jewish house because there are certain Judaica objects, which you will find in every Jewish house." [Rachel Keene]

4 (a) What are the main symbols used in Jewish art?
(b) What is Judaica? What purpose does Judaica serve? In what sense is Judaica a form of religious expression?

Tiles in an 11th-century mosque in Pakistan. In the patterns used by Islamic artists the circle represents infinity and eternity, since it has no beginning and no end. It also represents Oneness and Allah. The neat, repeating geometric designs point to the mathematical order behind the created world.

Islamic art and architecture are distinctive. Muslims never make images of people in their religious art. They use geometric designs and calligraphy (decorative writing based on the script of the Qur'an) to express their religious beliefs. Arabic is the only language used for Islamic calligraphy since this is the language in which Allah revealed the Qur'an to the Prophet Muhammad. Calligraphers use a special pen (a calmus), and write from right to left. So their writing arm moves towards the heart, drawing the words of the Qur'an into their life.

5 Design your own geometric pattern. Use a sheet of squared paper, a ruler, a compass, and pencils to make a design of repeating patterns.

An icon painter, Father Kallinkos, at Stavrovouni Monastery in Cyprus, 1994.

6 What special qualities do you think an icon painter needs to possess? Do you think an icon painter has to be a holy or spiritual person? Why might some people think so?

In Christianity art is used to teach, to express belief, and to glorify God. This function of art is clear as soon as you walk into an Orthodox church. Orthodox Christians use icons in their worship, both at home and in church. The word "icon" comes from a Greek word meaning "image". Icons should be "read" like books, since each one is painted in a specific manner. They have been called "windows into God", because contemplation of them encourages spiritual insight.

Religious art is not limited to paintings and architecture. In Japan, Zen Buddhists create gardens, which are then used to help them in their meditation. Many Zen gardens are unchanging – there are no flowers that fade or leaves that fall. The only changes that happen occur in how a person looks at the garden. Zen gardens can be made up of sand or gravel, water, rocks, mosses, and sometimes a tree. Many Zen monks were famous garden architects.

One way of telling the Hindu story of the Ramayana is through dance.

How would you describe this Zen Buddhist garden? What feelings does it create in you – for example, does it make you feel peaceful or agitated, warm or cold? How might this garden help a Buddhist become calm and meditate?

Religious and moral themes in the media

The media are all around us – newspapers, magazines, television, videos, the Internet. They have a powerful influence. Here is what the Dalai Lama had to say:

"Now for the media. I respect them very much and I appreciate the fact that they interfere with everyone's business! From time to time some public figures might abuse their position, showing neither moral principles nor self-discipline. There should be no discrepancy between the external appearance and the inner life of an honest person. In such cases, I think the media alone have the power to verify and expose such behaviour. Journalists are notoriously nosy and do their job well. [Furthermore] I think that if we did not expose all the evils of society, such as drugs, murder, sexual abuse, and exploitation of children, innocent people would still continue to suffer from them daily. On the other hand, I reproach them for attaching too much importance to the negative aspects which can greatly discourage the human mind." [The Dalai Lama, *Beyond Dogma: the challenge of the modern world*, Souvenir Press, 1994]

7 Study the quotation from the Dalai Lama. Why can the media be both positive and negative? Do you agree with the Dalai Lama that journalists have a responsibility for researching into the private lives of important people?

Television

A survey in 1991 found out that, on average, children spend 21 hours per week watching television. The same survey discovered that on average fathers spend 25 minutes per week (3.5 minutes per day) and mothers spend 38 minutes per week (5.5 minutes per day) in genuine conversation with their child or children. It is clear that the television has a big influence in the lives of today's young people.

"Consider the power of television, and the millions of people who live . . . inside television . . . Television has become the physical universe that people now relate to, and the mental universe as well . . . Millions live off the same television images." [Brenda Lealman, educational researcher, in E. Lang and R. Best, ed., *Education, Spirituality and the Whole Child*, Cassell, 1996]

8 Where do you get your ideas from? How large an influence do television and videos have in forming your ideas? Has television ever changed your mind on an issue?

9 How many hours of television and videos do you watch each week? Keep a time check for the next week. What do the results tell you about the importance of television in your life? What would your life be like if you did not have a television?

10 What does Brenda Lealman mean when she says, "Millions live off the same television images"?

In a way, television acts as a teacher, helping to shape people's view of life and their ideas of what is right and what is wrong. But what values is television promoting?

11 Watch television for three hours one evening. Make sure that you watch a soap like *Brookside* or *Friends* and some advertisements. What lifestyles do the good characters in the programmes have? What values are being presented as "normal", "good", and "bad"? What do the advertisements tell you about the "good life"?

12 Imagine that you are a TV reviewer for your local newspaper. Write a review of TV morality. Do you think TV is being morally responsible in the messages it is promoting? Provide reasons to back up your opinions. Do you think soaps should take on board social and moral issues? Do you think they should take on religious issues?

13 No one doubts that TV is immensely powerful in today's society. However, people have different views on its power. Discuss each of the following statements:
"Violence on TV makes people more violent."
"Advertisers are convinced that advertisements change our buying habits."
"TV does not make our moral values. All it does is mirror what is going on in society."
"Sexually explicit scenes should only be screened after 9 o'clock."
"Video age ratings are a joke."

> «In a single telecast I preach to millions more than Christ did in his lifetime.»
> [Christian evangelist, Billy Graham]

Certain television programmes deal explicitly with religious material. So-called "God slots" such as *Heart & Soul*, *Songs of Praise*, *Everyman*, and *Heart of the Matter* are worship and religious affairs programmes. Radio programmes like *The Moral Maze* and *Pause for Thought* now reflect the fact that Britain is a multi-faith society.

Television and the other media are also tools which religious groups are using to spread their message. In some countries, for example the USA, religious groups have bought television channels. These are watched by millions of people each week.

14 Look through a copy of a TV and radio guide. Make a note of all religious programmes. What subjects are they concerned with? Watch or listen to one of these programmes and afterwards answer the following questions. What do you think was the aim of the programme? Who was the target audience? What did you think of the programme? What impact do you think it had? What view of religion did it present? What would you do to improve the quality of the programme?

15 "Television offers a prejudiced view of religious people. It stereotypes them and presents religion as an old-fashioned idea." How far do you agree with this statement? Give reasons for your answer.

16 Do you agree with Billy Graham that "television is the most powerful tool of communication ever devised by man"? If he is correct, what are the potential dangers of this tool?

17 Some films, such as *Schindler's List*, *Priest*, and *Fiddler on the Roof*, have a religious theme. Watch a film with a religious theme and write a review. What is the film's theme and what religious ideas does it explore? Why do you think such films have been popular?

The Internet

Today's telecommunications have made the world a global village. The Internet has made it possible for people to "talk to" others within seconds anywhere in the world. As with other forms of communications, there are positive and negative sides. There are concerns, including among religious groups, about the easy access the Internet gives to all forms of information, including, for example, pornography. There are few safeguards to protect the young from information which is considered harmful.

Agent Glenn Nick of the US Customs CyberSmuggling Centre is responsible for tracking down people who are abusing the Internet. His warning to parents:

"You can't just put a computer in your kids' bedroom, hook it up to the Internet and expect them not to run into trouble. That's like dropping your kids off at the playground at 7 a.m. and not coming back till 7 p.m. Anything can happen to them." [*Time Magazine*, 14 September 1998]

This is one artist's impression of how modern telecommunications lay a pathway before us, making all places accessible. What do you think of this view?

18 Do you think that the Internet is potentially dangerous? What do you think needs to be done to protect people from the dangers?

19 Imagine that you are an advertising company. You have been asked to design an advert which would encourage people to join a religion. Choose one religion that you have studied. Design an advert for that religion which encourages people to join. What message do you want to get across? What form of media will you use – newspaper advert, magazine colour supplement, television advert, a web site? Justify your choice.

Sample Coursework Tasks

The following tasks are not prescribed tasks but are suggestions to assist teachers in devising tasks and titles which are suitable for their own circumstances and candidates.

1 (a) Devise a TV programme that will portray the life of a religion in Britain today. Assume that it is being made on behalf of this religion, and that the aim of the programme is to show the best points of the religion. [15 marks]

1 (b) What might be the benefits of such a programme? [5 marks]

2 (a) Select one religion you have studied and discuss how the arts can be used to enrich worship. [15 marks]

2 (b) Do the arts enhance religious belief or are they a distraction? [5 marks]

Information on scriptures

Throughout this book, quotations from the scriptures of the religions studied have been taken from modern English translations.

Buddhism

The **Tripitaka** is the main collection of scriptures used by Theravada Buddhists. It is also referred to as the **Pali Canon**, because it was written in the Pali language. It is a collection of the teachings of the Buddha, written down, according to some sources, in the second half of the 1st century BCE. It consists of: (1) **Vinaya Pitaka**, rules for monks and nuns; (2) **Sutra Pitaka**, sayings and discourses of the Buddha, including the **Digha Nikaya** and the **Samyutta Nikaya**; (3) **Abhidharma Pitaka**, further teachings.

The **Diamond Sutra** is an important text of Mahayana Buddhism, written in Sanskrit, probably in the 2nd century CE. It is structured as a dialogue between the Buddha and a disciple.

The **Dhammapada** is a collection of 423 verses on morality and mental discipline. It was probably compiled in the third century BCE.

If you want to read more of the Buddhist scriptures, we recommend *Buddhist Scriptures* translated by E. Conze and published by Penguin.

Christianity

The **Bible** is in two parts: the 39 books of the **Old Testament** (which is almost the same as the Jewish Tenakh) and the 27 books of the **New Testament**.

We have quoted mainly from the *Good News Version*.
If you want to read more of the Christian scriptures, we recommend this or the *New International Version* or the *New Revised Standard Version*.

Hinduism

The **Vedas** are four collections of hymns: the **Rig Veda**, **Sama Veda**, **Yagur Veda**, and **Atharva Veda**. They were composed in Vedic, an early form of Sanskrit, and the oldest parts are thought to date from 1300-1000 BCE. However, in their present form, they are thought to date from the third century BCE.

The **Mahabharata** was composed from c. 300 BCE, being added to until c. 300 CE. One of its 18 books is the **Bhagavad Gita**, written c. 200 BCE-200 CE.

The **Laws of Manu** (**Manusmriti**) is a respected code of Hindu law, divided into 12 books. Scholars have dated it variously from 600 BCE to 300 CE.

If you want to read more of the Hindu scriptures, we recommend *The Bhagavad Gita* translated by J. Mascaro and published by Penguin.

Islam

The **Qur'an** is the main sacred text of Islam, containing what Muslims believe are the revelations made by Allah to the Prophet Muhammad. The Qur'an is divided into 114 chapters called "suras".

The **Hadith** are records of the sayings, actions, and life of the Prophet Muhammad. There are six collections of Hadith, dating from the 9th century CE.

If you want to read more of the Islamic scriptures, we recommend *The Holy Qur'an* translated by Yusuf Ali and published by The Islamic Foundation.

Judaism

The Hebrew Bible, the **Tenakh**, is divided into: (1) the **Torah** (Law); (2) the **Nevi'im** (Prophets); and (3) the **Ketuvim** (Writings). The Torah became scripture between the end of Babylonian exile in 538 BCE and the separation of the Samaritans from Judaism around 300 BCE. The Nevi'im was accepted as the word of God by the end of the third century BCE. Which books should be included in the Ketuvim became finalised by the end of the first century CE.

The **Mishnah** is a collection of political and civil laws finally collected around 200 CE. It is divided into sections. E.g. **Mishnah Makkot** deals with legally imposed judgements. **Mishnah Abot** (also called **Pirkei Avot**, or the Ethics of the Fathers) contains sayings of the rabbis. **Mishnah Berachot** deals with the correct form of blessings before and after eating.

The **Mishnah Torah** (by Moses Maimonides, 12th century, Spain) presents the rulings of the Talmud as a comprehensive code of Jewish Law.

The **Yorah De'ah** is a code of Jewish law written in the 15th century.

If you want to read more of the Jewish scriptures, we recommend *Tenakh, the Holy Scriptures* (Jewish Publication Society); the *Jerusalem Bible* (Koren Publishers, Jerusalem, 1989); the *Mishnah-Mishnayoth (Hebrew English Edition)*, translation and notes by P. Blackman (Judaica Press, Gateshead, 1973, third edition); and the *Talmud: Hebrew-English Edition of the Babylonian Talmud*, translation and notes by I. Epstein et. al. (Soncino Press, 1962).

Sikhism

The **Guru Granth Sahib**, known as the **Adi Granth** ("first book") when it was first compiled by Guru Arjan Dev, in 1604, was finalised in 1705.

The **Rahit Maryada** is the Sikh Code of Conduct compiled in 1945.

If you want to read more of the Sikh scriptures, we recommend the translation by Dr Sant Singh Khalsa at http://www.sikhnet.com/s/GuruGranthSahib.

Index